FOURTEEN CLUBS
AND THE
AULD CLARET
JUG

FOURTEEN CLUBS
AND THE
AULD CLARET JUG

The Caddies' Inside Stories of Winning the British Open

NORMAN DABELL

Contemporary Books

Chicago New York San Francisco Lisbon London Madrid Mexico City
Milan New Delhi San Juan Seoul Singapore Sydney Toronto

Library of Congress Cataloging-in-Publication Data

Dabell, Norman.
     Fourteen clubs and the Auld Claret Jug : the caddies' inside stories
of winning the British Open / Norman Dabell.
        p.   cm.
     Rev. ed. of: Winning the Open. 2000.
     ISBN 0-8092-9331-5
     1. British Open (Golf tournament)   2. Caddies.   I. Title.
GV970.3.B75 D33   2001
796.352'66—dc21   2001028566

Contemporary Books

A Division of The McGraw·Hill Companies

This edition is published under license from and was first published in Great Britain in 2000
by Mainstream Publishing Company (Edinburgh) Ltd.
7 Albany Street
Edinburgh EH1 3UG

This edition first published in 2001 in the United States by Contemporary Books, a division
of The McGraw-Hill Companies.

1 2 3 4 5 6 7 8 9 0   LBM/LBM   0 9 8 7 6 5 4 3 2 1

ISBN 0-8092-9331-5

This book was set in Bembo
Printed and bound by Lake Book Manufacturing

Cover design by Nick Panos

McGraw-Hill books are available at special quantity discounts to use as premiums and
sales promotions, or for use in corporate training programs. For more information, please
write to the Director of Special Sales, Professional Publishing, McGraw-Hill, Two Penn
Plaza, New York, NY 10121-2298. Or contact your local bookstore.

This book is printed on acid-free paper.

Contents

CONTENTS

Foreword
A Tribute to Jeff "Squeeky" Medlen

I t's much easier to win a tournament that doesn't mean much to you. When you love a tournament so much, it makes it harder for you to win. My caddie, Jeff Medlen—known affectionately as Squeeky—knew how much it meant to me, how much I loved the British Open, how much I'd relish the prospect of winning it. Of all the times he'd caddied for me, he knew that winning at Turnberry was the most meaningful day of my golfing life.

We had a very special relationship, Squeek and I. The chemistry was right. We worked hard to improve how he caddied and I played. And we always said what we felt. That was what was brilliant about Squeek, not manipulating me but understanding me completely. And I understood him so well.

There were shots I hit under pressure alongside him that proved so important in my career, not necessarily the ones you might have seen on the television, like a crucial three-iron to the last to make a cut in a tournament. It could have been a particularly difficult line, you'd have to maneuver the ball, but you'd hit it perfectly. He'd remember that shot. Squeeky could remember them all.

There was always something for us to talk about and he was a wonderful companion. All the hours I spent on the golf course with him makes it hard to not have him with me any more. He was with me for such a golden period in my life. And it's left a big hole in my life.

Nick Price

Acknowledgements

Here "we" go again—another book of caddie yarns, this time giving an insight into how the Open Championships unfolded through the eyes of the men and women who carry the bags. Opens were won and lost on their advice and, quite rightly, they are entitled to credit all the action with how "we" did it. Incidentally, it's always "we" until someone three-putts or fluffs a chip. Then it's "he."

A huge thank you to all the hard-working "rake-rats" who co-operated with me for this selection of Open Championship stories from the end of the 1970s to the close of the millennium. You were magnificent. As I've said before, there was no way of doing it without you.

My gratitude to Nick Price, too. Nick provided me with a touching and revealing chapter from the other side of the player–caddie relationship. He very kindly agreed to relate his story of 1994 at Turnberry, where he won the Open with the late Jeff "Squeeky" Medlen.

And to my fiancée Sharon, thanks for your understanding (all those spoiled dinners!) when I got too immersed in the mill.

Introduction

Caddie—probably corruption of *cadet* and then *cady*, "a person employed to carry golf clubs and perform other services." The first record of a "cady," an odd-job man on a golf course, can be found in the accounts of the Marquis of Montrose in 1620. He wrote in his books, after playing the Scottish east coast links: "Payment of four shillings to the boy who carried my clubs." That was a small fortune in those days, because as late as the 1940s lads would be paid only a shilling a day for their services, while their senior caddies would be expected to carry out myriad other duties, too. The top caddie at a club was ostensibly the golf pro, greenkeeper and club-maker. His wages were not that lucrative. Nowadays, a trusted tour caddie, with a top-class professional, wearing sponsored clothing, headgear and shoes, can expect to average over £1,000 a week. He is no longer an odd-job man but a consummate professional.

Just a glance through the curriculum vitae of the bagman who accompanied Paul Lawrie to his dramatic victory at Carnoustie, the last Open Championship of a millennium, will show how far we have gone down the fairway in the past 20 years. Paddy Byrne, the son of an Irish expatriate based in the Middle East, had no real experience of caddying until he met Lawrie six months before the Scot's remarkable victory in the 128th Open Championship. He bears no resemblance to the weather-beaten, hard-drinking men who used to line up at St. Andrews, Royal Lytham and St. Anne's, Royal Birkdale—or any major golf club around the world for that matter—hoping for a day's work on the links. Paddy, only 23 when he began work for Lawrie at his then home,

INTRODUCTION

Dubai, in the year of the Scot's amazing 1999 Open triumph, is a far cry from the grizzled, stubble-chinned, veterans who thought nothing of sleeping under a hedge before washing in a stream and then reporting for work on a growling stomach whose only fill the night before had been ale and whisky.

While Paddy Byrne, a notable name indeed among the caddying cadre, had a full education and has embarked on what is now a well-accepted and potentially lucrative professional career, caddies of earlier years often cut short even rudimentary schooling—and earned just enough to maintain a nomadic lifestyle.

Jacky Lee, Peter Thomson's faithful bagman for two Open Championships, used to augment his caddie wages by stepping into the ring as a prize-fighter to earn enough to keep himself and his caddying brethren in food and drink on the days when there was no golf.

Now the modern caddie can expect to earn a retainer of at least £500 a week, more if he or she is experienced, and then a percentage of the master's winnings. That is normally 5 percent for making a cut (when the player qualifies for the final two rounds of a tournament to actually earn prize-money), 7.5 percent for finishing in the top ten, and 10 percent for winning the tournament. That can make caddies like Alastair McLean, Colin Montgomerie's long-serving associate, with his master for seven successive European order of merit titles and more than 20 victories in that time, a rich man.

Bernhard Langer's right-hand man Peter Coleman was the first man to place caddies not only in the limelight but in the bank manager's good books. The former railwayman—he is also credited with introducing the measuring wheel to provide totally accurate yardages to the greens from the fairways—bought a Porsche when Langer won his first U.S. Masters in 1985.

Taking it a stage further, Jerry Higginbotham, who was by Mark O'Meara's side for the American's 1998 Open success and at Augusta with O'Meara three months before when he took the U.S. Masters title, invested his percentages in real estate and restaurants.

The former-day "rake-rats," however, would probably not begrudge their modern brothers and sisters their improved lot, for the caddie job description has changed totally. Whereas it used to be just the basics—read an occasional borrow and carry the bag—nowadays a caddie has to be on his toes even hours before he takes to the course. No longer will an observation like "I think it's slightly straight sir" suffice when there could be half a million pounds resting on the advice.

INTRODUCTION

The job entails being there at the clubhouse well in advance of the player to get the equipment ready for action. It means at least an hour practicing before the round begins, ensuring everything that the weather demands is in the bag—rain gear, towels, several gloves. Balls have to be plentiful and all the same compression; appearance has to be immaculate. These are just the fundamentals.

Yardages have now become the most important part of the job and the ability to instinctively know which is the right club for the distance to be covered. The player may already have it in mind which club—often they don't—but the caddie is there to confirm and explain why it should be so. While the good caddie will already have walked the course, found out where the flags are placed on the greens for that day and worked out where the trouble lies in relation to bunkers, deep rough and water hazards, they do have it somewhat easier nowadays than their predecessors. To get their man to the green, the old caddie would "eyeball" the yardage, that is, look at the distance away from the green and judge which club should be used. Now there is an ever-burgeoning industry in providing yardage charts, a booklet of yardages and maps for each hole, which has sprung up on the golf tours. Caddies like Graham Heindrich, who took some time off from his operation to caddie for Jean Van de Velde in the Ryder Cup at Brookline, spend several days before tournaments providing the yardage charts in numbers to greatly assist club selection.

However, if that is one job made easier, there are plenty more that have to be done to be a successful caddie: psychologist, clairvoyant, weather forecaster, agronomist, dietician, conjurer—none of these would go amiss.

Maybe such a job description is what Mary Queen of Scots (who is said to have first mooted the idea of a caddie, when she returned to Britain after her marriage to the Dauphin, later Francis II of France) had in mind in the sixteenth century. The golf-fanatic queen employed pages, or "cadets," to respond to her every whim on the golf course.

Perhaps nothing much has really changed after all, the modern caddies might tell you. One aspect of caddying that certainly has not changed, even if the methods of getting to tournaments have gone from hitch-hiking to flying by Concorde, is the nomadic existence. If it's Tuesday it must be Turnberry—or Augusta, or Dubai.

1979 ROYAL LYTHAM AND ST. ANNE'S

Severiano Ballesteros with Dave Musgrove

Severiano Ballesteros	Spain	73 65 75 70 283 (par 71)
Jack Nicklaus	USA	72 69 73 72 286
Ben Crenshaw	USA	72 71 72 71 286
Mark James	England	76 69 69 73 287
Rodger Davis	Australia	75 70 70 73 288
Hale Irwin	USA	68 68 75 78 289
Graham Marsh	Australia	74 68 75 74 291
Isao Aoki	Japan	70 74 72 75 291
Bob Byman	USA	73 70 72 76 291
Bob Charles	New Zealand	78 72 70 72 292
Masashi Ozaki	Japan	75 69 75 73 292
Greg Norman	Australia	73 71 72 76 292

"He paced it back and says to me: 'Where is the ball?' I say, 'Under the car somewhere.' Then they all sorted out where he could drop—on the tractor path. He hammers the ball at the green, lands on the bit he wanted to stop on and the ball finishes up 15 or 20 feet from the flag. Then he holes the putt. No matter what anybody else says about his drive at the 16th, it was all deliberate and planned."

4

Never mind the fairway, show me the parking lot

Severiano Ballesteros had shown his intent three years earlier when, as a raw teenager, he burst on to the world golfing scene with a brilliant performance in the Open Championship at Royal Birkdale. Ballesteros had to settle for a share of second place in 1976 with the mighty Jack Nicklaus behind winner Johnny Miller. By the time Englishman Dave Musgrove took over the Ballesteros bag, it seemed only a matter of time before the charismatic Spaniard would lift the Auld Claret Jug.

That time arrived, on the Lancashire links of Royal Lytham and St. Anne's as Ballesteros clinched the Championship which will forever be known as the "Parking Lot Open."

There was less luck involved in Ballesteros's typically wayward driving, however, as Musgrove reveals. Musgrove, an affable philosopher, will occasionally trot out a quotation from Shakespeare or Dylan. The quote will fit the moment, such as Musgrove's favorite analogy for carting fifty pounds or so of golf bag for four or five miles around a golf course (he apologizes to Rudyard Kipling): "If you can meet with triumph and disaster, and treat those two impostors just the same—you'll be a caddie my son."

Since 1955, when he was 12 years old and first picked up a golf bag, Musgrove has had plenty of chance to observe those twin impostors. While his friends were keeping themselves in movie money and sweets by working newspaper routes, Musgrove's rounds came on The Nottinghamshire golf course at Hollinwell near his home in the coal-mining area of the Midlands, Kirkby in Ashfield. That served him well two ways. Not only did he keep himself in movie money and sweets but he picked up enough tips to become a single-figure handicap player and to this day retains single figures.

At first, Musgrove's caddying was only part-time as he pursued a draftsman's career with the Coal Board, but that did not stop him facing the first of those twin impostors, disaster. Or, rather, bitter disappointment. In 1971 in the Open Championship at Royal Birkdale, Musgrove had the much-sought-after bag of the hugely popular Argentinian Roberto de Vicenzo. Vicenzo looked very likely to pull off his second Open but his and Musgrove's hopes were dashed on the unlucky 13th in the third round, where a three-putt took the South American golfer out of the race.

Musgrove caddied for Vicenzo intermittently for several years and then, in 1972, having taken voluntary redundancy from Rolls-Royce Aerospace "for the call of the open road, instead of the office"—and "the chance to earn a big fat check now and again"—he decided to work the fairways full-time. This was with another Argentinian, Vicente Fernandez, and it was Fernandez who was to provide the link between the English bagman and Seve Ballesteros. First, Musgrove found success with Fernandez when the little Argentine player clinched the 1975 Benson and Hedges International at Fulford.

Among the players Fernandez led home were Manuel Ballesteros and his younger brother Severiano, only 18 years old and in his first year on tour. One year later, Musgrove and Seve were together when he took over the youngster's bag at the French Open, having lost a job through Fernandez breaking his finger. When Manuel Ballesteros asked Musgrove to caddie for his brother it was the start of a memorable four years for the pair of them.

"Roberto had written to me and asked me to carry for him in the 1976 Open at Birkdale. Loads of people had let him down over the years and I didn't want to be one of them, even if I did have a bag that week with Seve if I wanted it. So I got my mate Dick Draper to caddie for Seve—and I thought I was going to live to regret it when he was leading and looking for all the world as though he was going to win. In the end he finished second to Johnny Miller but it was a great performance, especially his putt on the last in the final round to make sure he tied with Jack Nicklaus. I could see he'd got plenty of guts.

"Even in 1975, when he came to the Open, Roberto recognized how good Seve was. And then before the 1976 Open—just what I wanted to hear after I'd given up his bag!—Roberto said: 'There's Johnny Miller, Jack Nicklaus, Tom Weiskopf and Seve; all the rest of us are here to make up the numbers.' My gut reaction was the same and it didn't take long before Roberto's words came back to me.

"Well, he didn't quite do it that time but I knew it wouldn't be long. I first saw him at the 1975 PGA Championship at Royal St. George's, which he won. There he was lashing away at balls on the practice ground, not holding back on anything, long legs and a big pair of hands. He was standing a long way from the ball, giving himself plenty of room. I saw the name on the bag and looked at him amazed. I asked his age and I was astounded.

"He continued to astound me for the next four years. It's no good me saying they weren't difficult years. Seve can be a very hard taskmaster. I was with him to the end of 1979. I felt I'd served my sentence when we parted company."

It did not take long for Musgrove and Ballesteros to click, with victory in the Dutch Open, and by the time the 1979 season came along, the partnership could boast eight titles. If there was anyone who followed golf and had not been made aware of Ballesteros by his fourth campaign, then they were following the wrong tournaments. However, Ballesteros had shown he could win a major, so to really show he was here to stay he needed to go up that extra rung and claim one. The Open Championship would really place him among the stars as, at 22 years of age, he became the youngest winner of the Claret Jug in latter times.

Ballesteros served notice that he was ready. His build-up to Royal Lytham was ominous as he took the English Classic title at The Belfry the first time it was played, and finished runner-up to Sandy Lyle in the Scandinavian Enterprise Open in Sweden, a tournament he had won the previous year. Seve was bang on form.

"The Belfry was cold and wet for the English Classic. That gave us a taste of what was to come at Lytham. The fairways were far worse than they are now. Say what you like about The Belfry and the Ryder Cup, if it wasn't for the 9th, 10th and 18th holes, it would be as average as I think it looks. The 10th fairway was covered in clover and the ball was uncontrollable. I know Seve's legend about him and the 10th at The Belfry and the plaque there commemorating his shot to the green, but it was almost impossible to get anything out of it that week. You either finished in the back bunker or short, in the water. Seve won with an under-par score somehow.

"I remember one day, on the eighth, there was a little dinghy turned over on the lake and he hooked his tee-shot, hit the boat—and came out on the fairway . . . The Shape of Things to Come!

"We went to Sweden to play the Scandinavian Enterprise Open and he played really well there. But Sandy played just that bit better and Seve had to take second place. Ironic, that, because Seve won an event and Sandy came second in it, just before the 1985 Open.

"There was a week off in between and I hoped Seve would keep his form for Lytham. He was playing and competing really well. He should have been on a real high, but you can never tell with Seve. When he wins he turns up the next week as if nothing has happened. And he used to look as though he didn't have a penny to his name. That's the difference between Seve and others. It's what's always set him apart a bit, I suppose. Winning can destroy a lot of people. The occasion and the competition from the rest of the field never bothered Seve. It's the same with the course he might be playing. It can be the worst layout imaginable, but he'll go into it 100 percent whatever. He never worries about winning or who he plays with, treats everyone exactly the same. They are all fellow competitors and he doesn't bat an eyelid, whoever they may be. He didn't when he was 18 and he wouldn't nowadays, whether they are superstars or if he's never heard of them. He knows they can all play brilliantly or badly and they can all be beaten . . . 'If you can walk with kings and keep the common touch.'

"At Birkdale in 1976, for instance, somebody asked him in the press tent if he was worried about playing with Johnny Miller [the eventual champion and someone right at the top of the golfing tree at that time]. His brother Manuel interpreted for him and he answered for Seve by saying, 'Worried? We could go out now and play and it wouldn't bother me.' He meant it as well.

"I have to laugh every time I think of Seve's early press conferences and how he is now, with his great command of English and his amazing vocabulary. Seve used to be asked long, drawn-out questions that went on and on. Manuel would appear to be explaining to him forever and ever, and then Seve would seem to be replying forever and ever. Then Manuel would answer by saying: 'Yes!'

"For the 1979 Open, Seve appeared to be giving it 101 percent. Roberto waited for him every morning and they practiced together. Roberto offered Seve some sound advice. He told him: 'You have to know what it's like playing these links. When the wind changes, it's as if you have never played the hole before. It can change in its nature so much.'

"I was glad he listened to only Roberto in the end. He was getting too much advice from all quarters, each one of his brothers for a start.

"Although Seve was hitting the ball all over the place in practice, nothing unusual in that, he was all the time figuring out which side of the fairways to miss on a lot of holes, and places where he felt he couldn't go at all. He found loopholes in the rough, if you like. He knew there were certain places you could go and, no matter how far off the mark, have a chance of making the green. There was no fluke to Seve's playing out of the rough in the 1979 Open Championship. He knew what he was doing all right.

"And it wasn't just checking out the rough. He concentrated on bunker play a lot. I'd told him that the best bunker players, people like Player, Charles and Thomson, always won at Lytham, Jacklin as well [there are 365 bunkers at Royal Lytham], so it would be as well to bear that in mind. He said to me, 'I am the best bunker player here.'"

Ballesteros made sure he was going to remain thus. Right up until teeing off for the first round, the Spaniard was tinkering with his bunker play. But it was never going to be Lytham's sand that would provide the problems for Ballesteros. His penchant for going for broke with every drive was a recipe for exciting golf, just what the spectators delighted in watching, for his magical saves and birdies from nowhere made the sort of golf they had come to see. Ballesteros would not let them down. Vicenzo had also advised Ballesteros not to hold back, to play aggressively. His Argentinian mentor sent him off with the immortal phrase: *"Tienes las manos; ahora juega con tu corazon"*—"You have the hands; now play with your heart." Ballesteros would not let his "Uncle Roberto" down, either.

"In the first round we teed off with Ken Brown and Lee Trevino, quite something because of Lee's reputation and his previous Open wins, of course. Seve and Lee got on like a house on fire, but you couldn't understand much of the chatter between them. It was the coldest week imaginable for July in Britain and the so-called summer. In fact, Trevino was so cold he still had his pajamas on underneath his golf gear. In those days Seve hit the ball as hard as he could. It's no wonder he had back problems, even then. He'd stand there and lash at it and then expect to hole every putt.

"He was pretty erratic and certainly didn't hole every putt on the first day and shot a 73. That left him way off the lead. Both of us felt there were better things to come if he could get the driving a bit straighter and he could hole a few putts."

The first-round leader was a real surprise package. Essex-based Scot Bill Longmuir was the man who somehow mastered a wind that had even confounded the great Jack Nicklaus. Indeed, Nicklaus, tongue in cheek, refused to believe not only Longmuir's amazing round of 65, which at one time had the Briton dreaming of the elusive 59 when he went out in just 29 strokes, but that there was such a person. "You guys have made up the name," snorted Nicklaus when told about Longmuir's three-shot lead over the field. The Golden Bear had only managed a 72 to be seven off the pace.

Longmuir's performance was to strike a chord in Ballesteros's mind when the Anglo-Scot again led the first round in an Open the Spaniard went on to win—St. Andrews in 1984. Ballesteros, despite insisting he was not a superstitious golfer, felt there might be some kind of omen in Longmuir's performances, so before the 1985 Open he sought out the Briton to "bond," in the hope that a little range chat might work again for him. If he saw Longmuir's name on the leaderboard again, then there was every chance the Ballesteros name would again be etched on the Claret Jug.

On this occasion, as in 1984, Longmuir faded away. His weekend returns of 77 and then a crushing 82 plummeted him down the field.

An opening round of 68 by Hale Irwin, though, put the reigning U.S. Open champion into an ominous second place, as he too mastered the difficult conditions. Irwin, also the 1974 U.S. Open victor, dreamt of becoming one of the few men to hold the championships either side of the Atlantic in one year. Ballesteros had some catching up to do. It wasn't long before he caught right up, even with his driver refusing to cooperate, as he matched Longmuir's course record of 65.

"Well, he ditched the driver he'd used for the first round. I don't think he'd played with it more than half a dozen times. He seemed to be rotating five or six drivers in the hope that he might suddenly find the magic weapon that would keep him straighter off the tee. In the second round, the driving was not much better, despite going back to one of his old drivers. In fact, I got so fed up with him missing the fairway, I said to him at one stage, 'Why don't you try closing your eyes and hitting it?' But the putts did start to drop. Not until the back nine, though. He came back in 32 [four under par] and was really on a roll when he birdied 11 and 14 and chipped in at 15. I thought, 'If he can birdie 16 now, we're on for a 66,' but the putt lipped out. He birdied 17 and 18 instead. It's a tough finish at Lytham and the wind was howling against us most of the time as well. The birdie on the last was a beauty. He's on a downslope of a grassy bank and he punches a five-iron to just over a yard. Those that said Seve played badly all week ought to remember shots like that.

"The point is, though, no matter how badly people say he played that week and still won, he'd actually got it all worked out. Everybody's going to miss a few fairways. Tom Watson was just as erratic in 1983. That's his game—and he's no mug. Seve was not as lucky as people think he was. It was all well planned."

His magnificent score—even if by now the Americans in particular were beginning to label him "Lucky Ballesteros"—was more to do with his amazing recoveries from all over the course and a short-game which was to become legendary. A few pundits, though, were beginning to realize that Ballesteros's weaving around the Lytham links was not all wayward driving. He was actually budgeting for his errant shots and plotting his way round like a navigator. With Irwin carding a second 68 to capture the lead, Ballesteros's first target had to be the bespectacled American. The two did not exactly see eye to eye, as Musgrove remembers.

"For the last two rounds we played with Hale Irwin, who was a couple of strokes better and leading the tournament at six under. At that time, nobody used to talk much about Hale, and he didn't use to sell himself that well. I felt he was a good bloke, straight up. A lot was said at the time about him and Seve being at loggerheads. Hale was made out to be the bad guy playing against Seve, especially because of one of their clashes in the World Matchplay at Wentworth, but I don't know about the bad guy image. Seve's always been convinced the Americans have got it in for him anyway, but he's said that about the French, the Italians, the Japanese!

"Anyway, if you look at Irwin's final two rounds—75 and 78—they weren't going to beat anybody. Mind you, both Seve and Irwin played badly in the third round. But you're never going to do a good score at Lytham when it feels like three degrees below freezing and there's a gale blowing, are you? Everybody was wrapped up like it was the Arctic out there. You couldn't feel your hands—and that was me. Goodness knows what it was like trying to hit a golf ball and trying to get some feel. And Seve's back was a real pain. The cold really got to it and it troubled him so much that we had to go and find a physiotherapist.

"We started very badly, choosing a one-iron at the second instead of risking a driver. It didn't work because the ball ended up in bush, completely unplayable. There was no place to drop so it was back to the tee and a double-bogey. Things didn't get much better straightaway but Seve rallied a bit before the turn but then let it slip again. They both got round in 75. It was a real struggle but I seem to remember only a couple of players were in the 60s for the third round, so there was really no ground lost at all. The crowd was on Seve's side, good and proper. The gallery was completely behind him, all of them, shouting 'get in,' even when he was going to miss a putt by six feet."

Perhaps the crowd finally got to Irwin. Perhaps Ballesteros got to him. Whatever, the American's hold on the Championship started to slip as soon as the final round began. From being two strokes behind Irwin, Ballesteros took control very early on. Then he had to repel all boarders as a bevy of players jostled for the Auld Claret Jug. There was no holding back off the tee still, however, as Ballesteros stayed true to Roberto de Vicenzo's philosophy.

"It started to look good as soon as we got under way in the final round and Seve was really motoring by the time we stepped on to the third tee. He birdied the first from about 20 feet to be only a stroke behind Hale, and Irwin ran up a double-bogey six on the second. We'd decided on a two-iron at the second, bearing in mind what happened the day before, and made a safe par, so that was that, Seve in the lead. I can remember the scoring vividly because in those days I had to mark all the cards. I remember putting Hale down for the six—then the card blew into the bunker on the second and I had to go chasing after it.

"As well as Seve's good start, he dropped a shot early on. But he also birdied one of the two par-fives, the seventh, and that came along just right because we weren't having it all our own way. It seemed they all started challenging him for it—Isao Aoki, Rodger Davis, Ben Crenshaw and Jack Nicklaus. I was constantly checking the leaderboard. Seve obviously knew what was going on and what was needed. He never flinched. I remember him saying, 'Maybe we don't have to worry about Hale so much now, but there are two or three others we'll have to watch out for.'

"It's a strange thing. You don't usually see the rest of the tournament. You only see your one match, only your two players. Most of the time you have no real idea what's happening anywhere else. You'll see a name come up on the leaderboard, then it might disappear. You think to yourself, 'I wonder what happened to him?' After a while you forget him. Then you hear the crowd roar and a new name comes up on to the leaderboard and you wonder whether he holed a long putt or chipped in. Was the board wrong? It never is, though, at the Open.

"Anyway, Aoki came and went, then Crenshaw came up. Davis came up and I think took over the lead, but then he double-bogeyed the 14th and we were back in front again. We did know that at least. Seve just kept hacking along.

"On the sixth hole he was miles left and we hadn't got a clue which club to hit in because he was in uncharted territory. But he made par somehow and he says to me: 'It is him with the biggest heart who will win.' He meant he'd got the bottle to win.

"I don't know whether that was in his mind at the 13th. A lot of smart people have put the 13th down to luck. They tie it in with how Jack Nicklaus was unfortunate not to win and how the 13th made all the difference. But they tend to forget that on the first day Nicklaus holed in one on the fifth—and Seve hadn't even started his round by then. Then on the second day, Nicklaus put it stone-dead on the fifth, so he's taken just three shots there. Maybe he was unlucky on the last day, but come on . . . You have to think about what's happened every day in an Open Championship. You take your luck as it happens.

"The 13th was certainly a killer hole, though. He'd taken different clubs each day, but never gone for it. It's a short, dog-leg, par-four and the conservative, sensible way is to play an iron and a wedge. The only way to make the green is to miss the bunkers but that means a drive of 300 yards. I remember the wind howling behind us and him saying to me: 'We'll go for it today.' I might have expected him to do so in the previous rounds, but this time? I ask you. Twenty-two years old, leading the Open, six holes to go—and he's going for broke, going for the green!

"Well, he smacked it into the hill very nearly 300 yards but the ball didn't quite make it. It caught the top of the bunker and went in about 60 yards from the flag. He needed to chop down on the ball and chose a wedge. He came out of the bunker with a fantastic shot but the ball screwed off to the right of the green and went down off the mound, instead of falling towards the flag, as he was expecting it to. He was about 12 feet away now and the putt went in for a three. That really got him going, punching the air, he was really fired up. To birdie with a long par-four coming up was a great bonus. He could easily have bogeyed the 13th.

"He three-putted the 14th, so the 13th hole birdie meant even more then. A television crew came past us on its way to the 15th and the guys on board told me that Crenshaw—who was our nearest challenger then—had double-bogeyed the 17th. Seve always wants to know what's going on. If you can tell him what's happening with the other players, he's happy because then he knows what there is to do. Those that aren't winners don't want to know what's happening to anybody else. As soon as they see their names on the leaderboard they worry themselves to death until their name's gone off the board. Then they're all right again. I said to Seve: 'Crenshaw's just double-bogeyed the 17th.' 'Oh,' he says, then smashes the ball off the 15th tee, up over the hill and goes running after it down the other side. His second shot was in the rough on the left, but a long way down. Then he chips stone-dead.

"At the 16th, there's a tractor path between two fairways, where they park the cars. Seve's drive was 60 yards from the front of the green and about 40 yards from the middle of the fairway, in among the parked cars, but he was on the right side. Don't forget all his careful planning, studying the rough beforehand. This meant he was now coming back into the wind. From the fairway, you couldn't stop the ball where the flag had been positioned. If you played it out to the left of the fairway it was down wind and a difficult shot.

"He walked up to the green and found a softish spot to land on. He didn't bother too much where the flag was. He was just interested in where he was going to land the ball and hold it. He paced it back and says to me: 'Where is the ball?' I say: 'Under the car somewhere.' Then they all sorted out where he could drop—on the tractor path, which was, in effect, fairway. He hammers the ball at the green, lands on the bit he wanted to stop on and the ball finishes up 15 or 20 feet from the flag. Then he holes the putt.

"I knew he'd got it then because he was three shots clear. He'd hit exactly the shot he'd wanted to—a high cut to gain maximum distance with the wind and finish on the right. He'd spotted that the rough out there wasn't too bad if he'd gone in it, because it had all been trampled down by the spectators. That was the way to come in. He knew he could get it on the green from there.

"No matter what anybody else says about his drive at the 16th, it was all deliberate and planned.

"On the 17th, the bunkers are on the left, so Seve missed the fairway to the right and hacks over all the trouble up the right, pitches on. The crowd are all shouting 'get in.' They really are all behind him now. It was ten years since Jacklin had won and they'd adopted Seve.

"Then there was a big cheer from the 18th and and we thought it was Nicklaus who'd holed for a birdie. But the board didn't change. We were puzzled. What had happened was that Mark James, who was playing with Nicklaus, had missed the green, shanked his chip right across the green, but then taken a train ride to get the putt for a four. But the noise put Seve on his guard and he putted conservatively on the 17th, well conservatively for him, for a four. In fact, he'd probably have been happy with a five.

"Now we came to the 18th. The only place, really, you haven't to go is right and in the bushes. Seve hit a three-wood and hooked it miles! He was nearly on the first green. He says to me: 'What's over there?' I say: 'I don't know. I've never been over there before.'

"By this time I'm like the ice man and he's still at boiling point. He hacks forward after asking me if it was a five-iron. I'd agreed it was. At that stage I'd have agreed to anything just to get in. It comes up just short of the green, but he can putt it and he says: 'I can take four putts from here and still win.' I say: 'No you can't, because I've got a bet on with one of the caddies that the winning score will be under par. So you need to make four.'

"He whacked it up and got it. I won. Harry Carpenter came up to interview him and asked him about the last putt. Seve said: 'My caddie told me I had to get it!'

"There were no great celebrations after Seve's win, not for him anyway. He wasn't a great partygoer. Me and my mother stayed the night at Seve's place and watched the Open on television. The next morning Seve and all his gang had gone."

1984 ST. ANDREWS

Severiano Ballesteros with Nick de Paul

Severiano Ballesteros	Spain	69 68 70 69 276 (par 72)
Bernhard Langer	Germany	71 68 68 71 278
Tom Watson	USA	71 68 66 73 278
Fred Couples	USA	70 69 74 68 281
Lanny Wadkins	USA	70 69 73 69 281
Greg Norman	Australia	67 74 74 67 282
Nick Faldo	England	69 68 76 69 282
Mark McCumber	USA	74 67 72 70 283
Graham Marsh	Australia	70 74 73 67 284
Sam Torrance	Scotland	74 74 66 70 284
Ronan Rafferty	N. Ireland	74 72 67 71 284
Hugh Baiocchi	S. Africa	72 70 70 72 284
Ian Baker-Finch	Australia	68 66 71 79 284

"As we came off the 17th green, Seve said to me: 'There's going to be a playoff, Nick.' I said: 'Not if we birdie the last there won't be. Make a three and there won't be any need for a playoff, Seve, because the trophy will be yours.' I guess that might have got him thinking positive again. That's exactly what he did. There was no need for a playoff."

The catcher in the rye

A
n earlier sporting career in baseball gave Pennsylvanian Nick de Paul
the sort of quick eye a good caddie needs and the ability to assess a
situation in a flash. It also gave the quiet—and subsequently long-
suffering—American his little hallmark in golf. He became known as the caddie who could catch the players out. De Paul's penchant was to catch his
master's golf balls on the practice range with the same baseball glove he had
used in his former career, fastening on to all shots, from sand-irons to full-
blooded drives, with an unerring eye and a pouch like a major league out-
fielder. His amazing trick used to brighten up practice ranges from Augusta
to St. Andrews, not only for Ballesteros, who never ceased to be amazed at his
bagman's feats, but the goggle-eyed watching gallery who flocked to see the
remarkable warm-up routine.

That routine was perfected in the early 1970s when de Paul forsook the bat
for the bag, his first pro being George Archer, who lived on a farm. Their
practice area was a huge field that was also full of cattle, so de Paul needed to
be alert to save the beasts from damage if Archer's aim did not live up to his
name.

De Paul may have looked like a circus act, but he was no clown. Not only
did he accompany Ballesteros to his dramatic second victory in the Open
Championship with an exhilarating finish at St. Andrews in 1984, de Paul was
also by Ballesteros's side for two successful Ryder Cups, 1985 and 1987, and
carried for ten other tour successes.

Their relationship began in 1981, one year after Ballesteros had won his first Masters and ten years after de Paul had begun his caddying career at the age of 30. After working for Archer for three years, de Paul had looked for pastures new in the shape of Australians Bruce Crampton and Rodney Marsh. When Marsh began to wind down his U.S. Tour events, de Paul jumped at the chance of working for Ballesteros after the Spaniard and his Open-winning companion of 1979, Dave Musgrove, and subsequently another Englishman, Pete Coleman, parted company.

"Seve asked me to do a few tournaments for him in 1981 when he came over to the States and I was pretty thrilled by that. He'd won the 1979 Open and I knew what kind of a player and prospect he was, so it was a great thrill to be asked to work for him. He was a real demanding guy, as everyone knows. But what we caddies liked about him was his determination. We knew he was going to try his hardest over 72 holes, come what may. He had such a lot of natural talent to go with his spirit. Even if you were five behind with five to go with Seve, he still thought he could win. And he very often still did! There's nothing pumps up a caddie more than a guy who thinks like that. Seve gave me plenty of headaches over the years. Seve gave you hell every other hole, it seemed, complaining about everything from golf to life in general, but you have to take the abuse. That way, he's not batting on his own. It's all part of the business of being a caddie."

Despite all the brickbats de Paul had to suffer, there will always be the bouquets of success to remember, the victory at the Home of Golf in 1984 being the American caddie's fondest memory. Many years after their triumph over a Tom Watson at his peak and arch rival Bernhard Langer at St. Andrews, de Paul said: "He's quite a guy. I hope somewhere down the line I'll have the opportunity of carrying the sack again for him."

Ballesteros and de Paul proved an irresistible pairing at St. Andrews. The American caddie had the onlookers at the range transfixed with his catching trick. His master had everyone transfixed on the golf course. De Paul had a premonition his player would win, even though the season leading up to the Open Championship had only been moderate for Ballesteros, and was left kicking himself for not backing his hunch.

However, de Paul could be forgiven for not following up his gut feeling, for Ballesteros had been in despair of his game by the time he went to The Belfry in the week before the Open Championship. While at the Midlands of England course, soon to be the scene of European Ryder Cup triumph, and where one shot in particular—his outrageous gamble at the 10th hole—enhanced the Ballesteros legend, he finally got his swing right. Then, in practice at St. Andrews, he honed it to perfection.

Two other men knew Ballesteros was getting back to his best. His close friend Vicente Fernandez, the Argentinian journalist turned golf pro, and another great acquaintance, Jaime Gonzalez, Brazil's top golfer, oversaw the Ballesteros swing in the days leading up to the Open.

At the Lawrence Batley International, Fernandez noticed Ballesteros was "reverse-pivoting" in his swing. The little Argentinian was sure that was the key to his friend failing to break 70 in any regular tour event in nearly six months.

Fernandez and Gonzalez continued their work with Ballesteros as soon as they got up to St. Andrews. By the time practice was over, Ballesteros had rid himself of his problem, which was effectively "turning too much instead of just transferring my weight." When de Paul joined up with his master, he could sense he was caddying for a new man.

"I should have had a bet on Seve before the Open. I could have got odds of 10–1 and made a fortune. He was getting help from Vicente Fernandez and it seemed to be working. Seve was striking the ball so well at The Belfry in his practice at the Lawrence Batley International the week before the Open that I should have known he was going to do something special. You could have got those good odds because he'd had a poor year until then—by his own high standards. While he didn't score very well at The Belfry, you could see he was just tuning up, going through every type of shot and working on his game. He was thinking about the Open all the time, even though he gave his usual 100 percent to the tournament he was playing that week. It was just that he put that bit extra into practice. His game was coming together.

"I reckoned St. Andrews was a hooker's course as well. All the trouble is on the right. In those days Seve rarely used to lose his drives to the right. It was just made for him, I felt. As it was, I nearly didn't get the chance to make a start with Seve. With being at The Belfry the week before, I had hoped to be travelling with him directly in a private plane after the tournament finished but, with it being only a four-seater, there wasn't enough room for me. There was nothing for it but to take the bus from Birmingham to Dundee. The night I went up, the bus wasn't due to leave until 11 P.M., so I left my luggage at the left-luggage office at the bus station and went for a meal. When I got back—crazy. The office wasn't open again until the next day. I couldn't go without my luggage so I had to get a driver to break into the office for me. It was a good job he did. If I'd had to wait for the office to open the next day I'd have missed the first round at St. Andrews.

"Even with making the right bus, I didn't arrive until 9 A.M. on the morning of the first round. I just had time to walk round the course and refresh my memory. I'd caddied there in 1978, but I needed to get my bearings and also get some feel for the links and the way it was playing. I was worried that everything had been such a rush and that I might not be fully prepared when we teed off, but I need not have worried. Seve was in complete control in the first round. It was as if he was at home at St. Andrews.

"The first thing I noticed when I got there was that the rough was pretty high, higher than I remembered it the last time. And it started to blow just a little when we went out in the afternoon, even if it was a perfect sunny day. Seve hardly put a foot wrong. I can't remember once having to discuss a club or study a line with him. If the others had realized just how totally he was in charge, they would all have been jittery. He was in a great mood, too. His mother and his girlfriend at the time, Carmen, now his wife, of course, were with him for the week, and he seemed totally relaxed. The front nine was an absolute cruise and by the time we got to the 17th he was four-under.

"Seve's never been one to find the Road Hole intimidating, not on the surface anyway. He just feels it's about the most difficult hole in golf. It stopped his momentum every day until the final round. He went for a cut off the tee but it didn't come off that well and he finished up in the heavy stuff. It took a four-iron to try to get there but he didn't make it and stayed in the rough. It was a pretty awful lie still and he only just got over the Road bunker with a real job on to avoid three-putting. To show just how much he was in control, though, he ran his first putt around most of the edge of the bunker down to about six feet and holed the second putt. That was some bogey and it made him just as happy as with his birdies. In fact it felt like a birdie in the finish.

"We just missed out on a birdie on 18 so that meant a 69 instead of the 68, but even though the slightly disappointing end to the day cost him a share of the lead, it didn't change my thinking that he was going to be there at the finish."

Ballesteros has always been a great believer in "destino," his way of explaining why he had lost one tournament but won another. It was, he believed, not through his performances that trophies were won or lost, but through fate. If it were meant to be, then it would be. Certainly, that adage seemed to be

20

the case when he had decided at the last minute to change a flight from Madrid to Santander that year, flying home in the evening after jetting in from the Million Dollar Challenge. The flight he had originally booked on crashed on the runway with all passengers lost.

His performance at Sun City in the same Million Dollar Challenge also came when the Ballesteros form was in a trough. Was St. Andrews going to be another case of the Spaniard somehow overcoming seemingly insurmountable swing problems?

He lay fifth after round one over an arid Old Course as he mastered "Burn" (the Old Course first) to "Tom Morris" (the 18th), rarely bothered by the trials and tribulations of such holes as "Ginger Beer," "Heathery," "Hole O' Cross," "Bobby Jones" or "Cartgate," the traditional names for what, to most players, are formidable tasks.

Only "Road" stumped the maestro. Its imitation railway sheds (soon to be gobbled up by the Old Course Hotel) bordering the course on the right meant a blind drive with 200 yards–plus carry. Waiting to greet any errant drive which did not fall foul of the buildings was the wispy and clinging heathery rough. Waiting to greet any approach that caught up in that tangled mass was the Road Hole bunker, a chasm that would be more at home in the landscape of the Somme. Waiting to greet any approach that was hit too aggressively was the hungry road itself, nestling under the much-peppered wall guarding the confines of the course. The Road Hole appeared as a course architect's folly, not even the best way of making do when the links had run into the town. It had been many an Open aspirant's nemesis. It would, and will, continue to be until some Philistine decides to dig it up and try again. In 1984 it proved to be the watershed for two players in particular, Severiano Ballesteros and Tom Watson.

On Friday, the question on Ballesteros's mind, and on his caddie's, too, was, could they master the Road Hole in the second round? Could "destino" be in the cards again?

The leaderboard was certainly giving off omens. Scotland's Bill Longmuir was one of the three leaders at 67. When Longmuir led at Royal Lytham and St. Anne's in 1979, Ballesteros went on to win. Was this a good omen? Ballesteros, an eclectically superstitious man who would not use a number three ball because he considered the number unlucky and who had lucky last-day colors of blue—dark for Opens, light for Masters—felt it was. Or so he did later when the following year he invited Longmuir for range practice, hoping the Scot would lead again after his tuition and encouragement!

With Longmuir in the lead were Greg Norman and Peter Jacobsen. The trio were a stroke better than Ian Baker-Finch, 23 and playing his first Open. It was to prove a crushing disappointment for the young Australian as his quest for a maiden victory on his début ended with his second shot of the day in the final round. Jacobsen and Longmuir, too, fell away, but Ballesteros remained in contention. His 69 left him two off the lead, sharing fifth place with Tom Kite of America and—to Ballesteros's delight—the man who had helped with his swing, Jaime Gonzalez. If Gonzalez was getting it right, he must know what he was talking about, thought Ballesteros—and bagman de Paul.

"Seve was in a great mood again when we set off for the second round in the morning. After our work on the range [de Paul only just failed in his ultimate goal, a 'grand slam,' that is, to catch every ball Ballesteros hit at him on the range] I was confident his swing was still in great shape as well.

"It was a bit windier than the first round and it gathered force after we got through the front nine. The fairways were dry, bone hard and unpredictable but Seve found very few problems. He was coasting—until we got to the Road Hole again. Seve said to me, 'A par at least this time, Nick.' I hoped so. He deserved a good score. I was hoping for a 66 then we wouldn't be far off the lead that night. Things didn't work out too well again, though, on 17.

"He seemed to have got the drive away okay this time but the wind was coming at us and his ball drifted into the rough again. The wind was really causing problems by the time he hit in a six-iron. It was never a five but the wind caught the shot and knocked the ball down into the Road bunker. Seve did well again to make a five because he needed to knock a four-footer in for only bogey. There was a little bit of chewing out this time, but I think Seve knew he hadn't committed himself as well as he could have for the second shot. A 68 was still a great round."

That left Ballesteros three strokes adrift of the new leader, the remarkably unruffled novice Baker-Finch, who moved to ten under par with a splendid second round of 66. Ballesteros now shared second place with Nick Faldo of England and the now veteran former twice Open Champion Lee Trevino. Longmuir hung on a further stroke adrift.

Ominously for Ballesteros, the player he feared most—if he ever dared allow himself such a thought—was on everyone's shirt tails. The previous year's Open Champion at Royal Birkdale, Tom Watson, was looking to equal Harry Vardon's record six Open Championship titles. He played in the worst of the wind that blew in from the Eden Estuary but lay only a further shot back on five under par with fellow Americans Fred Couples and Lanny Wadkins.

The gauntlet had been thrown down for the Ballesteros–Watson duel. But would everyone be confounded by a player not only new to the Old Course but new to Opens altogether? Baker-Finch gave little sign of relinquishing his lead in the all-important jockeying third round.

Once again, however, the infamous Road Hole took its toll on Ballesteros to hold the Spaniard in check by Saturday night.

"It was another day of unpredictable bounces but Seve handled it perfectly. We picked up three birdies and 14 pars with just one bogey. No prizes for guessing where we had the bogey. The 17th of course. It was a similar story to the day before, into the left rough, and he did tremendously well to drop only one shot. At the time Seve was real angry but he calmed down quickly enough. In fact, I heard he had a joke with the press later, at least I hope it was a joke. I wouldn't have fancied playing the 17th for a fifth time. He told the press conference he was determined to make at least one par at the Road Hole and, if necessary, would come back out on Monday and play it again if he didn't par it on the last day.

"Well, history says he didn't have to come back and play it again, but it cost him another 69 in the third round. It still didn't stop me feeling he was going to win. I just felt he was so determined that he was going to be there or thereabouts at the end. It would probably all depend on how Tom Watson went. But Seve let me know how he felt on more than one occasion that week. He wanted to win at St. Andrews so badly that he wouldn't let anything get in his way."

After Ballesteros's third-round 70 it was that man Watson in his way, and that young man Baker-Finch. Watson's 66 contained just one bogey, seven birdies and ten pars, to share a two-shot lead with Baker-Finch, who carded 71, on 11 under par. Ballesteros shared third place with Germany's Bernhard Langer. They were to be the quartet around which the embroidery of success in the 113th Open Championship was woven.

Watson had had a great stroke of fortune right at the first hole when his approach pitched short of the Swilcan Burn, but then decided against treachery and leaped forward on to the green instead of diving into the brook. A grateful Watson never looked back from there and put himself well on his way to that goal of a sixth Championship. Baker-Finch would not be so lucky at the first in the closing round.

Ballesteros and caddie de Paul, though, had half their minds on their playing partners, Bernhard Langer with caddie Pete Coleman, for the final round. By now Ballesteros and Langer were deadly enemies on the course and even off it they were aloof, a minor feud which reached its zenith in the autumn when Ballesteros beat the German in the World Matchplay. For the moment, Ballesteros looked upon his first task as being to make sure he played better than Langer at the start to gain an early advantage. It did not quite work out as he planned, at least not immediately.

"We woke up to yet another fine day for the final round. I was relieved because I knew Seve would play his best with the sun on his back. When it's windy and cold it does affect him. He'd had back problems for several years. So the weather was good and he looked good, wearing his lucky dark blue color.

"Bernhard Langer got the first blow in by hitting a great shot over the Swilcan Burn at the first hole to only a few inches—about a foot, I guess—and he birdied to go one shot nearer the lead straightaway. We could only make par. Pete Coleman was caddying for Bernhard and Pete had caddied for Seve for a time, so I'm sure he was thinking it was one-up to them. I thought, 'Things are going to be tight this afternoon. Bernhard will give nothing away.' I know Seve was thinking the same.

"But a little matter of a birdie wasn't going to unsettle Seve and he got straight back on the job, and that was to get back at Bernhard, hitting some lovely shots into the green. The putts didn't seem to want to drop, though. We did get a birdie at the fifth and that got that one back at Bernhard. That seemed to put Seve in good spirit. The important thing, though, was that we were closer to the lead.

"Baker-Finch had had an unlucky start by spinning back into the Swilcan Burn at the first and when I checked the leaderboard we were a stroke behind Watson, level with Langer, so there was all to play for now. Seve was really focused. He didn't even let some wiseacre upset him in the crowd on the sixth when he turned to me and sort of groaned that his drive had gone in the bunker. Somebody in the gallery thought it was funny and Seve tore him off one. He didn't let it rattle him, though, and then we found we weren't in the bunker anyway and made par all right.

"I knew a putt would have to drop before long and it came at the eighth, the par-three [178 yards]. Seve hit a great five-iron and left himself an eight-foot putt. He sank it and turned to me with a real glint in his eye and said something like, 'About time. Now let's go.' Within a couple of minutes I saw from the leaderboard that we had at last gone to the top, the first time in the week.

He was relieved to see that one go in because the ten-footers he can usually knock in just would not go in that day. He just couldn't get a putt of any decent length to fall and I felt it was getting to him. He missed a birdie chance on the tenth by three-putting after nearly making the green, for instance, for only par. I tried to help out by looking at the putts but he didn't really need me. What he needed was a bit of luck on the roll.

"We got just the opposite at the 11th, where we dropped a shot and went back to ten-under and off the top of the leaderboard. It's a short hole, 172 yards, and Seve left it short. We both thought an eight-iron would be enough with the wind, but it needed a club more and his ball rolled back off the green. He used the putter and nearly ran it up to the hole, but it stopped on top of the hill and he made a four. I expected some kind of blast but Seve was obviously deeply focused and surprisingly there was no huge inquest over the eight-iron. What made it worse, though, was when we knew that Watson had picked up a shot at the same hole and gone back in front. By then I thought it was going to be tough to beat Tom.

"But, as we played the 13th, I changed my mind and thought it might just be down to Seve and Bernhard, who was still only a stroke behind us. That was because Tom Watson looked to be in big trouble with his drive at the 12th. I looked back and saw that he was. Tom never should have taken a driver at the 12th because there's a lot of trouble near the green, which can be tempting to go for because it's less than 320 yards in length. I think he'd tried to make a certain birdie, but he'd come unstuck. He'd hit into the heavy gorse and I honestly thought he was going to take a seven because he had to take a penalty and his drop was going to be difficult. That would really take the heat off—Tom Watson gone. That would be a huge bonus if we only had to worry about Langer.

"Somehow, though, Tom managed only a bogey five when I had a chance to look at the leaderboard again. I couldn't believe he'd done that. And he got the shot straight back at the 13th. It was a real slugging match now with Watson. He was back in front and it seemed there was not much Seve could do about it. I was still only thinking about winning. I just knew it was going to be tight, but—and I know it's easy to say with hindsight—still felt Seve could do it. He was so wrapped up in what he was doing, so determined to win. There was a kind of aura of it about him and I was definitely carried away with it, I don't mind admitting.

"We stayed with Watson, though, because at last Seve dunked in a long one. It was all of 25 feet at the 14th, the par-five. He played the hole really well, because it's so tight on the right with the wall and path running so close. The putt was a real lift for us both. At last we'd sunk a decent putt. We were level—but it was playing on my nerves. I don't know what it was doing to Seve but he looked cool enough. And he still looked mighty determined.

"My nerves were really jangling when we got to the Road Hole. That was understandable, bearing in mind what had gone on for the three previous days here. Mess up now and we were handing it to Watson, or Langer. Each day we'd driven into the left rough and finished up taking bogey fives. Three fives and they were all great bogey fives. Each one of them could have been double-bogeys and, one of the days, even worse.

"I wasn't absolutely brimming with confidence, but there was nothing wrong with Seve's tee shot this time. It was still about the same distance as the last two rounds so we knew it was a six-iron. He hit it smack on the green this time, no problem. What a cool customer! I can't even remember the length of the putt we needed to make par, I was so relieved to be away from the hole without any damage this time. We'd made our first four of the week there and that was that. Relief. I know that Seve joked about it afterwards, saying he was very happy to par the 17th this time because that meant he didn't have to come back on Monday! Myself, I was quivering with excitement, I don't mind admitting that either. We were up there and a birdie at the last might just be enough. When I thought about it afterwards, the Road Hole was definitely the turning point."

Turning point it was—for Ballesteros and Tom Watson, the only conceivable winners now, with Bernhard Langer spent and on his way to a share of second place. Watson had clinched the previous year's Open with a magnificent approach with his two-iron at the 18th at Royal Birkdale. That very same iron would now cost him his chance of that elusive sixth Championship and, unless he can defy Old Father Time, his place with Harry Vardon in the history books. His caddie Alfie Fyles would never discuss why they chose the two-iron after Watson hit a pinpoint drive over the mock railway sheds. Watson has never said much about the choice, either, only that the aim was to keep the ball low and perhaps there was a mistake in the distance to the flag when the pair weighed up the options.

In the event, Watson's over-clubbing—bearing in mind Ballesteros only a few minutes before had hit in a six-iron after a good drive—produced the inevitable. His ball flew to the wall over the road and his Open chance flew out of the window with a bogey. As he was playing from the shadow of the wall, Ballesteros was hitting the 18th green in two. When Watson stood over his lengthy putt to try to save par, an earth-shaking roar came shuddering down across Grannie Clark's Wynd, over the Swilcan Bridge and down the course to the Road Hole. Watson knew the worst. The putt was missed and within seconds the scoreboard showed the American he was two strokes behind and without an eagle on the last would have to settle for second best this time. Caddie de Paul surged through the peaks of triumph in a dream, but a dream which remains vivid in his memory.

"As we came off the 17th green, Seve said to me: 'There's going to be a playoff, Nick.' I said: 'Not if we birdie the last there won't be. Make a three and there won't be any need for a playoff, Seve, because the trophy will be yours.' I guess that might have got him thinking positive again. That's exactly what he did. There was no need for a playoff. He won the British Open.

"While we were walking on to the 18th green, I looked behind. I'm not sure whether Seve did. I saw Watson in trouble. He'd gone through the green and he looked as though he was playing from right up against the wall. Seve had hit a perfect drive at the last, left-center of fairway. He then only needed a pitching-wedge and he hit it straight at the pin to about 18 feet or so. I thought it was even closer when he hit it because it was covering the flag all the way.

"I'll never forget the last putt as long as I live. It was a right-to-left turn up the hill and he hit it perfectly. It was in all the way—or so I thought. To me it seemed to hang on the right lip for at least two or three seconds before it dropped in. Agonizing. People tell me it wasn't anything like that sort of time, but it was real suspense for me because things go through your mind. 'If it doesn't drop it could be a playoff or if Watson sinks the putt we could still lose.'

"Anyway, it dropped and when it fell there was an almighty roar. Seve was very excited. He was pumping his fists. It must have had an effect on Watson. He had a big putt on 17 anyway, and he didn't make it. There was no way we could lose now. Seve was even more excited when he realized what Watson had done. The celebrations started all over again!

"It was time for me to disappear. I wanted Seve to have the stage to himself. He'd earned it. He'd got to have his moment. He was determined to win at St. Andrews and he'd done it. He's quite a guy."

1985 ROYAL ST. GEORGE'S, SANDWICH

Sandy Lyle with Dave Musgrove

Sandy Lyle	Scotland	68 71 73 70 282 (par 70)
Payne Stewart	USA	70 75 70 68 283
Bernhard Langer	Germany	72 69 68 75 284
David Graham	Australia	68 71 70 75 284
Jose Rivero	Spain	74 72 70 68 284
Christy O'Connor Jr.	Ireland	64 76 72 72 284
Mark O'Meara	USA	70 72 70 72 284
Anders Forsbrand	Sweden	70 76 69 70 285
D.A. Weibring	USA	69 71 74 71 285
Tom Kite	USA	73 73 67 72 285

"It was always going to have to be inch-perfect—to carry the little ridge and then pull up. He could have run a low one up and then he'd have probably gone 15 or 20 feet past. He decided to throw the chip up. It looked as though it was going to be just that bit short and sure enough the ball didn't quite get over the rise. He thought he'd blown it, I know."

Like chalk and cheese

English caddie Dave Musgrove made it two wins in seven years with two different players when he accompanied Scotland's Sandy Lyle to victory over the dunes and hay of Royal St. George's in another tough Open Championship which was again hit by bad weather. It was the first time a Briton had lifted the Claret Jug since Tony Jacklin in 1969.

The way to victory was decidedly different to Musgrove's success with Severiano Ballesteros six years before. But then again, working for Lyle was a whole different ball-game. "Caddying for Sandy was different again to caddying for Seve," says the bluff but kindly Nottinghamshire bagman. "Seve wore himself out week after week. He put so much into it and expected so much every time. Sandy was so much more relaxed. It didn't take so much out of you. He even sometimes brought me a cup of tea before a round! After Seve's win at Lytham I was worn out for a week. You could talk to Sandy about lines for putts and which irons to hit. With Seve you were sticking your neck out telling him how far it was to the green. Of the two Opens, Sandy never looked like winning until the end; Seve had it won a long, long way from the end. The night after Sandy won he was in the marquee that was holding his celebration dinner, with his apron on. He was cleaning up and wishing everyone would go so he could get some peace and quiet. After Seve's 1979 win he vanished on another crusade, went off to beat another army, save another universe."

Musgrove left Ballesteros soon after their win together at Royal Lytham, having "served my sentence." He moved to fellow Englishman Michael King and then another Spaniard, Manuel Calero. Then Musgrove decided to make a play for Lyle's bag when the Scot decided to ply his trade in America. Lyle, the son of a teaching professional, had cut his amateur teeth in Shropshire before becoming one of the quartet of '70s, '80s and '90s European superstars alongside Ballesteros, Nick Faldo and Bernhard Langer. Naturally, with Lyle in the ascendancy in the golfing world, it proved a difficult task to land the bag and Musgrove had to bide his time before the no-nonsense ex-draftsman teamed up with the soon-to-be double-major champion.

Lyle won the European order of merit in 1979 and 1980 and it took two more years before Musgrove and Lyle paired up, but they then became a formidable partnership. Together they won the Open in 1985 and the 1988 U.S. Masters, coupled with numerous European Tour successes. Musgrove helped Lyle to his third order of merit in 1985 and they completed two victorious Ryder Cups together in 1985 and 1987. Musgrove's greatest disappointment with Lyle came in 1989. He was there in the room next to the telephone when Lyle told Tony Jacklin not to pick him for the Ryder Cup match at The Belfry in 1989. That was virtually the end of their success story together, before their parting in 1990.

"Sandy was going to the U.S. Tour and I asked if I could carry for him the next year, but everybody was asking so I didn't get very far. I still went to the States in 1980 to try my luck, though, and caddied for Andy North [the 1978 U.S. Open champion and, ironically, again American Open champion in 1985, the same year Lyle won the Open with Musgrove]. I got plenty of chance to talk to Sandy throughout that year and struck up an acquaintance with him.

"The following year Calero looked like getting in the Ryder Cup side but he had to finish in the top two at Fulford in the Benson and Hedges International. Sandy was already in the European side. I got talking to him again when you could see Calero was struggling to make it and I said I might not have a bag for the Ryder Cup. Sandy then asked me if I'd like to caddie for him for the 1981 Ryder Cup at Walton Heath. He had Jimmy Dickinson caddying for him but Jimmy caddied for Jack Nicklaus in the Ryder Cup.

"Now Jimmy doesn't go abroad, I thought, certainly not to the States, so if I do a good job at Walton Heath, there is every chance I might be able to land the job full-time with Sandy in future. And that's just what happened. I started caddying full-time with Sandy in 1982.

"I had survived my time with Seve, so I reckoned anybody else would be a piece of cake to work with. Walking with Seve down the 18th at Lytham was a fantastic memory and I was keen to do it again, with Sandy this time.

In my first year with Sandy I thought he was going to come up trumps straight away in the Open. He had his chances at Troon in '82 when Tom Watson won. Sandy played with Watson in the third round and Tom played so badly he convinced himself he wouldn't win. A lot of them did fancy their chances that year. Peter Oosterhuis and Nick Faldo could have won it. Bobby Clampett led for a long while and it looked as though they couldn't catch him at one stage. Then there was Nick Price, of course. He only lost it over the last few holes. Sandy definitely can be counted as one of those who could have won the Open in 1982. He played well enough at times to show it was in him anyway and I was very optimistic about Open Championships. I thought, 'Just give us the right breaks and he'll do it, because he's got the bottle for it.' You need plenty of bottle.

"Funnily enough, though, the chance of winning in 1985 was far from my mind at one time. There was definitely no indication a couple of weeks before the Open that Sandy was going to do well. In the Irish Open at Royal Dublin Sandy wanted a four in the first round at the 18th to shoot an 89. He hit his second shot at 18 out of bounds—and walked in. That was our early lead-up to the Open, although the wind was horrendous at Dublin. The ships in Dublin Bay were bobbing about like corks and the last man to equal par on that first day had gone out at 11:30 A.M. We went out at 2 P.M. It was awful.

"The plan was to come home from Ireland, have a week at home, play in the French Open, The Belfry (Lawrence Batley International) and then the Open. But because of his Dublin escapade, Sandy said he'd have to go to the Monte Carlo Open, the next tournament, to try to pick up a bit of form and get his swing right. It meant me having to dash back to England because my passport was at home. I hadn't taken it with me to Ireland because you didn't need it. Also, we'd got no tickets for Nice.

"Well, it proved worth all the kerfuffle because we finished third in Monte Carlo and Sandy was swinging well—chuffed with his game, really. Things were looking up after the gloom of Dublin and I felt much more optimistic about his Open Championship chances. It was on to St. Germain for the French Open straight afterwards and Sandy kept his form. He was second. Seve won and Sandy came second. It was just the opposite before the 1979 Open. I thought, 'Well, that might be a good omen.' And if we weren't going to win, at least I'd got second place wrapped up at the Open! Sandy really finished well at St. Germain. Seve was miles in front but Sandy wouldn't lie down and he birdied the last four or five holes to finish second.

"At The Belfry, Sandy had three good rounds and got into a position to win. But I think he had it on his mind that it wasn't a good idea to win the week before the major. He thought it was a bad omen to do that and he'd already won the tournament twice before. He didn't let it worry him in 1988, though, when he won the Greater Greensboro the week before the Masters!

"Off we went to St. George's. A couple of years before, when Seve won the PGA Championship there, Sandy's chance of winning went when he lost a ball and two shots after hitting a television cameraman. So he felt St. George's owed him something.

"He played his practice rounds with Bernard Gallacher, Neil Coles and Tommy Horton. You couldn't get a more unassuming half-past-eight four-ball. But when you get to know them, and it takes years and years, they're marvelous company. We played with Gallacher and Coles first and then Tommy joined us after he'd qualified. We only had about six people watching us most of the time. We got to the 18th on one of the days and there's Greg Norman and Jack Nicklaus who'd taken five hours to get round. We'd done it in less than four, had a bit of lunch and had more practice during that time.

"Ivor Robson, the starter, was waiting for Sandy every morning that week. He gave him his usual lecture. 'Listen, Sandy. You can do it. You can win this. Don't worry about the others.' Good old Ivor. He was a real Sandy fan. I could see him peering over the crowds every day for Sandy.

"Sandy played really well for the first two days but the greens were very strange and unkind to him. We seemed to agree on the lines and everything looked right when he stood over the ball. Then it seemed to wander off in all directions whenever he made the putt. So he didn't hole a lot of putts. At St. George's, though, nobody's going to shoot anything spectacular. Least ways that's what you normally thought about Sandwich. That was not counting Christy's [Christy O'Connor Junior, the first-round leader] 64. That was an incredible score. Christy talked the ball in that day all right!

"Everybody talks about the five Sandy made on Sunday night at the last hole and they'd never remember that he started the week with a bogey five. He missed less than a two-foot putt at the first in the first round. He still shot 68, driving better than I'd ever seen him drive before. It was with a driver he'd acquired from Eamonn Darcy only a month before. It only worked for him that week, though. A few weeks after the Open it was consigned to the Lyle trophy case at home in memory of its loyal service during the week at Sandwich. That was because after the Open he couldn't hit a fairway with it!

"He felt a 68 was just about the worst he could have got out of the round, driving like that. As well as that miss at the first, he missed five more putts of around the six-foot mark. A 66 would have been a fairer score for the way he played in the first round."

Unsurprisingly, O'Connor Junior, the silvery-haired nephew of "Himself," the legendary Christy O'Connor, led the first day by four strokes. Lyle took up a share of second place with David Graham and two young Britons, Robert Lee and Philip Parkin. The 64 by O'Connor equalled the best opening Open round and bettered the famous 65 shot by Henry Cotton at the same venue exactly half a century earlier.

Leader O'Connor benefited from the better conditions, as did Lyle. For some, St. George's that year meant wind and rain which sapped the very soul from their swings as mother nature went through her card. Those players who teed off in the afternoon of Thursday and then, as the start times reversed the next day, on Friday morning, suffered badly in the squalls and from the luck of the draw. Among those players was Seve Ballesteros with a round of 75, 11 shots off the lead. Caddie Musgrove made a mental note. His theory about Ballesteros and Lyle finishing first and second before an Open and all its portents had been blown away in the wind, a wind which blew so strong it left great swathes of flattened sea-grass hay in St. George's most exposed heavy rough, giving the course an unkempt appearance after two days, like a huge unmade bed on the Kent coast.

Eventually, the inclement weather would take its toll on everyone, refusing to relent. The often horrendous conditions ensured St. George's, which was already considered one of the toughest par-70s in the world, would be the real winner.

"On the second day, the weather was just as bad as it had been in the afternoon the day before, but we missed most of the really bad stuff, didn't get the worst of it. That first hole haunted Sandy, though. This time he took a six on it, double-bogeyed it. He skied his tee-shot and didn't hit enough club for the second, went in the front bunker and couldn't get out. We had our ups and downs throughout the day. Sandy battled well and nearly salvaged his awful start. He could have easily let it all get away from him after a start like that.

"There was a lot of talk about the weather and the luck of the draw and you had to feel sorry for those that got the worst of it both days. But that happens all the time. In the end, it all comes out in the wash. You get lucky draws and unlucky draws. To get a bad draw in an Open, though, is a bit hard to bear.

We heard about players not able to hit the 17th green with a driver and a three-wood in the morning, the wind was so strong. When we played it, Sandy hit a driver and a three-quarter nine-iron to avoid going through the green!

"Sandy shot a 71 and that was about right for the way he played. It gave us a share of the lead because Christy had fallen away. We were on top with David Graham, leading by a stroke from Christy."

Lyle led with the Australian Graham by a stroke from O'Connor, who posted 76 in the second round as he failed to find the touch he had conjured up on the opening day. The American D. A. Weibring (he never used a first name) shared second place with O'Connor but the most significant second round belonged to Germany's (then West Germany's) Bernhard Langer.

Langer had triumphed in the U.S. Masters a few months earlier and the ice-cool Teuton looked in scintillating form, ready to go one better than his finish at St. Andrews the previous year. His 69 at the height of the terrible weather in the second round was, arguably, a better achievement than O'Connor's 64 in the first round. The 69 brought Langer within two strokes of the lead, within two strokes of his Ryder Cup partner Lyle. Caddie Musgrove felt that Langer would be the one to watch now.

"The talk everywhere was about Langer. He was in great form that year. He'd won the Masters and he was probably the best golfer in the world at that time. How he managed to shoot 69 in the weather he got on Friday . . . We spent a lot of time with Bernhard over the years. He was the coolest customer and very, very shrewd, wouldn't leave anything to chance, the sort of bloke you wanted on your side—not having to beat him to win the Open. Pete Coleman, his caddie, and me have been around together a long while as well. I thought Bernhard would be the man to beat. And in the end, I wasn't far out. He made us sweat in the finish.

"It was the weather which caused the problems in the third round most of all, though. We'd had a 3:15 P.M. start and we'd only played one hole when the end of the world looked as though it had come, rain lashing like there was no tomorrow. We had to shelter in the tent of the Royal and Ancient Golf Club (known as the R. and A.), the organizers of the British Open, while it passed over. The waiting around didn't affect Sandy's concentration because he played the first nine really well to level-par. The first let us off this time and he was looking good at the turn, although David Graham was playing that bit better. He was well ahead of us until he dropped shots at the end. Sandy didn't play nearly as well over the back nine and finished up three-over with a 73, lost a fair bit of ground.

"Sandy felt as though he'd played steady enough, though, and he wasn't that disappointed. Bernhard was looking as though he really was going to do it this time. He shot a 68. Him and David Graham were now up on top. We were three strokes behind now. Even with Langer looking dangerous, though, you felt it was anybody's Open. There was Woosy [Ian Woosnam] up there. It was going to be a really interesting last day. I said to Sandy, 'At least you're going to be playing with Christy tomorrow. It's a good draw.'"

Langer and Graham (who managed a 70 despite his late dropped shots as the shadows lengthened) at one under par, led by three strokes over Lyle, O'Connor, Woosnam and American Mark O'Meara. More Americans, Tom Kite and Peter Jacobsen, were a further stroke back.

However, the way St. George's was playing and the way the weather threatened to prevent anyone making a charge through the field it seemed as though three shots would be far too much to recover. When leaders Langer and Graham immediately bogeyed the first in the final round, though, the field closed in. Caddie Musgrove had his eyes on all corners of the course.

"In front of us were Tom Kite and Peter Jacobsen. They were in the thick of it as well. Kite was the danger at the start, but he took a six on the tenth. We could see it. He missed the green on the right and needed a good putt to even make his six. That was him gone, we felt.

"At the 10th Christy says to Sandy: 'If either of us two can come back in two under par, we're going to win this. A couple of birdies and we can do it.' Christy was playing unbelievable golf, but nothing would drop for him. I reckon he could easily have shot 64 again in the last round, but he just could not hole a putt. Christy's words came back when Sandy has putts for birdies on the 12th and 13th holes but misses them both. Nobody was really clear, though, so I hadn't given up hope. I nearly did after the drive on the 14th, though."

At least six players were in with a chance of victory. American Payne Stewart had been the player to mount the last-day assault this time and threatened to beat the odds and come through the field to win. Overnight leaders Langer and Graham were still there. O'Connor could not be discounted. Spaniard Jose Rivero had also surged through to burst into contention. Woosnam had gone but O'Meara still hung on.

It needed something special to separate one player from the rest. Lyle found that something special at the long 14th hole, one of only two par-fives at St. George's. The hole is tight on the right with a boundary fence running all the way up the first part of the hole. On the left lay the hungry dune-grass rough. Up ahead, the stream which splits the fairway about halfway was not given the name "Suez Canal" for nothing. The only way of making the wide, flat expanse of green is to go by way of "Suez." There, Lyle played a shot that has gone down in Open legend, a shot bagman Musgrove will remember all his life.

"It looked as though no one wanted to take the 1985 Open Championship. When Sandy hit his drive into the left-hand rough at 14 I thought that included us. You have to play on the left because out of bounds is so tight right, but Sandy overdid it. He turned his right hand over far too quickly and the ball also got a huge kick left through the lighter rough into the real heavy, so we looked stuffed. It's knee-deep and reedy, horrible stuff. He never even thought about doing anything else but get back into position. All he can do is hack it out sideways and we're still short of the Suez Canal. He's still got 220 yards and the wind's causing problems. I thought, 'Good luck, mate.'

"We decided on the two-iron to get to the green but it's going to have to be pure. He catches it absolutely superbly. In fact, it was a bit long and right and the ball finishes up just off the green about 45 feet away. He ran the putt down and even halfway it looked in. It went in like a good one. Birdie. And it could have been bogey or worse. I'll never forget. Now we were in with a shout."

The birdie took Lyle into a share of the lead, with Stewart set to post a three-over-par target, Langer and Graham his arch rivals on the course and playing behind, knowing just what they had to do to prevail. Now it was time for Lyle to prove that he had the right stuff. He certainly had the power and it needed to be unleashed at the very next hole if he were to leave himself an easier approach. Imbued with the delight at holing the 45-footer on the 14th and marking a birdie down on the card when his Open could have been lost, Lyle mastered the 15th. It brought the big Scot close to tears as he took the lead again for the first time since early in his third round, and it left caddie Musgrove dry-mouthed.

"We knew how tight it was and just what another birdie at this late stage could mean. I think the 15th is the hardest driving hole of the lot into the wind but Sandy hit a fantastic drive, wasn't much short of 300 yards. He outdrove Christy by 50 or 60 yards. In fact, Christy's hitting a wood for his second shot and it was going way to the left. From the right you have a chance but from the left no chance. Christy's caddie is desperately shouting 'fore' because the ball's heading for the gallery. Christy tells him to shut up because he wants it to hit the crowd!

"Sandy then hits a six-iron for his second shot, which shows you how long his drive was. The hole's nearly 470 yards long, normally wind against. He had a choice of two shots and he played the most difficult one—the one that would make his ball stop better and hold. He cut it in perfectly to leave himself a putt of about 12 feet.

"He holed that and he knew he had a chance of winning then. I could see he was filling up and I hoped it wouldn't get to him. We said a few things to each other—I don't even remember what, because it was a bit of a daze for me as well—and he soon got his composure back. He needed to because the pressure was immense then.

"The 16th, a short hole, was playing very long. It was the downfall of David Graham. He went into the right-hand bunker, the one you shouldn't go in. Sandy came up short on the front of the green, but he made his three. He's still in front.

"He thought he'd got too much club on the 17th for his second shot so he didn't hit it all that hard. It was a five-iron. He came up short of the green after being in the left-hand semi-rough with the drive.

"As if we didn't have enough to think about, we also had the performance of the streaker, of course. This naked body just came flying out of the crowd. Peter Jacobsen took great delight in tackling him but we had to wait while it was all going on. Sandy was a bit cheesed off because he couldn't see whether it was a man or a woman running about with no clothes on. What a thing to happen so close to home when you're on for winning the Open!

"Well, Sandy kept his nerve and two putts kept him in front but he was in the rough again at the 18th. After the drive he turned to me and held out his hands. 'Look. They're steady, no shakes,' he said."

It was not the drive which was to cause Lyle agony at the death, however, but his third shot after missing the green and landing his ball in the dreaded "Duncan's Hollow." When he watched aghast as his ball almost returned to his feet after his floated chip left him agonizingly short of surmounting the little summit of the green, Lyle thought he had blown his Open chance. He needed great courage and acumen if he were to surpass the three-over-par target set by Stewart earlier. That could only be done if he took no more than two more shots and reduced the damage on the final hole to only bogey to outdo Stewart.

But even that might have only been good enough for a playoff. Langer and Graham still sat on his shoulder. If the calm German, especially, could turn it on at 17 and 18, then Lyle's number might be up anyway. Conscious of Langer's experience in winning at Augusta in the April, Lyle feared for his chances now. As if in supplication at the altar of St. George's, the Scot sank to his knees, his face buried in the hollow and his visor, wrenched from his head, slammed into the quilt of rough which had betrayed him.

Lyle had to regroup, thought his caddie. The Scot did so admirably and forever cast out the doubt that he might not have the courage to win a major. Musgrove has the final moments etched forever in his memory.

"This time he was in the right-hand rough, just the semi-rough, but an awkward shot because we've got to go over one of the St. George's 'hog's-backs' [ridges] on the way in. It was so tough to keep the ball on the fairway. Over the back of the 18th hole is out of bounds, so you don't want to over-hit. You don't want to go in the bunker on the right short of the green, either, where Graham finished up.

"So Sandy decided to play it left-to-right. He hit what looked to be a tremendous shot and the wind should have done the business for him and pushed it back left-to-right, but it didn't. He was coming out of the rough and the ball was flying too hard. It hit the green and finished down in the hollow with the flag just over a little rise. It was always going to have to be inch-perfect— to carry the little ridge and then pull up. He could have run a low one up and then he'd have probably gone 15 or 20 feet past. He decided to throw the chip up. It looked as though it was going to be just that bit short, and sure enough the ball didn't quite get over the rise. He thought he'd blown it, I know.

"You have to give it to him—he had enough about him to get it right the second time. It left him about a three-footer and he made it. There must have been so much pressure on him at that point. In the end it was a great five, but Sandy looked terrible. He really feared the worst. But he needn't have done. Langer and Graham had taken the heat off with bogeys and they needed to birdie the last to get into a playoff with him. It's history that they didn't make it. Graham went into the bunker and Langer went through the green. He nearly chipped in, though, and that gave us a few trembles.

"A lot went through my mind while we were waiting for Langer and Graham to finish off. I knew that if Sandy won it gave him exemptions in the States the next year; the U.S. Masters, Tournament of Champions, World Series, all those. It won't be just this week when it all means so much to both of us, I thought, it's the doors it opens. It could mean the U.S. Tour and an attractive career for me as well as him. It was a fantastic feeling for me when he held up the Jug.

"The first thing Sandy said when we met up again after the prizegiving ceremony was, 'Come back to the house.' He had press conferences to do first. I got two pints of beer. I was thinking, 'I bet nobody has thought of giving him a beer.' I carried the pints past security guards, R. and A. officials. It was like Fort Knox. But I got him his beer in the press conference.

"After all the formalities were over, I followed Sandy back to his home in my car. I was supposed to be going back to my home but I finished up driving to Lyle Towers with his clubs—and the Open trophy, the Claret Jug would you believe!

"Sandy had to play in the PGA Benevolent Society pro–am the next day at Sunningdale. It was the best thing that could have happened to him. He was out of the way of everybody. There were only about six spectators. After Sandwich, it was just as if you'd gone deaf! There was no spectator noise. He played reasonably well, made four or five birdies, and we headed back to his home. By the time we got back, there was a marquee in the garden. His wife had invited the press and a load of friends, such as Faldo, Gallacher, Horton, Queenie (Michael King), and Neil Coles. Queenie made a speech, of course. He said, 'We've all come today because Sandy Lyle won a competition.' Then, unlike Queenie, he got lost for words.

"Winning the Open gave Sandy inspiration. It gave him confidence to win the Masters later on, knowing he was a world-class player. Soon after St. George's he shot a 65 and 64 in the Benson and Hedges International and won it. Then he came second after losing a playoff, for the Glasgow Open.

"It was a lot different after Seve won his first Open. The next time he played after the Open was also the Benson and Hedges, at St. Mellion. He played the worst he'd played for ages and shot a 79. Winning the Open just seemed to give Seve more pressure to win."

1986 TURNBERRY

Greg Norman with Pete Bender

Greg Norman	Australia	74 63 74 69 280 (par 70)
Gordon J. Brand	England	71 68 75 71 285
Bernhard Langer	Germany	72 70 76 68 286
Ian Woosnam	Wales	70 74 70 72 286
Nick Faldo	England	71 70 76 70 287
Severiano Ballesteros	Spain	76 75 73 64 288
Gary Koch	USA	73 72 72 71 288
Fuzzy Zoeller	USA	75 73 72 69 289
Brian Marchbank	Scotland	78 70 72 69 289
Tommy Nakajima	Japan	74 67 71 77 289

"I said: 'Greg, you're playing too fast. You're real nervous and you need to slow down a little.' I don't know whether I got through. He's still walking kind of fast, so I grabbed his sweater from the back and pulled on it to slow him down. I said: 'Whoa! Walk my pace. Let's talk.' He said: 'Pete. You're absolutely right. Why try and pressurize myself into losing it? Let's have fun.'"

Choker? Who's a choker?

G reg Norman had not earned the sobriquet "Great White Shark" because of his sun-bleached hair, nor his magnificent set of molars. It was not because he came from the land of the formidable denizens of the deep. Norman hunted trophies like a shark and preyed on tournaments around the world. He did it very successfully, too. But the really big prize had eluded him ever since he earned his nickname in 1981, when the player who told the world he liked shark fishing in the Great Barrier Reef led the Masters after two rounds. Major honors had been denied him devastatingly in 1986 by the time he came to a wild and woolly Turnberry for the Open Championship.

The Great White, at 31 years of age, was at a zenith in his graph of success in 1986—in fact he led all four majors going into the final round that year—but his graph of luck and misery in the majors thrice slumped to a nadir that year. The one exception came at the Ailsa course hard by the Firth of Clyde.

Norman had allowed the U.S. Masters title to slip from his grasp right at the very last hole, which he bogeyed, pushing his approach into the gallery to lose by a stroke to Jack Nicklaus. At the U.S. Open he should have won after leading by three strokes with only six holes to go of the third round. At the end of that third round, his concentration apparently broken by the reaction of the crowd who wanted an American champion, he took only a one-stroke lead into the final round. The slender lead soon evaporated and Norman finished a distant 12th behind winner Ray Floyd. Then, in the U.S.

PGA Championship, Norman was to be defeated by the first of two heart-sinking, sickening chip-ins, which denied him two major title chances in less than nine months. This time it was Bob Tway holing out from a bunker to steal Norman's major prize at Inverness. It would happen again the following year when Larry Mize was the culprit at Augusta.

While the Australian was pitied for the way lady luck seemed to turn her back on him, by the time he came to Turnberry in 1986 the snipers were calling him a "choker" when it came to the major championships.

After the crushing disappointments of Augusta and Shinnecock Hills, Norman was desperate to prove his critics wrong. His caddie during those two major misfortunes was an American, Pete Bender. Bender was equally desperate for success. He believed, with the right application, Norman could prove that he was not only the best player in the world but too good to be a choker. It would not be through lack of inspiration or experience from the caddie if Norman were to let this major chance slip by.

Experience was something of which Bender had plenty. By the time he and Norman strode out to take on the wild Ailsa links, Bender had been caddying for 18 years, some of that time carrying the bag for arguably the greatest player of all time, Jack Nicklaus. He had tasted the bitter tang of defeat at the death and he wanted no more of that—for himself but mostly for the man with the crunching swing and the deadly irons.

Bender picked up his first bag at the tender age of 18. Born and raised in Santa Cruz, California, he lived near Monterey, where the Bing Crosby tournament was held and it was there where he began a long-serving caddying career.

"When I got out of high school I wanted to be a caddie, so I picked up bags at my local club. A lot of members told me I was very good—I could pull clubs well and read greens—so I should try going to the Bing Crosby to work for a pro in the tournament. I did. In the 1968 Bing Crosby I carried Frank Beard's bag. We got on real well and I had a lot of fun that week. The following week the U.S. Tour moved to Los Angeles for the L.A. Open and Frank asked me to caddie for him there. That was how I got started.

"After nine or ten tournaments with Frank I moved on and caddied for Tom Shaw for three years, from 1969 to 1971. I felt I was working my way up the ladder and my next player was Jerry Heard, who was a real good player in the 1970s. I was with Jerry for four years, from 1972 to 1975, and I learned a lot from him. For instance, we didn't have yardage books when I started with

Jerry and with him I learned how to use them. In 1975 I left Jerry, and not long after, joined up with Lanny Wadkins, whom I worked for from 1976 to 1980, when I was ready to move on again.

"I couldn't move much higher then because I got the opportunity to work for Jack Nicklaus. I was with Jack for nearly two years and during that time I first met Greg Norman. I had my greatest thrill up to that time, working for Jack in the 1983 Masters. It was really exciting as Jack finished sixth, shooting a 67 on the last day. That was the highlight of my career up to then.

"We played practice rounds with Greg and for some reason I got talking and joking with him a lot. We got on good together. Suddenly, Jack was playing less and less on the tour, and so Greg asked me if I'd be interested in working for him. I said I'd have to think about it. I was playing hard to get, you see. Well, I did think about it—for about an hour! I called Greg up to say 'yes' and he asked me how would I like to start work for him at Muirfield Village in the Memorial the following year? Even though the Memorial is Jack's own tournament, I decided to quit Jack after the last event of 1983, the Chrysler Invitational, and start fresh with Greg the next year.

"At first it looked as though I'd made a big mistake. Jack won his tournament at Muirfield Village and we missed the cut. Afterwards we flew back to Greg's house and we spent the next few days working really hard. Then we went back out for the next tournament, the Kemper Open, which we won. After that we never missed a cut together. We really did work well as a team.

"The big year was 1986, though. We led all four majors and won the Kemper Open again, as well as the Las Vegas Invitational. The way Greg played that year, he could have done the slam [the elusive grand slam of golf, winning all four majors in one year, a feat not yet achieved by anyone].

"The way Greg played in 1986 it seemed everything would come his way. But he let the Masters slip out of his hand at the finish. He gave it just a little too much right hand playing the four-iron into the last, looking for birdie when he could have at least had a chance for a playoff with Jack if he'd parred. The doubts must have crept in even then. At the U.S. Open at Shinnecock Hills, he played the best I ever saw him play, even better than the British Open that year. We played our main U.S. Open practice round with Jack Nicklaus and after it Jack shook his head and said, 'I've never seen a guy play so good. If Greg doesn't win this tournament, then there's something wrong.' Greg was driving superbly, hitting good irons, chipping well, and his putting was great. I didn't think we could go wrong.

"In fact, everything did go according to plan, until the third day—when the crowd got to him. They were pulling for the other guy and he was definitely put off by it all in the end. He'd looked as though he was going to cruise it after 12 holes and then everything got on top of him. The rest's history. He just disappeared at Shinnecock Hills. Greg was real hurt by what happened at the U.S. Open. But now he more than ever wanted to win the British Open.

"When we got to Turnberry we found the rough was going to be a major influence on the tournament. And especially a major influence if the wind got up or the weather turned sour. The fairways were so narrow and the rough was so high. It was really thick even just off the fairway and a lot of players complained about it. We just listened and said nothing to them. Greg and I liked it that way. I believed he was the best driver in the game and I didn't think there was a guy on the U.S. Tour who could drive as far and as straight as he could. I felt the same way about the week. We knew the course would be in his favor if he drove well, drove anything like he had done all year so far. If he drove well then I was in no doubt he would play well all round. It would just increase his confidence to know that other players might be struggling with keeping the ball in play out there.

"We tried to be real loose before the tournament. I didn't want him to be too uptight or tense, so I kept the jokes coming. As well as the joking, we just went out to enjoy the practice. I'd throw a ball in the bunker and then bet him a Coke he couldn't get up and down. I tried to keep his mind off the real tension before a major championship gets started. We worked the same routine each day for our practice rounds—some relaxed play on the course, some hard work on the range before and after the rounds. We played a practice round with Jack Nicklaus again and Jack said pretty well much the same as he did at Shinnecock Hills: that if Greg didn't win then it wouldn't be because of the way he was playing. His only problem might be his confidence. That's what Jack felt.

"I wanted a good start and a bit of luck with the weather. I prayed the weather would be on our side. It had started to turn really nasty on the Wednesday night, so it was fingers crossed when I woke up on Thursday morning. Sometimes you can draw the wrong straw with the weather and then you're finished. Well, we didn't draw the short straw, but not the long one either. It was cold and windy and the course was playing long and tricky. It was tough to make pars and every time we did we were tickled to death.

Birdies were definitely hard to come by. We were quite happy to take a 74, four over par. That put us in about 15th to 20th place, quite a handy start."

The gray day and cold wind put an end to anyone bringing Turnberry to its knees. Only the little Welsh pocket-battleship Ian Woosnam mastered the par of 70 to lead by a stroke. To do that, Woosnam needed to come home in 31, a feat thought impossible by most of the field. Whereas wedges had been the approach club at many practice holes, players sometimes now needed one-irons. England's Nick Faldo, Gordon Brand and Robert Lee, along with the Swede Anders Forsbrand, proved that they were used to such adverse conditions.

Many were not, although it was strange that the previous year's champion at St. George's in similar conditions, Scot Sandy Lyle, could not cope with the dune-grass rough and left himself much to do to stay in the tournament. American Craig Stadler shot an 82 and then pulled out, claiming that his injured wrist had been incurred while trying to extricate himself from the clinging, damp hay. Another one to all but fall by the wayside was the man who eventually gave the American gallery its wish at Shinnecock Hills a few weeks beforehand, Ray Floyd. He shot a 78. Even Norman had—perhaps jokingly, though with a measure of intent—contemplated suing the Royal and Ancient Golf Club if he were to injure himself. Playing partner Jack Nicklaus had a poor start, so it left him a mountain to climb if he were to have any hopes of adding to his remarkable triumph at Augusta at the age of 46.

Norman was a sleeping giant, however, felt caddie Bender. The giant awoke and inflicted a body blow on the Ailsa course.

"Greg's 63 on the second day was a fantastic round, but really he let it get away from him. He three-putted the last hole for bogey. He had a long putt for birdie and a 61. How he wanted that 61.

"The round started off pretty slowly and we were even after five or six holes. It was around the middle of the round when Greg started to string the birdies—and an eagle—together. He suddenly picked up shots before we turned for home. There was no holding him then. It really started to light up at the 10th and 11th when he made a couple more birdies. A big crowd had started to gather as Greg got on a real head of steam. I was pumping him up, and he responded. I said: 'Come on. There are a lot of birdies left out here still,' and he just kept making them. The crowd were really worked up by it.

"I try to caddie aggressively, like Greg plays. I wanted him to shoot for every flag. But I didn't have to push too hard that day. Everything was going his way, or so it seemed. It was all automatic. Once Greg got going, I didn't have to say too much.

"When he nearly knocked the flag out at the 14th the gallery was going wild. Then we had an eagle chance at the 17th. He really torched a five-iron to only about 12 feet and we were both thinking, 'Hole this one and birdie the last and it's a 60.' Greg was really excited and the crowd went totally hushed for the putt. But he just missed it, so we now needed to pick up one more shot on the last and it was a 61.

"It was a shame we finished as we did. Greg hit a good drive and then put a three-iron on to the green, knocked it on to about 35 feet. I tended the flag for him and I could tell he wanted the putt so badly. He said to me, 'Pete, I want this one. I want a 61.' But it wasn't to be. He ran the putt by about three feet and then pulled the one coming back wide. He was real upset at that. So was I. It would be tough to say he was disappointed with a round of 63 but there's no doubt the last hole left a bitter taste in his mouth.

"Now he had a big lead, though, and we were really in business, leading in a major for the third time out of three, not bad. We'd played with Ray Floyd—that was a real ironic draw, wasn't it?—and Raymond shot a 67 in the second round after starting with a 78. Nobody knew just how good Ray's round was because they were all talking about Greg's 63."

Shooting seven under par at Turnberry is always going to cause some leapfrogging up the leaderboard and Norman's magnificent 63 hauled him from a share of 16th place into a two-stroke lead at three under par over Gordon Brand. Nick Faldo, whose time would soon come, shared third place a further two strokes back, with Japanese Tommy Nakajima, the man who had once seen his Open hopes sink in the sand of the Road Hole at St. Andrews.

Norman might have been dejected at missing out on the 61, disappointed as well at missing the Open Championship record 62. But he was elated at giving himself a chance of putting right the mixture of bad luck, bad focus and inadequacy that had cost him the two previous major titles.

However, any thoughts of getting anywhere near his magical 63 when he woke up on Saturday morning blew away on the wings of a stormy day in Scotland. Only the sentinel lighthouse watching over "Bruce's Castle," the ninth, and "Dinna Fouter," the tenth, refused to bend in the gale. Even the tall and muscular Greg Norman had to stoop to fight the ferocious squalls.

His lightweight caddie Bender nearly got blown away altogether. Norman's lead, however, budged but did not crumble.

"We'd had some pretty awful weather already, but the third round was the worst of the week. The day was brutal. I remember trying to hold the umbrella against the rain and the wind was gusting over 40 miles an hour. If I hadn't had the golf bag on my shoulder I would have taken off with the umbrella!

"Greg shot another 74 and we were as glad of it as in the first round. We struggled coming in, making four or five bogeys. But they were good bogeys. Greg had said before the tournament that the secret of winning might be in not taking worse than bogey. That definitely applied to the third round. Some of the holes even we couldn't reach in two on the par-fours. They were playing so hard and long. We just kept our heads down and tried not to make mistakes.

"The most exciting thing about the day was getting off the 18th green! Neither of us could wait to get the round over. We were so cold and miserable. Tommy Nakajima wasn't either of those things. He'd come on strong towards the end of his round to pull up to within a shot of us. It was some 71 Tommy scored that day."

Nakajima's mastery of the wind and wet, unusual for a Japanese, whose fellow countrymen normally loathe the unpredictable British climate, brought him alongside Norman for the final round. To soar only one stroke behind Norman, Nakajima even overcame a double-bogey at the 16th which forced him off the top of the leaderboard as he scrambled like a fighter pilot to protect his score.

The man from Japan was Norman's chief threat, with Gordon Brand and Ian Woosnam three adrift of the lead. That appeared to be it for potential winners because Nick Faldo, Gary Koch of the U.S. and Spain's Jose Maria Canizares lay six strokes off the pace.

Norman was on the brink and he knew it. Later he was to say he deliberately kept himself nervous for the final round so that he would stay in touch with reality instead of allowing himself to drift mentally, as he felt he might have done during the U.S. Open. Caddie Bender might have to combat those nerves, however.

Also, Norman was still seeking perfection in his quest to be the first Australian Open Championship winner since Peter Thomson in 1965. He had been given a tip by his practice partner Jack Nicklaus the day before, all about getting the grip right, especially in such bad weather. Norman discussed such matters at length with Bender on the range before the fateful last day. He was determined not to lose his grip this time on a major.

For the Great White Shark and his American caddie, a little local advice became the logic of the final round. The Scottish king Robert the Bruce is said to have built a castle at Turnberry, near to the ninth hole which is named after his edifice. Of course, it is Robert the Bruce who watched the spider in the cave before regrouping to defeat the English at Bannockburn, thus coining the immortal lines, which could have been written for Greg Norman: "If at first you don't succeed, try, try again."

"There was a lot of pressure on Greg for the fourth round, and that made his eventual win even greater. He so much wanted the major and he wasn't going to be short on trying, even if it still didn't come off for him. We talked a lot about trying your best and if it wasn't good enough then there wasn't anything he could do about it. You do have to be careful not to try too hard, though.

"The press and the experts had put the monkey on his back that he couldn't win a major, that he seemed to be 'choking on Sundays.' But we got some of that pressure off right away, and I think it proved very important as far as the way the tournament went from then on.

"We had a one-shot lead and for the par-four start we hit a one-iron off the tee because it's a real tight hole. You just have to lay it up. Well, we knocked it on and made four but poor old Tommy had a bit of a disaster. He somehow three-putted from only three feet and made double-bogey straight off at the first hole. That helped us a lot. It opened up a three-shot lead going into the second and that gave us a nice little cushion to work with.

"When we came to the third hole I thought we were going to need some of that cushion. It's a long par-four and Greg hit his second shot into a greenside bunker, some way from the hole still. Tommy was on the green. It was a long, long bunker shot that Greg had to play, and into the wind, but he hit it great. It took one bounce and rolled right into the hole for birdie. Tommy looked at us and shook his head. He couldn't believe it. At that moment I think he felt that it was Greg's day.

"This opened up a four-shot lead, but at the fifth Greg hit a bad second shot and chipped up, missed the putt and dropped back to only three ahead.

It worried him a bit, but it wasn't here that he looked nervous and gave me reason to be concerned. That came at the seventh tee, on the par-five.

"He hit a low, snap duck-hook off the tee, which I have seldom ever seen him do. Right then, I knew something was wrong. With having all those years' experience I know when a player is nervous or choking, whatever people want to call it. His ball had gone into deep rough and I noticed he was walking toward it much faster than usual. And he was talking to me much faster. I said to myself, 'Oh boy. It's getting to him. He's feeling the pressure.'

"Anyway, we've been a bit lucky. Although our ball is in high rough—and I mean high because it's up to Greg's knees—we've caught a good lie. So he can hit a pitching-wedge back on to the fairway. He knocked it on to the fairway, hit his third shot on to the green and then two-putted for par.

"As we were walking to the next hole I tried to think of the right things to say to him, so I said, 'Greg. Do me a favor. You're playing too fast right now. You're real nervous and you need to slow down a little. You're the best player here and you'll win this golf tournament, but you've got to take your time and enjoy it. Don't rush it. Don't be nervous. I'm here to help you.'

"I don't know whether I got through. He started walking away and he's still walking kind of fast, so I grabbed his sweater from the back and pulled on it to slow him down. I said: 'Whoa. Slow up and walk my pace. Let's have fun. Let's talk and let's just have fun.' I changed the subject and thought of a joke. He started to laugh and joked back. He said: 'Pete, you're absolutely right. I've got this won. Why try and pressurize myself into losing it? Let's have fun.' He seemed relaxed again, and I told him, 'Right. Now hit a good shot and just relax.' He did just that.

"At the next hole, the eighth, another long par-four, he hit a four-iron second shot about eight feet from the hole. It was a great shot. He made birdie to open up a four-shot lead, according to the leaderboard. I looked at him and winked. He looked over and winked back. I knew from there on in he was going to win. He'd settled down.

"The tee-shot at the 14th was the only one to give me concern from then on in, and in the finish it was the hole everyone will probably remember as the one which finally sealed Greg's win. He drove on the right and into the rough, but he again caught a good lie. I think I said it was a six-iron but maybe we chose a seven. I gave him the yardage and he hit his shot right at the flag. It was perfect. It took one bounce, hit the flagstick and dropped about three feet from the hole. I remember walking up the fairway to him and saying to him, 'You're not that good!' He looked at me and hit me on the shoulder. I said, 'Were you aiming at that flag?' He said, 'Of course I was.'

"Whether he was or wasn't it was great to have a shot like that at that point. Everyone will remember how good Greg's golf was that week when they think about a shot like that. He made the putt to open up a five-shot lead.

"At the 15th he knocked it on to the green comfortably but we had a long wait because poor old Tommy was in trouble again. He'd hit his ball into the creek and he had to take a drop. We sat on the grass, in fact I think we even stretched out, near the green. Greg said, even then, 'Pete I'm still nervous.' But this time I think he meant excited-nervous because I think he knew he was going to win his first major at last.

"When we got to the 17th, the last par-five, he hit his third shot about three feet behind the pin, but he turned to me and said: 'You know, Pete, I'm so damned nervous I can't see the line to the hole. You'd better tell me where to hit it and how hard.' I said: 'No problem.' He knew he had the tournament won but he was so high he couldn't line up a three-foot putt! When it was his turn to putt I told him: 'Inside right lip and soft. On the toe.' When you hit a putt on the toe of the putter it kills it. It doesn't go very far normally because you can't really hit it very hard. Greg said: 'Okay,' and then stood over his putt. He was hardly able to hold the putter. He knocked it three feet past! So I said, 'Knock it back into the heart of the hole.' He did. Another small crisis was over.

"We went to the last. He wanted to hit a driver off the tee but I said: 'No, no, no. You don't need to hit a driver. Hit a one-iron short of the bunker, then we can probably hit a four-iron in. Let's not do anything silly like knocking it out of bounds.' So he said, 'Okay,' took a one-iron, left it short of the bunker then knocks his four-iron second on to the green. That's the last I see of Greg Norman for some time.

"The crowd really closed in on us. It was pretty hectic—and scary. I got bowled over twice and lost sight of Greg completely. When I finally got back alongside him at the green he was really excited. I was really happy for him because now he'd answered his critics, answered their questions: could he win a major? Also, he'd silenced all the doubters. He wasn't a choker. He two-putted to win by five with a 69. Nobody was really in sight of him at the finish. He left them for dead. We hugged and I told him how proud I was. Then he had to check out his card and his score and he was gone.

"He threw a small private party at the Turnberry Hotel and he invited me. He was in seventh heaven, so excited. I stayed about half an hour. I felt I really shouldn't be there. I was only the caddie. So I sneaked out of the party.

"Greg went out on the course with Laura [his wife] about eleven o'clock that night and sat on the bleachers [grandstand steps] on the 18th with a bottle of champagne, while he went over his round again. He's such a nice guy. Would you believe he took the Claret Jug to a New York jewelers and had an exact copy made up just for me?"

1987 MUIRFIELD

Nick Faldo with Andy Prodger

Nick Faldo	England	68 69 71 71 279 (par 71)
Paul Azinger	USA	68 68 71 73 280
Rodger Davis	Australia	64 73 74 69 280
Ben Crenshaw	USA	73 68 72 68 281
Payne Stewart	USA	71 66 72 72 281
David Frost	South Africa	70 68 70 74 282
Tom Watson	USA	69 69 71 74 283
Nick Price	Zimbabwe	68 71 72 73 284
Craig Stadler	USA	69 69 71 75 284
Ian Woosnam	Wales	71 69 72 72 284

"Next week at the Open, Nick was swinging really good. His whole game looked bristling with confidence. He said to me: 'I just feel it's all coming right just at the right time. I feel that something's going to happen this week.' There were definite signs that something was in the wind."

Par will do nicely, thank you

Andy Prodger may have often looked at his former boss Nick Faldo and not only seen his own alter ego but the golf champion he always really wanted to be, rather than someone carrying a bag for one. The unassuming but gregarious bagman's two major triumphs with the patrician, reticent Faldo, the dogged maiden Open victory at Muirfield in 1987 and the dramatic, nerve-fraying playoff success in the 1989 U.S. Masters, have, at least, provided some golfing fulfillment for the tough little Englishman.

Prodger was a golf professional himself and had aspirations to achieve just the sort of success that Faldo accomplished while the pair were together. He worked for the Ryder Cup brothers Bernard and Geoff Hunt as an assistant at the Hartsbourne club in Hertfordshire and practiced with other Ryder Cup stalwarts such as Peter Dawson and John Garner in the 1970s.

In 1973 Prodger decided to try his hand at qualifying for the Open Championship at Troon. It was on the Scottish coast that Prodger's playing ambition suffered its first major blow. After playing in the first qualifying round he never got to hit a ball in the second. On his way to the course he was injured in a car accident—with his caddie—and never made it to the tee. Other disappointments would follow before he decided to change ranks, pick up the bag and hang up the professional clubs. Prodger found he was far better at caddying than he could ever have been at playing.

His caddying career began in 1980 and he soon found success by teaming up with Faldo for the first of two periods. They picked up two significant titles together, the 1980 and 1981 European PGA Championships. Their relationship came to an end in 1982 but Prodger carried on sharing victories with his players in the four-year split, among them Craig Stadler and Tom Purtzer, top Americans, and in a World Cup with England's Howard Clark, the individual title of 1985. He also did part-time duties for Gary Player and Bernhard Langer.

It was the second term, from 1986 to 1989 which proved so successful for Prodger and Faldo, however, as they marched to victories in two majors, won the World Matchplay and paired up for two Ryder Cups.

Diminutive Prodger took the bag as Faldo took on the mantle of Britain's golfing hero. That hero status was founded at Muirfield, the home of the Honourable Company of Edinburgh Golfers, the club that founded the original Rules of Golf in 1744. A fitting place for the best British golfer of the modern era to begin his major-winning feats.

"When I first started playing in tournaments I was playing well but nothing would go right for me. Tournament after tournament I'd miss the cut by one or two shots each week. I'd had enough in the end. It made my mind up for me. I was never going to be good enough to make the grade as a touring professional, which had been my great ambition from the age of 15 when I first got a job on a driving range.

"It was a really low part of my life. Around 1978 I quit my job with the Hunts at Hartsbourne and then started a period of my life I really try to blank out. I tried everything—engineering, factory work—but what I needed was a fresh-air life. I was never an indoor bird. So I tried window cleaning. That didn't work out either, even though I was at least outside. I still had the golf bug.

"Then in 1980 I got chatting to a chap called Stan Fancourt, ironically the caddie who was with me when I had my car accident in 1973 trying to qualify for the Open at Troon. They used to call him 'Stan the Man' at Hartsbourne, where he used to do a bit of spare-time caddying.

"Stan persuaded me to play truant from my job—which was so boring I can't even remember what it was at that time now—and take a fortnight's holiday with him in Italy where he was going to caddie for Craig De Foy. Craig had played for Wales in World Cups and he was a really good pro, so that impressed me.

"It took two days for us to get to Rome where the tournament was being played and, of course, I hadn't got a bag. I was hoping for somebody as impressive as Craig De Foy but seeing as I was just there on the off chance I knew that would be a bit of a long shot. I did, at least, know a couple of the players out there because I'd caddied for Roger Fidler in the 1977 Open while I was still an assistant and also carried Florentina Molina's bag. He was an Argentinian on the tour at that time.

"What happened, though, was quite fantastic. I noticed Nick Faldo was pulling a trolley and it made me curious. I found out that he'd fired his cad-die John Moorhouse and then he'd tried a German lad on the bag. But he'd only lasted the practice round! Everyone seemed to be avoiding Nick. To tell the truth, I think they were all a bit scared of him. I might have been, too, if I hadn't have been so new to the game, I suppose.

"Well, I took the bull by the horns and approached him. I asked him if he'd give me a chance and I was very pleased, as well as a bit flabbergasted, when he said he would give me a try-out. We had a good tournament. I'm not sure who was most pleased when we finished fourth. Anyway, Nick was pleased enough to ask me to to Madrid and caddie for him there.

"I said I'd love to do the job but he wouldn't see me for a couple of days because I couldn't afford to fly to Spain from Rome and I'd have to take the train. Nick said, 'I'll pay your air fare and then you won't have to worry about long train journeys.' So I flew to Madrid with him. I couldn't believe my luck.

"We didn't do quite so well in Madrid but we were hitting it off really well and he was happy enough with the way I worked to offer me a job for the rest of the year. I jumped at the chance. It was my opportunity to have that fresh-air life. Okay, it wasn't the same as playing but that was never going to work out. It was time to take a fresh path in my life, I felt. It was a real crossroads for me when I took that trip with Stan to Rome.

"What a year 1980 proved to be for Nick and myself. He won the PGA at St. George's and finished second on the European order of merit. Without sounding big-headed, Nick was so thrilled with my caddying that he told everyone on television in an interview that, 'Andy Prodger has been great. He's helped me with my putting particularly.' I'd suggested changing some little thing—the way he was lining up, perhaps, or his stance—and Nick was over the moon. We really hit it off and Nick turned round to me and said, 'Stick with me, Andy, and I'll make you a millionaire.' I said, 'Stick with me Nick and I'll make you a multimillionaire!'

"In golf, and especially with caddie–player relationships, things can change pretty quickly, though. Although we won the PGA again the next year, by the Lancôme Trophy in the autumn things were definitely not at their best between the two of us. Nick said to me, 'We don't seem to be communicating very well. I need a change. I'm not going to say we won't get back together, but we need a break from each other.'

"So we split up towards the end of the season and I then went over to the States. I'd got a bee in my bonnet about playing over the Pond after going there with Nick to play a few tournaments on the U.S. Tour. I became a 'parking-lot caddie' that is, I used to wait in the parking lot each tournament in the hope of picking up a bag.

"Chi-Chi Rodriguez was one of my jobs for a time but he got cheesed off because he couldn't compete with the younger players. Then Tom Purtzer won the Phoenix Open with me on the bag and I also got my first taste of Augusta with Tom. He was lying third in the Masters at one time and that gave me my first urge to be with a major winner. When Nick Faldo asked me to go back on the bag for him in 1986 I didn't realize it but that major dream was going to come true pretty quickly."

Prodger once again came to a crossroads. He expected to caddie for the extrovert American Mac O'Grady for the 1986 Open at Turnberry but that did not materialize. As he had made the trip back from America, however, he decided to stay on in Europe. Faldo, who had tried to prize him away from the U.S. Tour previously, got his wish. The pair joined up for their second term.

Faldo had also reached a crossroads about 18 months before they began their second spell. Sure that his own swing would not stand up to the pressure of winning a major—and he had often been close to winning—he had sought the help of the swing guru David Leadbetter to rebuild his method and technique.

The combination of Faldo, Leadbetter and Prodger was to reap a huge dividend at Muirfield, especially on a tortuous final day when all the faith Faldo had built up in trusting Leadbetter's methods was put to its stiffest test.

"Nick and I started working together again in July 1986 but we didn't do much until the following year. He was still going through the swing change with David and he'd not really done anything, certainly hadn't had a win, since the '84 season. It was a big step to take but Nick felt he needed it. He virtually went back to square one with David and the whole swing change took two years. In the end he'll tell you it was all very worth while.

"Our first win was in the Spanish Open at Las Brisas. Before that, we played in America in the same week that the Masters was on. It was a tour event for the players not competing at Augusta and it was a real non-event as far as both of us were concerned. It wasn't that Nick didn't put his back into it because he shot four rounds of 67 and finished second. No, it was because he knew he should not have been in Hattisburg, Mississippi. He should have been in Augusta, Georgia.

"He vowed, there and then, he'd never play in a tournament like that when there was a major on. His view was that a man of his stature shouldn't be playing in what was, after all, a second-rate event, while the Masters was on.

"Well, he was soon going to take care of that problem! In a few weeks he was going to earn an invitation to the 1988 Masters.

"At the Scottish Open the week before the Open at Muirfield, Nick brought in David Leadbetter to correct a fault. Nick was hitting the ball too low and David told him to swing under more and finish higher. This seemed to work very well for Nick. It only seemed to need David to be on hand to see a transformation with Nick. Just having David there seemed to give him confidence and Nick showed signs of playing really well.

"Next week at the Open, Nick was swinging really good. His whole game looked bristling with confidence. He said to me: 'I just feel it's all coming right just at the right time. I feel that something's going to happen this week.' There were definite signs that something was in the wind.

"When we saw who we were drawn with in the first two rounds both Nick and I were delighted. It was Nick Price and Ray Floyd. I knew we were in for a couple of enjoyable days as soon as I heard Nick Faldo say to Nick Price, 'Have you heard this one, Nick?'

"They spent the whole of the opening round telling each other jokes. Not many people know that Nick Faldo fancies himself as a comedian and practical joker [over the years they would find out that Faldo has a somewhat 'rare' sense of humor—thanking the press 'from the heart of my bottom,' when he next won at Muirfield]. He doesn't give off that kind of air, but get him with a mate like Price, there's no stopping him. And he was always playing tricks on people.

"We played late on the first day and I went round in the morning spotting the pin positions, trying to get a feel for the course so I could give the right information to Nick when we were under way. We birdied the first couple of holes and we were on top of the world. The joke session helped to relax the two Nicks and everybody in the group played well. It needed something to brighten the day up, that's for sure. It was pretty awful weather by the time we got out, wet and blustery and pretty unpleasant all round later in the afternoon.

"They seemed to inspire each other. We shot a 68 and so did Nick Price, so the jokes obviously worked both ways. That was three-under and that was fine. Rodger Davis had gone crackers and shot a 64 but we were well in the hunt."

Davis had indeed "gone crackers," his seven-under-par return earning the Australian a three-stroke lead. Lying second was the remarkable Lee Trevino, showing there was life in the old barking dog yet, 15 years after he clinched his last Open Championship title. Faldo, Price and two more Americans, Larry Mize and Paul Azinger, held third place, four off the lead.

For Mize, it was part of an unforgettable year. Three months earlier he had defeated Greg Norman and Severiano Ballesteros in a memorable play-off at Augusta, chipping in to clinch the U.S. Masters. In the end, though, it was Azinger who would be the American to run the closest to a maiden Open title.

As Andy Prodger remembers, however, it was a more senior American who provided unlikely inspiration for Faldo to contend. It was early inspiration on a windy and drenching second day at Muirfield, when much of Prodger's time was spent keeping his player dry.

"Whatever good feelings we got from the first day soon disappeared in the second round. It was a real job keeping the grips dry and constantly finding dry gloves. The weather was pretty foul all week. It wasn't just the weather that caused a bit of early depression, though. We were in trouble from the start because Nick put his tee-shot into a bunker at the first and he couldn't hit his second shot very far. That left him deciding for a long time which club to use for his third shot.

"He was a good while making his mind up which club to hit. I gave my opinion but, of course, it was a big shot so early in the game. Nick didn't want to double-bogey straightaway. Well, he finally decided and did manage to hit the green. When we got up to the green, Floyd said to Nick, 'I thought you were never going to play that shot.' I was really surprised to hear him come out with that. He'd obviously got a bit fed up waiting for Nick to play.

"It was a significant remark in the 1987 Open because it acted like a kick up the behind to Nick. Give him his due, Nick didn't react. In fact, Floyd's comment seemed to inspire him more than upset him. He said to me something like, 'I'll ignore that remark and the best way to treat it is to play well.' Nick was out to make Ray Floyd eat his words and get his own back. Well, he didn't quite make him eat his words because Floyd actually outshot us 68 to 69 but the group again played well in the wind and rain."

Paul Azinger's second 68 earned the lanky American a one-shot lead at six under par over Faldo. Another American, Payne Stewart, shot a 66, and now two Australians were in the frame: Rodger Davis, who had quieted down with a 73, and the dark horse Gerard Taylor.

Despite the Australian challenge, the 1987 Open was developing into an America-versus-Faldo scenario. This was especially so in the case of Floyd and Faldo, whose first hole altercation remained in both memories for years—especially when it came to Ryder Cups. Leader Azinger, too, found that the 1987 Open would give him need to settle a score with Faldo over the ensuing years, even though his main grievance should have been against the Muirfield gallery.

This was particularly so when the pair were rivals for the 1993 U.S. PGA title, eventually won by Azinger. Azinger, who fought and won a battle with cancer, used his bitterness of 1987 to inspire him in many a Ryder Cup clash, not only against Faldo but against anyone from Europe, it seemed.

When the third round began, however, there was only comradeship for caddie Prodger to contemplate. Faldo, too, must have been full of bonhomie. Saturday was his thirtieth birthday.

"It was good news for me that we were playing with Paul Azinger for the third round because Paul's caddie was a good friend of mine, Kevin Woodward [the Zimbabwean who caddied for Nick Price in 1982 and for Ignacio Garrido in the 1997 Ryder Cup]. Although Kevin and I were friends, it was strictly business out there. Nick had got the blinkers on now, so there were no jokes, there was no idle chitchat. On with the job. He has tunnel vision when he's doing well.

"The weather was lousy again, in fact it was absolutely terrible earlier on but it had eased off slightly by the time we went out in the afternoon. When I'd checked the pin positions in the morning, I'd decided it was going to be somebody already under par who would be in position to win the next day, as opposed to somebody coming through the field. That was because I just couldn't see anyone scoring really well enough in the bad weather. Sandy Lyle had the best round of the day by shooting 71 in appalling conditions. He never hit more than a one-iron off the tee, his caddie Dave Musgrove told me that night.

"Paul started badly, bogeying the first. It was one of the few times that day he didn't get up and down out of trouble. That put us level on top with him. But then he started to go well and he got in front again. He seemed to play that first nine better than the back nine, every day, if my memory serves me well. He just wasn't at ease with the back nine—it seemed. It was certainly so in the last two rounds. That was another significant factor in Nick winning. Nick was just as comfortable on the back nine at Muirfield in 1987 as he was on the front nine.

"There was another significant thing happened that day and it was on the back nine. On the 13th we were warned for slow play. It was like water off a duck's back to Nick. He hardly turned a hair. But I'm sure it upset Paul.

"Paul just got the edge at the finish, though. He holed a great putt on the last for a five. We both shot 71s because Nick hit a poor second shot on the last and he took bogey-five as well. By Nick bogeying the last it meant he wouldn't now be playing in the last group, which was now Paul and David Frost. We were paired with Craig Stadler."

The atrocious weather of the third round did indeed prevent anyone mounting a charge through the field. It was so rough and wet, with winds 40 m.p.h. plus, that the Royal and Ancient Golf Club decided to shorten some of the holes so that players had a fair chance of reaching fairways. An idea of the awful conditions can be gained from the fact that 26 players teeing off at the height of the bad weather in the morning failed to break 80.

Azinger's 71 in the calmer, more benign conditions of the afternoon allowed him to hold his one-stroke lead over Faldo and, now, South African David Frost. Because of the "first-one-in-last-one-out" rule, Azinger, at six under par, played with Frost, who was five-under like Faldo, but finished his third round before the Englishman. Would that prove to be another one of Prodger's "significant" factors?

Faldo's playing partner for the final round was the "Walrus" Craig Stadler, the man who missed the tiddler of a putt which had gone a long way to precipitating America's Ryder Cup downfall at The Belfry two years earlier. Stadler was one of Andy Prodger's players in the period between working for Faldo. They had won the Swiss Open together in 1985. Stadler shared third place at four-under with Tom Watson and Payne Stewart. Raymond Floyd was three-under. Now, Frost excepted, it really was Faldo versus America!

It was time for Faldo to show that his near two years swing change with David Leadbetter was all worth while. A cold, damp and foggy Muirfield would be the final test that week. Level-par on day four might not be a spectacular way of proving your coach was right. But it might just be good enough to win you the Auld Claret Jug.

"It wasn't a very nice day again. This time there was a good old Scotch mist and it was damp and cold. We just kept parring everything, 18 straight pars, as everyone knows. But they weren't just ordinary straightforward pars. Some were real scrambles and they gave me hundreds of gray hairs that day.

"Nick got up and down three times from bunkers, at the seventh, eighth and tenth, and those saves were really crucial. The eighth will live in my mind for ever. I don't know whether it will in Nick's. He had a shot out of sand of about 35 to 40 yards into the wind, which is probably one of the toughest shots in golf. Nick put it to a yard from the pin. It was a brilliant shot. I was really elated. I said to him, 'Great shot, Nick,' but he hardly showed any emotion. The blinkers were really on now.

"The birdies just would not come, though. We'd had a couple just stay on the lip and we—well I was, for sure—were getting desperate. To make it worse, Paul had got three shots ahead according to the scoreboard. He'd gone to eight-under, playing the first nine really well again. I had a feeling he'd get edgy after the turn, though.

"We had to do something, though. Nick asked me to read putts with him but still nothing happened. He was perplexed. He said to me: 'I'm hitting good putts, Andy, but they're not going in. Do you think I'm not supposed to win this?'

"He must have really thought that at the ninth, the par-five. We were between clubs. He wanted to hit a four-iron in but I thought that would never get up to the hole. I was searching for birdies and eagles with Azinger going great guns. So not getting there was no good to me. I said: 'Hit a three-iron. If you get a soft bounce with your four, you're going to have a very difficult chip left. Give it a chance to get there.'

"In front of the ninth green there are several ridges and he hit one of those on the down slope. His ball bounced through the back of the green! He didn't get up and down for the birdie. He blamed me all right, but he didn't say a lot. I knew I was taking some rare old stick mentally, though.

"He didn't let it affect him for long, although he did put his second into the bunker at the tenth. He got up and down again and this was a really tough hole, 475 yards but still a par-four. Most players bogeyed it on Saturday and Sunday.

"We still couldn't get that birdie putt to drop. On we went, par after par, until we got to the 16th hole and I thought, 'This must be it now.' It's 188 yards, a short hole, of course, and Nick hit a really great tee-shot to about five or six feet. You could feel the crowd willing it in. But it didn't make it and I was beginning to think it was slipping away."

A tough finish and the added pressure of winning his first Open played on Faldo's nerves. It also played on the nerves of the man who looked for all the world as if he would be the débutant on the winner's rostrum—Azinger.

The slim American had built a three-shot lead by the time he turned for home, relishing the front nine holes again. However, Azinger, as Prodger predicted, found the incoming nine holes a much tougher proposition. His lead melted to only one stroke. By the time the pair played the fateful 17th with about 15 minutes between them, Azinger was head to head with Faldo. They were the only conceivable winners.

At first, Prodger thought that missing the penultimate chance for birdie could have cost Faldo victory, even with Azinger now only a stroke in front. But Faldo's swing stood up. Azinger's did not, and nor did his course management. Two bogeys to finish by the American decided the destiny of the Auld Claret Jug—and, arguably, the career of Nick Faldo.

"The feeling that the Open was slipping away from us was even more pronounced when we could only make par on the 17th. It's a par-five and you're always looking for a four on any par-five. You take par when it's a tough day, though, and as long as your main opposition isn't running away. We saw that Paul was only a stroke in front. It was a very brave putt of Nick's to save par anyway. Maybe par wasn't bad after all.

"As it happened, the way Paul played the 17th he'd have taken par, in fact grabbed it with both hands. Fortunately for us, unfortunately for Paul Azinger, he drove into the bunker on the 17th, the one place you must never be. If he could relive that shot, I'm sure he'd never take a driver off the tee. It lost him the Open."

Azinger had ignored the advice of his caddie, who had pleaded with him not to take a driver at the 17th. He had found a deep fairway bunker, yawning in the Muirfield mist as if weary of being ruffled by miscalculating mortals and designed to punish impetuosity.

There was no hope of gaining the green in two. Azinger could only pitch out sideways. He missed the green in three and ran up a six. Azinger and Faldo were level as Faldo played the final hole.

"We had a birdie chance at the 18th. Nick hit a fantastic shot into the green. It was a five-iron and the ball never wavered off line an inch, I'd swear—a fantastic shot under such pressure. We had a putt from quite a long way away, but it was a birdie chance all the same. You could feel the tension of the crowd. They all wanted him to make it.

"The ball was never going to go in the hole for birdie that day, though. Nick tried to get that last one with all his heart, tried too hard, in fact, because the ball went over three feet past, maybe about four feet. It was a great save in the finish when he holed the putt. The relief!

"We were just walking off the 18th when the crowd started fidgeting. That was because the scoreboard was changing. When Paul's score at the 17th came up and they could see him and Nick were now level the crowd were close to erupting. While Nick signed his card at the recording area I stood beside the 18th green, my heart in my mouth.

"I watched Paul play his second and I'm sure he was just like us on the ninth, in between clubs. He made a terrible swing of what I believe was a four-iron [it was a five-iron—maybe it should have been a four] and pulled the ball into the left greenside trap. I walked over to check out how it was lying—my mind was running even if my legs were walking. I looked at his ball and thought to myself, 'He might be pretty good at getting up and down out of bunkers and he has been all week, but he's going to have his work cut out here.' It's easy to say in hindsight, but I thought, 'We've won this now.'

"But he darned nearly did it and nearly got up and down for a playoff. His bunker shot wasn't that good but his putt for par was. Only a fraction harder and it would have made it.

"All this time Nick was in the scorer's hut, watching the action on television. It must have been terrible for him, all the tension. He was with his wife Gill and baby Natalie watching it all. I believe he had a cry in there when he knew he had won. Who could blame him? He came out fairly composed, though, before the presentation.

"To be frank, I was a bit upset with the way it finished. It was great to win but I was disgusted with the way spectators cheered Paul's bad shots and when he went into the bunkers at the end. I spoke to him afterwards and apologized for the crowd—as if it was my fault! He just said, 'Well you can't help it. That's just life.'

"But the Royal and Ancient Golf Club, or the Muirfield captain, remarked on it during the presentation, about the unsporting behavior of some sections of the crowd. It was an unsavory ending to a great day for me.

"Another thing that was a disappointment for me was missing the traditional breaking through the ropes and the pursuing spectators at the end, getting the police escort through the crowd to the last green. I hope I've still got it to come.

"The crowd cheered us in, of course, but it's not the same as coming down the last with a sure winner. Sandy and Dave [Lyle and caddie Musgrove in 1985 at St. George's] had it the same. You do regret missing the buzz."

"Well, Nick collected the good old Claret Jug and I stopped to think, 'What does this mean to Andy Prodger?' It meant I was now one of the few. I was now alongside such caddies as Dave Musgrove (Lyle and Ballesteros), Willie Aitchison (Trevino and Vicenzo), and Jimmy Dickinson (Nicklaus).

"But I didn't have much time for celebrating in Scotland. I'd promised my mother I'd buy her some new central heating and the only time it could be fitted was the coming week, so I needed to go home that night because the workmen were coming round on Monday.

"My celebration consisted of a few beers with my caddie friends at Edinburgh station and on the night train. Nick flew down the next day to play a charity pro–am but I couldn't caddie for him because I was with the central heating workmen.

"Looking back on the week, I think David Leadbetter's swing change was important. So was the way Nick could relax on his opening two rounds. It was good to do that before the pressure came on. Maybe Ray Floyd stung him into action, too. Paul's unease on the back nine was critical and there were other points; Nick changed his putter at the last minute, for instance.

"But that last round of 18 pars told in the end. When the pressure is on you still have to make those pars. Nick Faldo was very successful at that."

1988 ROYAL LYTHAM AND ST. ANNE'S

Severiano Ballesteros with Ian Wright

Severiano Ballesteros	Spain	67 71 70 65 273 (par 71)
Nick Price	Zimbabwe	70 67 69 69 275
Nick Faldo	England	71 69 68 71 279
Gary Koch	USA	71 72 70 68 281
Fred Couples	USA	73 69 71 68 281
Peter Senior	Australia	70 73 70 69 282
Isao Aoki	Japan	72 71 73 67 283
Sandy Lyle	Scotland	73 69 67 74 283
David Frost	South Africa	71 75 69 68 283
Payne Stewart	USA	73 75 68 67 283

"When we got to the green we could see the ball had run off down into a hollow and was nestling in the rough on a down-facing slope. I said to myself, 'This isn't good. We need to get up and down for two to make sure of winning. This isn't an easy shot.' Seve then produced a magical shot under pressure. It was perfect weight and he nearly holed it."

Never mind the parking lot, show me the yardage

When Severiano Ballesteros played an Open Championship he had an even greater will to win, one that transcended even his normal determination to succeed. The Championship was dear to his heart more than any other tournament and Seve was arguably more dear to the gallery's heart in the 1970s and '80s than any other golfer. When Ballesteros arrived at the 1988 Open Championship there was nostalgia to go with the desire. It was at Lytham where he had clinched his maiden major title in 1979.

Nine years earlier, Ballesteros had prevailed with a mixture of swashbuckling golf and uncanny course management at the Lancashire links. On the bag in 1979, marveling at his outrageous circumnavigation of not only the fairways but the myriad infamous bunkers, Ballesteros had the pithy Englishman Dave Musgrove. In between, in 1984, it was the respectful former baseball player, American Nick de Paul, who brought Ballesteros in at St. Andrews.

For 1988, hard taskmaster Ballesteros had another Englishman on the bag. He was a former insurance man whose main job was to map yardage charts—Ian Wright, the man with the nickname "Two Bags."

It was Wright's penchant for turning out accurate yardage charts and his reputation in course management that first attracted Ballesteros's attention after he had parted company with yet another of his long-suffering bagmen. Wright earned the sobriquet "Two Bags" after he caddied twice in one day at an earlier tournament of 1983, the year he decided to give up trying to be a successful insurance agent, having already forsaken a career in television repairs. His caddying career began at Royal St. George's in the European PGA Championship—a tournament won, fatefully, by one Severiano Ballesteros!

Wright's first taste of the Open Championship came in 1984, ironically another tournament Ballesteros went on to win. Wright caddied for the Scot Brian Marchbank. They were the first to birdie the legendary Road Hole that week. It did not inspire Marchbank enough and he missed the cut.

The nearest the Yorkshire bagman got to Ballesteros that year was watching him practice. In fact the eager Wright, a supreme enthusiast for the game and an eight-handicap golfer in his own right, spent many an hour watching the greats of golf practicing at St. Andrews that week, and used up all the space in his autograph book. Within four years he would be alongside one of those greats, marching down the 18th fairway to ecstatic acclaim for his player.

The English bagman achieved those heady heights in his first year with Ballesteros, in fact only a few months after joining up with the Spanish maestro in 1988. Ballesteros, ever the superstitious golfer, thought he had found a lucky charm, for he had been in a minor slump until teaming up with Wright.

The Yorkshire caddie was no rabbit's foot, however. Their relationship was initially spectacular but fairly short-lived. Soon after shouldering the blame for Ballesteros's grave error with his doomed three-iron approach at the 18th in the 1989 Ryder Cup singles defeat to Paul Azinger, a shot which left the Spaniard in the lake, the pair parted company.

That Wright had taken the slings and arrows of Ballesteros's misery in the Ryder Cup only highlighted the philosophical and mild-mannered Englishman's motto for a caddie: "Learn to plan in advance, know the danger, know your player's limitations, know his strengths—and expect a rollicking when he gets it wrong."

Eamonn Darcy, the genial and well-liked Irishman who could be a tartar to his caddies, inspired Wright's philosophy when Darcy sacked him just before the 1985 Open at Royal St. George's. Darcy had a good week at Sandwich but Wright, who had taken veteran Maurice Bembridge's bag, got no further than the first two days of the major once again.

While there was bitter disappointment at losing the Darcy bag in 1985, it was to be a landmark year for Wright. While caddying for Vicente Fernandez in the Epson Matchplay at St. Pierre, the little Argentinian practiced with Ballesteros. Wright had met Ballesteros officially. When, at the end of 1987, Fernandez recommended Wright to Ballesteros, the relationship was formed.

"I was caddying for Magnus Persson at Las Brisas on the Costa del Sol when Vicente came up and asked me if I wanted to caddie for Seve. He'd had to act a sort of go-between or it would have looked as though Seve was trying to poach me. Players won't do that to each other. I asked Magnus what he thought and he was great about it, telling me to go ahead because I wouldn't get an offer like that very often in my lifetime.

"After I'd told Seve I'd definitely like the job and he told me he'd be in touch, I heard nothing and I decided he'd changed his mind, so I took a job with Carl Mason. We were at El Prat in Barcelona early in the 1988 season and Carl missed the cut. Dave Whelan, who came from quite near my home in Redcar in the northeast of England, was pulling his own trolley but he was leading the tournament after the first two rounds, and he asked me if I'd like to do the weekend. Well I wasn't called 'Two Bags' for nothing!

"Dave only went and won the tournament, beating Nick Faldo, Barry Lane and Mark Mouland in a playoff. Then Carl and I had a win the following week in the Sunningdale Foursomes. Seve was far from my mind at that stage.

"When we were back in Spain in April, though, two caddies who had recently come back from America—Greg Norman's caddie Steve Williams was one of them—told me that Seve had been telling everyone that I would be working for him this year. I said that it was the first I'd heard of it and that it would be nice if he told me.

"Later on I was sitting in the clubhouse having a meal, with Carl only a few feet away, when Seve came into the lounge and asked me if I was working for Carl all year. I could feel Carl's eyes boring into me. What could I say? I told Seve I was committed. He turned straight round and walked out. I thought, 'I've got to do something about this. I might be throwing away the chance of a lifetime.'

"Soon after I saw Seve in the locker-room, so I took a deep breath and said, 'Right. Let's talk again about me caddying for you.' He told me he wanted me to have a four-week trial period with him, starting at the PGA Championship at Wentworth next month. If it all worked out then I'd have the Open Championship with him at the end of the four weeks. We discussed wages and I thought it was a good deal, although I'd be paying for my own flights and accommodation. Some top players include air fares and hotels but mostly you have to foot your own bills, so I was happy enough with that. I then had to break the news to Carl.

"Well, I served my trial period, did the PGA Championship, French Open and Monte Carlo Open and then he was going to take the Scottish Open week off to prepare for the Open Championship. In fact, after the French Open he told me I wouldn't have to worry about the rest of the trial period.

"I felt I'd survived okay when he started talking about other tournaments for the rest of the year. It wasn't a bad little start. We finished tied second in the PGA Championship, fourteenth in the French Open and third at Monte Carlo. Not bad for Seve and not bad for yours truly as far as the shekels were concerned!

"I think one of the reasons that we got on well together right away was my interest in yardages, and my books. Also my temperament. When I first started the yardage books I had about 30 players buying my books, which were a bit basic, all hand-drawn. I used to measure up on a Monday, draw them up straightaway and then photocopy them. By 1986 I had 70 players buying the books. I'd work all through the night making up the booklets, very tiring when you consider I was also caddying. Others used to do the yardage books but I think I might have been the first to do it on a week-to-week basis. Even the top pros used to buy my books, including Greg Norman, Bernhard Langer and Sandy Lyle. It was nice they had faith in me.

"Seve was one of the few who didn't take my book, though. But he was interested. I think it was my reputation with the books which first put him on to me. Then when we worked together, he knew at least that I could work out how the course was planned—and that the yardages should be correct!

"Also, Seve has a tremendous sense of humor if you can bring it out of him. It even stretches to my Yorkshire jokes. It could come in handy to break his thoughts with a joke, to stop him being too intense. It got him away from thinking about the bad shot he may have played two shots ago, and it relaxed him. When I'd watched him before working for him he'd started to look careworn, as if he carried all the worries of the world on his shoulders.

"Before I started work for him I sounded out a couple of his old caddies, very experienced men, Pete Coleman and Dave Musgrove. When I said to Dave, 'What's the best advice you'd give about working with Seve?' Dave said, 'Don't!' He warned me, and so did Pete, that I'd get blamed for everything. I figured it came with the territory.

"By the time we'd played three tournaments I felt I could handle it. We were very good foils for each other. I'm very quiet on the course, even placid. When he wanted to vent his feelings I just stood and listened, let him get his frustration out so that he might then relax and get on with it. On club selection, most of it was confirmation, but if he asked me which club I had to give a good reason for my choice. On reading putts, he called me in occasionally.

"After Monte Carlo, Seve went home to prepare for Lytham. He said to me, 'Make sure you're there on Sunday.' I was there all right. Seve decided he wanted to play nine holes, so after we'd registered we went out on to the course. Seve was hoping to avoid the public but there was no chance of that. Even at this stage of the week there were about 150 people following us for practice. It certainly gave me the flavor of what it was all going to be about. I'd already done my yardages, so I was prepared. We played a few holes on the first nine and then cut across to do a few on the back nine.

"That was quite relaxed. The next day the real hard work came as we worked out a strategy for each hole. We made a plan for each hole and how to play it and then varied it according to weather conditions, if necessary. I met Seve very early to talk about the practice round.

"He told me exactly how we were going to play, hole by hole. I made all the necessary notes, checked the yardages and particularly checked out the bunkers, distances to them and where they were most likely to be in play. Lytham is a mass of bunkers and if you can avoid them it's a key to getting a good score.

"We played with Sandy Lyle and Nick Faldo [the new Masters champion and the previous year's Open champion] and the crowds following us were just phenomenal. Right from the start people were encouraging Seve, getting right behind him even then. On the Tuesday we played a four-ball and Wednesday we didn't intend playing at all, just practicing on the range, chipping and putting, but Seve decided at the last minute to go out again for another nine. Weren't the crowds pleased about that? Then we practiced chipping and putting, fine-tuning. Seve spent a lot of time on the putting green on Wednesday. He normally spent an hour a day on his putting anyway.

"Then it was Thursday, the big day. Our tee-off time was 9:25 A.M. and that meant meeting up about an hour and a half beforehand, so he turned up about eight o'clock to practice. Putting got the most attention again. I double-checked the bag—two yardage books, in case one went missing, towels, spare gloves, a dozen balls, two sets of rain gear, bandages, and so on. It's quite a load, about 45 pounds in weight. Then we were off. I had a premonition that we were going to win.

"We had a great start, birdie, birdie, birdie, and I'm feeling as if I'm in a dream. We've gone two shots clear of the field after three holes. Seve took the course apart over those first nine holes and he birdied five of them. After the daze of the first three holes I started to settle down a bit, got my feet on the ground and started working instead of spectating!

"We found our first real trouble at the 14th. The first nine holes had been mainly downwind but on the back nine it was more difficult. The drive was just a little off-line and the ball settled on an awkward ridge in the semi-rough. Seve decided on a two-iron. He was going for it.

"With the ball lying a bit awkward, though, he pulled it left. The club caught the grass and turned it and the ball shot straight left into some pretty wicked jungle—heather, trees, gorse and God knows what. We were very lucky to even find the ball and it was difficult to locate where the green was, which direction from where we were. You just couldn't see over the bushes. It was going to have to be a penalty-drop because the ball really was unplayable. But from where?

"At this stage there must have been 300 people milling around, while we're first looking for the ball and then working out where to drop. I'm charging backward and forward through the crowd, bag still on my shoulder. What a mess! It caused me a big problem.

"There was one bloke who just would not move out of the way while I was trying to sort out the line in. I asked him to move because he was standing right over the ball, but he wouldn't budge so I shouted at him. He did no more than grab the bag and twisted it on my shoulder. I got him sorted out but it had given me a twinge. I hoped it wasn't anything serious.

"We decide the only sensible way we can play it is to take the ball back towards the sixth tee, where at least there was cut grass. I then have to work out the yardage to the green, so I go off, pacing right up to the green. It's 125 yards. We decide on a seven-iron.

"Seve then plays the most magnificent shot over the trees and scrub. He couldn't possibly see where he was going, or how far. We soon found out. He'd hit it to about five yards from the pin. He then sank the putt and made one of the greatest bogeys I've ever seen. It felt like a birdie. Seve was one of the few players in the world who could have played that shot and turned it into only a five.

"But it was also proof of how he thinks everything out so carefully. The whole thing took about 25 minutes. He made sure he wasn't trying to hack his way out of an impossible situation because it was real elephant and tiger country. Then to sink the putt as well. It wasn't an easy putt because the ball lay on a ridge.

"We both had a little smile to each other at that point. It was a real bonus to make the save and it kept us in good heart. That was just as well at the end because we had a few more anxious moments, like driving unplayable at the 18th—but still salvaging only bogey again. He shot a 67 and we led by two.

"I was worried, though. The twinge I felt after that unpleasantness with the spectator on 14 got worse as we went along and I was really struggling when we got in. I didn't tell Seve about it because I didn't want to worry him. I just went to my digs and had a long soak, hoping the problem would have eased in the morning."

Ballesteros's heroics at the 14th and 18th—where he admitted "I don't think Daniel Boone would have played from there" when asked about his remarkable saves—earned him a two-stroke lead over the American Brad Faxon and Australian Wayne Grady. Both his closest rivals would become Open challengers, particularly Grady the following year. Four players were a stroke adrift of the lead, among them Zimbabwean Nick Price, another man who consistently contended strongly in Open Championships.

A battle royal between Ballesteros and Price, which was to take dramatic twists and turns all week, had been set up. Wright, however, could not shake off his premonition. But, after waking up to find, gratefully, that the stiffness in his shoulder had eased, Wright's day on the course began fitfully. And he was soon to feel the sharpness of his master's voice.

"I was absolutely certain Seve was going to win. I'd never seen him hitting his long irons so well. Good iron-play at Lytham is crucial. But his putting was good, everything was good. There was just something about him, I'd seen it in the build-up, that gave me the hunch he was going to win. So I was full of confidence for the second round, especially as my neck and shoulder pain seemed to have eased. The soak got most of the stiffness out.

"We started the Friday round quite nicely, nothing like the day before but steady, and then at the third we brought the bunker into play. I got a real ticking off when Seve found the sand with his three-iron. The one thing we'd especially planned was to keep the ball out of the sand. It was the key to Lytham. The bunkers are killers, deep and hard to get out of. Most of the time there was no chance of getting on for two if you were in them. We could have saved par but the putt didn't drop from about ten feet.

"That was about the distance Seve got on for his eagle chance at the sixth but that didn't drop either. The ball seemed to drift a bit in the wind. But we did birdie both the par-fives so we were one-under at the turn. That shot went when Seve found the left rough off the tee on the 14th again. This time he didn't try for the green and played up short with a six-iron. Same result, though, bogey. We weren't getting the best out of the 14th, but then again it was probably the hardest hole.

"We could have dropped a couple of shots at the end as well, but Seve played some great recoveries to save pars on the 17th and 18th and that left him—and me—in good spirits. A 71 wasn't a bad score because it was a fairly tricky afternoon. It got very windy."

Nick Price's 67 had taken him a stroke in front of Ballesteros at five under par. The cream had certainly risen to the top on a leaderboard that featured most of the current top men from both sides of the Atlantic.

Ballesteros's playing partners were well up there. Nick Faldo shared third place with American Craig Stadler as the Englishman made his bid for back-to-back Open titles and the "Walrus" made his bid for a second major honor six years after his first, the 1982 Masters. They were three shots off the lead.

U.S. Masters champion Sandy Lyle matched Faldo's 69 to put himself in contention for a second major in the year, to lie four strokes away from leader Price. Two more Americans, Fred Couples and Bob Tway, the U.S. PGA champion the previous year, shared that spot with Lyle.

The weather was about to intervene, however. The mackerel skies and fickle winds were a prelude to a Friday-night deluge. The rain had eased by Saturday morning and the players down the field managed to squelch out on to the course. But when the heavens opened again before noon the course became waterlogged.

Play was abandoned and all scores cancelled. The luckless early players had to start again the next day. The leaders never set foot on a squelching course. Ballesteros and Wright had to find some way of keeping concentration at optimum to be at their best for a Sunday third round.

"When I walked the course first thing on Saturday morning I knew the tournament was going to be in trouble. It had poured down all through the night and the course was in a state already when I walked the 18 holes to check the pin positions. Already there were people laying down straw to soak up the wet but they were losing the battle. Then it started raining again and that was that. The water lay on the greens and on most of the fairways and I knew we wouldn't be going out.

"I phoned Seve and told him there was very little chance of us playing and that I'd keep him in touch. When I went back out they'd decided to abandon play and restart on Sunday. Now the big problem was going to be boredom. It became a long, tedious day, sitting around waiting for something to happen and it never did. That's very difficult when you're in the middle of any tournament but for it to happen in the British Open . . . I didn't see Seve until about one o'clock when he came and hit a few balls. He seemed pretty relaxed. The loss of play wasn't bothering him.

"It was a big relief to finally get under way on the Sunday. The bad weather meant the course was playing long. We were with Nicky Price, of course, and because of the abandoned play we were out in a three-ball. Craig Stadler was the other player in the group.

"We started with a couple of birdie chances but both went begging. Then at the sixth, a hole you look for birdie on, we hit trouble—and through no fault of our own. Seve pulled the ball left off the tee but it didn't look too bad. Then we found it had hit a spectator and disappeared into some bushes left of the fairway, just behind the ropes. Seve worked out all the things he could do. He decided he couldn't declare it unplayable because he wouldn't have a place to drop anyway, not one where he could have a full swing anyway. He opted to play a back-hand shot with an eight-iron and had a few practice swings.

"It was always going to be a difficult shot because the ball was right down in the undergrowth. Seve was on edge. He thought I was standing too close for comfort and told me to move. When he played the shot and only moved the ball about 18 inches, I feared the worst—and got it. He had a go at me for still being too close. He could see me out of the corner of his eye and he said he might have hit me if the ball came out at a funny angle. Then there would have been penalty.

"Well, he calmed down enough to play a much better shot back-handed the next time. It cost us a bogey but it could have been much worse if the second back-hand shot had stayed in as well. We could have taken eight or worse. The sixth could have been a major disaster. Seve's attitude, though, was how it was all week. He didn't let it upset him. He had a chirp at me for being too close and was absolutely right. His ball could have ricocheted off a branch or a root and the last thing we wanted was penalty shots. But he wasn't as ferocious with me over the incident as he perhaps could have—and had—been.

"I'm not one for saying that one shot changes a tournament; but I think the shots he saved on the sixth were crucial. It showed how he had taken it in his stride because he birdied the seventh, the other par-five, and we were only a shot behind Nick by the turn. He said to me at the 10th, 'We have to play better this nine or we lose ground.' I wondered if he was thinking about the 14th.

"We picked up another shot on the 13th and that really cheered us up. Seve was really relaxed and he even asked one of the policemen with our group how the Test match [cricket] was going while we were waiting at one of the tees. I needed to be relaxed myself because the 14th had been a thorn in the side so far. There was more than a bit of hope when I said to Seve before the drive, 'Nice, easy swing.' He did just that and we nearly made birdie. It was relief enough, though, to get off the green with par this time.

"Apart from escaping from a bunker for par on the next, that was about it. We shot a 70. Nick Price had gone well and he looked the biggest threat now, although Nick Faldo had appeared and he was always trouble. Craig had a real nightmare, though, and he was out of it."

So the Open Championship ran over to a fifth day. The Championship committee had hoped to try to fit in two rounds on the Sunday but a delayed start had put paid to that plan. Nick Price sailed serenely on and he held a two-stroke lead at seven under par.

The practice three-ball of Ballesteros, Faldo and Lyle were tracking him, though. Ballesteros and Faldo were the second-placed men, with Lyle a stroke behind at four under par. After the American challenge faded, the top man from the United States was Larry Nelson, at three under par.

Because of the weather and the danger of unfinished business, the players again went out in threes for the final round—leader Price, Ballesteros and Faldo making up the final trio.

As the leaders played the first nine holes, it looked anybody's title. The top four men fought tooth and nail and Fred Couples of America came from behind to challenge, back-to-back eagles early on giving him a chance.

However, as the afternoon wore on, it became a battle of attrition between Ballesteros and Price.

"Monday dawned and it was a strange feeling. I'd had a good night's sleep despite all the thoughts of what the last round meant, but now I had to get packed for going home before I could worry about what this afternoon was going to bring. I didn't change my routine because we had an extra day. I did all my preparations as usual. I still felt we were going to win.

"We practiced for one hour before the off, chipping and plenty more putting. We had a light lunch and then we were heading for the first tee. Seve was in his lucky dark blue. What followed was the most spectacular round of golf I'd ever been privileged to witness. At first it looked as though it was going to be a battle between six or seven players. Everyone seemed to be taking the front nine apart, according to the leaderboard. There were eagles and birdies flying in all directions. Fred Couples came into the reckoning; Nick Faldo, Sandy Lyle, they were all up there.

"We were very aware of the others bunching up and Seve had a couple of reasonable chances of birdies to try to put some pressure on the two Nicks and the players coming at us, but he missed them both, so the pressure was pretty tough at that stage. He kept calm, though, and the most he said was, 'I thought that was going to break,' or, 'I thought there was more swing on that.' He didn't panic and then, all of a sudden, we got going. Everybody had been having their charge, now it was our turn.

"Seve and Nick Price both made birdies and eagles and suddenly they were clear of the others because it wasn't happening for Nick Faldo. We birdied six and eagled seven. It was a great shot to the green by Seve at the seventh. A five-iron did it. Just six feet for the putt. By the time we'd birdied the eighth it was looking like a battle between Nick Price and Seve because they'd shaken off the field pretty well.

"Seve was still incredibly relaxed, though. I expected him to be more pumped up but he kept his head and he had a very calm manner on the back nine. He knew that the Open was going to be won and lost on the back nine.

"Two great putts, about 20 feet, both went in on the 10th and 11th for birdies and when we came off the 11th green it was a two-horse race, with Seve one ahead. At the short 12th, though, I was in trouble. It's a par-three of nearly 200 yards and I gave him the wrong club. He came up short. It wasn't the best of shots but he'd hit a four-iron and certainly it should have been a three, using the left-to-right wind. He normally hits a low left-to-right shot, and the green ran that way. I was horror-struck when the ball went up in the air and never looked like making it. Black mark to Wright [ironically just the opposite to the pair's problem at The Belfry in the Ryder Cup the next year!].

"This was when I really did get a mouthful from Seve. He didn't hold back, used some good old-fashioned Anglo-Saxon mixed in with some Spanish which I guessed meant the same sort of thing! I just couldn't afford to get mixed up in a slanging match at this stage or our chances could be blown, so I did what is commonly known as 'cocking a deaf 'un.' I just let him burn himself out and said nothing. If I'd offered my two-pennyworth the balloon would really have gone up. As it was, after he'd just missed the putt to save par, he stomped off to the 13th and just said 'stupid bogey.' It brought us back level with Nick Price.

"If it had been a special round up to then, from then on it became extra special. Pricey hit his ball to inches on the 13th. Seve hit his to about 15 feet and he really put the wind up me then. He was prowling around the green as usual—and then he suddenly asked me to read the putt with him. On reading putts, he called me in occasionally, but I hadn't been involved on the greens all that week. Well, we agreed on the line and I was very relieved. It went in. They were still tied.

"We then had the dreaded 14th. This time Seve missed the green with a three-iron after the ball caught a grassy mound. Then he came up too strong with a wedge—after I'd handed him his sand-iron—and couldn't get up and down. That made it three bogeys out of four. Luckily for us, Nick Price also dropped a shot there with a bad putt. We're still tied.

"Nick [Price] looked as though the putting was getting to him. I felt it could be the chink in his armor. He'd said he'd not putted especially well all week. He had a struggle to make par at 15, whereas Seve ran a long putt up stone-dead to make his. But in the end the breakthrough didn't come from Nick cracking because of the putting. It came through a magnificent shot by Seve at the 16th."

Ballesteros was at his watershed of 1979. It was at this hole that the Spaniard produced his "parking lot" tactic, driving on to a parking area under a car, purposely, he maintained, to give him a safe second shot to the green. This time Ballesteros had no need of parking lots after a safe drive with a one-iron. But he did use the same club to make the green as he had in 1979, a nine-iron. After much discussion, Ballesteros chipped with the club of destiny to just three inches. His nerveless nine-iron had, in effect, clinched his second Lytham Open.

"It was the shot of the round for me. But there was more to come. Pricey still didn't look too confident with the putter and the best he could do was par at the 16th, so we're now one ahead. At the 17th it could have been all over.

"I thought Nick Price was extremely lucky to stay on the course. His ball whacked into the fence around the practice range but he did really well to recover and save par. He hit a great one-iron and made the green for two putts. Seve hit a nice shot to the heart of the green and also made his par, so we're still one ahead.

"The 18th tee was a real heart-stopping moment for me, though. Seve drove down the right and I wasn't convinced it had avoided the bunkers [Tony Jacklin's caddie had the same needless fear in 1969]. Seve said anxiously, 'Is it past the bunkers?' I told him I was sure it was, although I wasn't sure.

"It made it a long walk down. All the while Seve kept saying, 'Are you sure it's past the bunkers?' I kept saying, 'Yes, it is,' but my heart was in my mouth. At last I saw somebody standing by the ball. Only then did I know we were safe.

"The plan then was to play to the left part of the green because the wind was coming over the top of the grandstand, left-to-right, and we knew it was important to keep left. It takes out all the trouble on the right, such as the bunkers. The green slopes left-to-right, too. I thought we had what could be a 'flying' lie and I decided I had to take into consideration how much adrenalin Seve would have flowing in him. We decided on a six-iron.

"He hit what seemed a really good shot but, from where we were standing, we couldn't see the ball finish because of a hillock on the left of the green. I thought it would have swung left-to-right and finished somewhere just past the flag. When we got to the green we could see the ball had run off down into a hollow and was nestling in the rough on a down-facing slope. I said to myself, 'This isn't good. We need to get up and down for two to make sure of winning. This isn't an easy shot.'

"Seve then produced a magical shot under pressure. It was perfect weight and he nearly holed it. Even now, when I watch it on video, I think it's going to catch the hole and drop. Once that happened, I felt great. I just knew there was no way Nick was going to hole his putt, which was a long one. He just never had a chance. He knew he had to hit it hard to get into the hole and there were no prizes for being short. Birdie was his only chance.

"It never looked like going in and went eight feet past. I felt really sorry for him when he missed the one back. That was sad for Nick, although it didn't make any difference to his second place. He'd played a really great round of golf and he'd done everything he could. I mean, a 69 and he'd lost the Championship. He must have felt sick. Seve's 65 was really just something out of this world.

"Everything afterwards is a bit of a blur. I remember shaking hands with Andy Prodger, Nick Faldo's caddie, and the next thing Seve and I were hugging each other in the middle of the green and tears were filling my eyes. I shoved the glove and ball in my pocket. They were mine for posterity. I'd promised a policeman my overalls for charity, so he got them. Then I was grabbed by a radio reporter and went straight on the air. I haven't a clue what I said.

"A guy who'd had a bet on Seve threw me a bottle of champagne down from the stand and I fought my way to the locker-room to enjoy it. Andy

Prodger, Dave McNeilly, Nick Price's caddie, and 'Barry the Judge,' another caddie, were the only ones left in there.

"While we sat there, Nick Price walked in. What can you say to him at this point? I just said, 'I'd really appreciate if you'd have a glass of champagne with me, Nick, for the way you played against us today.' He said he would. That showed the character of Nick Price. He must have been feeling terrible, but he joined in the celebrations.

"I never saw much of Seve. He went to talk to the press and to the presentation, which I watched from the locker-room. An hour later I got a message from him. It said: 'Can you bring my gear to the car?' When we met up in the car park, he said, 'Thank you very much. See you Tuesday.' It was hard for me to remember where we were on Tuesday!"

1989 ROYAL TROON

Mark Calcavecchia with Drake Oddy

Mark Calcavecchia	USA	71 68 68 68 275 (par 72)
Greg Norman	Australia	69 70 72 64 275
Wayne Grady	Australia	68 67 69 71 275
(Calcavecchia won after four-hole playoff)		
Tom Watson	USA	69 68 68 72 277
Jodie Mudd	USA	73 67 68 70 278
Fred Couples	USA	68 71 68 72 279
David Feherty	N. Ireland	71 67 69 72 279
Eduardo Romero	Argentina	68 70 75 67 280
Paul Azinger	USA	68 73 67 72 280
Payne Stewart	USA	72 65 69 74 280

"As Wayne was getting set up for his putt, Mark said to me, 'If he makes this, how many putts do I have to win?' I said, 'If he makes it you've got two putts to win. If he misses it, you've got three.' Wayne missed the putt. Mark said, 'I got three from here? That I think I can hit.'"

Someone didn't read the script

After a spectacular finishing round, the 1989 Open Championship script was going according to plan. The world number one golfer Greg Norman was surely about to prove his class and add the title at Royal Troon to the Open Championship he had sealed so succinctly three years previously. That, however, was reckoning without a partnership which had first formed itself at the University of Florida in Gainesville, that of burly professional Mark Calcavecchia and his long-time fellow student, friend and business associate on the bag, Drake Oddy. After a nerve-jarring showdown at Troon, the American duo had provided a major upset and created golfing history.

Calcavecchia became the first man to win a four-hole playoff for the Auld Claret Jug when he defeated the world's top golfer and the Great White Shark's fellow countryman Wayne Grady, one of the most in-form players of the time.

For the first time, too, since 1893 and William Auchterlonie, the Claret Jug's engraver had to etch 12 surname letters into the trophy. But while Calcavecchia was long on name he had never been long on staying power in an Open Championship. His unexpected victory provided the biggest surprise since Bill Rogers took the major in 1981. Calcavecchia had just not read the script.

However, to the discerning golf follower, was the 1989 success by Calcavecchia such a surprise? The American had looked for all the world set to pull off the U.S. Masters title the year before until Sandy Lyle produced his magical seven-iron from the bunker at the last at Augusta. And Calcavecchia had risen to number two on the American money list in 1989 with wins in the Phoenix Open and Los Angeles Open, before making the journey to Scotland for the third major of the year. Only money list leader Tom Kite and U.S. Open victor Curtis Strange were hotter properties than Calcavecchia from over the Pond.

Yet that year's U.S. Masters winner, Nick Faldo, was also more of a favorite for a Troon victory than Calcavecchia, and the defending champion, Severiano Ballesteros, would be certain to lift himself for the Open as he always did. World ranking leader Norman's record stood out on its own even with those giants of golf for opposition. Calcavecchia started as something of an each-way bet at best.

It was Calcavecchia's lack of experience in the British major that made his victory more of a surprise. The 1989 Open was only his third tilt at the title and the year before he had missed the cut at Royal Lytham and St. Anne's. But it was not just lack of experience. Calcavecchia hardly had his mind on the job all week. As the British newspapers were quick to point out, an expectant father was hardly likely to be in the running. The Calcavecchias were expecting their first baby and it was due that very week. How could the Nebraskan possibly concentrate on winning his first Open at only his third attempt with his wife likely to go into labor at any time?

It took an outrageous stroke of luck on one shot during the closing round, coupled with an exhilarating finish. Then it was his sense of purpose, once he had got into contention, that enabled Calcavecchia to defy the pundits and the psychologists and earn a place in the record books.

The winning partnership of 1989 was actually fashioned ten years earlier at college. Oddy had been studying at Gainesville for two years when Calcavecchia joined the University of Florida golf team in 1979, immediately spotted for his golfing prowess. While Oddy, the grandson of English immigrants, who clearly had a say in his first name, studied, his friend Calcavecchia played on the college team. Eventually, Calcavecchia left to turn professional while Oddy studied on and earned his degree. "I wasn't a bad golfer myself," says Oddy, "and at one time I thought of trying out for the team, but the coach wasn't keen on people going to class."

After graduating Oddy decided to do some part-time caddying for Calcavecchia in 1982. He enjoyed the life so much that in 1986 he became bagman and travelling companion for Calcavecchia, who was not keen on touring on his own. Two months after starting full-time Oddy helped his friend win his first U.S. Tour event, the Southwest Classic in Abilene, Texas. Calcavecchia added further victories in 1987 and 1988 and came desperately close to clinching his first major, defeated by Lyle only at the last hole at Augusta. Then the pals from salad days finally found the recipe for major success.

"Mark decided to come over to Britain a week early this time because when we played the other two British Opens we didn't get there until Tuesday morning, not enough time to get used to the conditions. Even by the Thursday Mark hadn't felt properly acclimatized. So we gave ourselves plenty of time this year and I'm sure that was a lot to do with how he played that week; it really helped a lot.

"We shared a room at the Caledonian Hotel and we had the staff there on standby because Mark's wife was expecting and we didn't know from day to day whether we'd be hopping on a plane back to Phoenix. We had the air schedules worked out for any time of day for us to get back in a hurry.

"Mark was in a hurry to get to the course on the Monday, though. He picked me up at the airport, we dropped my suitcase off at the hotel and then it was off to the course. It was vital for both of us because British courses are so different from American courses. You need a lot of inspection and hours of work to get things worked out. When we played in the States the only practice round we had was in the pro–am. Mark's not a mechanical player and he doesn't get much out of just playing and hitting. At places like Troon and Muirfield you have to play at least a couple of times from different parts of the fairways to have any idea of what they're all about.

"I'd read books on Troon but I never expected it to be so brown and dry. You expect the weather isn't going to be hot in Britain but that's how it was and how it had been for a few weeks, apparently. The course looked parched. The rough was a bit threadbare but to make up for that the course was hard and bumpy in lots of places. After the first practice round, though, Mark's impression was that he liked the course. He hadn't liked Lytham the year before. He was never comfortable with it and it wasn't much of a surprise that he didn't shoot well, made 76 in the first round at Lytham and then really hit the bottom with an 84. His good shots there didn't get good results and his bad shots got really awful results.

"This was different. Sometimes you just have a feeling. Mark felt he'd have more birdie chances here. That wasn't so much because he was hitting more greens than he used to but more that his short-game had really come on. At

Troon you had to hit a lot of different types of shot and on some holes you just could not go for the green. He felt he'd have an advantage around the Troon greens because he'd developed really good hands. That week he just happened to have an incredible touch around the greens, so his assessment in practice was right.

"On the Tuesday I did the yardages and then we played our next practice round with Curtis Strange, Mark O'Meara and Arnold Palmer. We played a competitive match and that was just what was needed to get him sharp. It was also relaxing and good for Mark that way, especially playing with Arnold. We talked with him about the last time he had won at Troon, about the way things were then—what the weather conditions were like and where he had hit the ball on certain holes. Remarkably, conditions were very similar in 1962, when Arnold won, to the conditions we had.

"Arnold had his trusty old caddie from St. Andrews with him, Tip [Tip Anderson, with Palmer for his victories of 1961 at Royal Birkdale and Troon in 1962 and also Tony Lema's caddie when the flamboyant American won at St. Andrews in 1964], and it was wonderful to hark back. It all helped get the feel of Troon. We teamed up with Mark O'Meara and we won money off Arnold and Curtis. We took great pleasure in taking the money off them and it took our minds off the coming tournament a little bit.

"There were plenty of serious moments, though, and we took a lot from the practice, took a lot in. The longest hole, the 577 yards sixth, played really short and even the Postage Stamp, the eighth, which we'd heard so much about, wasn't so frightening. You have to get the shot just right or you haven't got a shot, but in practice it seemed very benign. That was mainly because there was no wind and the wind provides 70 percent of the difficulty, a major factor at any British Open, I guess.

"Then there was the 17th. On the Tuesday in practice Mark tried to hit a couple of one-irons at the par-three 17th. It's 223 yards but he could hardly get to the green with a one-iron, so he had to make sure with a three-wood. It never played that long during the tournament and the most he hit for the tournament was a one-iron, when it was windy. The rest of the time it was two, three, even four-iron.

"The toughest conditions during the week were on Tuesday and at least when the wind did blow, it was in the same way as it blew in the practice round. At Lytham the year before it blew one way in practice and another in the tournament. That made the holes entirely different when we got into the tournament proper.

1979: English caddying doyen Dave Musgrove helps Seve Ballesteros with club selection during the "Parking Lot Open" at Royal Lytham and St. Anne's.
(ALLSPORT)

1984: Seve Ballesteros and baseball catcher Nick de Paul cross the St. Andrews Swilcan Bridge. (ALLSPORT)

1985: Sandy Lyle and Dave Musgrove muse over another tough St. George's drive. (ALLSPORT)

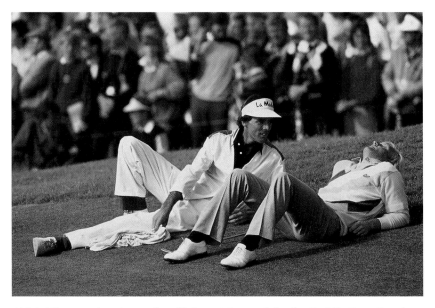

1986: The monkey is nearly off Greg Norman's back. Caddie Pete Bender and the "Great White Shark" bask before victory at Turnberry. (ALLSPORT)

1987: Andy Prodger keeps dry at Muirfield while Nick Faldo assesses the options. (ALLSPORT)

1988: "Trust me. That's the correct yardage," Ian Wright assures Seve Ballesteros at Royal Lytham and St. Anne's. (ALLSPORT)

1989: Friends from salad days, Mark Calcavecchia and Drake Oddy at the U.S. Open a month before triumphing at Troon. (ALLSPORT)

1990: Nick Faldo and Fanny Sunesson have to scamper to avoid being swamped by the St. Andrews gallery. (ALLSPORT)

1991: Ian Baker-Finch and Pete Bender study a line at Royal Birkdale.
(ALLSPORT)

1992: "Stand still, please." Sergeant Major Fanny Sunesson stands guard over Nick Faldo at Muirfield.
(ALLSPORT)

1993: Decision made. Tony Navarro approves of Greg Norman's choice at St. George's.
(ALLSPORT)

1994: "Try, try again." Nick Price and "Squeeky" Medlen near Robert the Bruce's Turnberry castle.
(ALLSPORT)

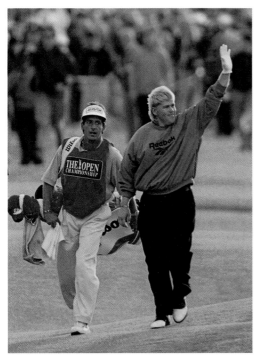

1995: John Daly salutes the "Home of Golf" and the St. Andrews gallery, while faithful caddy Greg Rita enjoys his master's triumph. (ALLSPORT)

1996: Tom Lehman and Andrew Martinez discuss the lie of the Royal Lytham and St. Anne's land. (ALLSPORT)

1997: Justin Leonard and Bob Riefke hope the ball has stayed out of trouble at Royal Troon. (ALLSPORT)

1998: Jerry Higginbotham (black cap toward the top, right) helps Mark O'Meara search at Royal Birkdale's sixth on a fateful Saturday. (ALLSPORT)

1999: Victory for a local hero. Scot Paul Lawrie congratulated by his bagman Paddy Byrne at Carnoustie after one of the most remarkable and bizarre British Open finales of all time. (ALLSPORT)

2000: A triumphant Tiger Woods completed the set by capturing the oldest major trophy, the Auld Claret Jug, at the "Home of Golf." (ALLSPORT)

"On the first day we had a steady round, nothing spectacular, scoring 71. The year before Mark hadn't had any fun and he'd vowed that, no matter what happened, 'We're going to have a good time the next time we play in the first round of the British Open.' We were pretty relaxed all the way round. We'd played pool the night before and chilled out because we hadn't had to start too early or too late for the first round, as had happened in the previous two British Opens. A three o'clock start, for instance, is hard for Mark because he's such an early riser.

"We didn't have too many problems and finished up under par. Mark watched some of the guys burning up the course. There always seems to be some guy who gets away in the first round. This time it was an English guy called Wayne Stephens. He got five shots ahead of us.

"But big tournaments aren't won in one round, no matter how good you score. The first round you're trying to play well but you just try to get into a decent position. You've come all that way so you don't want to start poorly and then have to grind it out to get back. If you start too aggressively then it can all go wrong. We felt we were well in touch."

It was indeed Wayne Stephens out in front and the Channel Islander kept his dream alive until late in the second round. A 66 earned Stephens, a player who had even toyed with the idea of giving up the game a few years earlier, his success was so limited, a two-shot lead.

There was a bevy of players at 68, including veteran Lee Trevino, bidding to add an Open title 17 years after his last British major victory. The most significant man at 68, however, was another Wayne, this one Australian Wayne Grady, who was destined to slug it out with Calcavecchia and Greg Norman at the death. Norman himself was one shot further back after a 69, with Tom Watson, who was again seeking that elusive record-equalling sixth Open Championship title.

Calcavecchia was well down the field and the bookmakers were offering even longer odds on him winning now. The stage had been set, though, for an epic and historic Open. Calcavecchia joined the party with a second day 68 but, as his caddie Oddy points out, it should have been much better.

"I don't think Mark played as well in the second round, strangely enough, as he had done in the first when he was three shots worse. He just scored well for his 68. He made what you might call some stupid bogeys, for instance where you miss the green on the wrong side of the pin. Most courses you can miss either side of the hole but at Troon that's not the case. The Postage Stamp is a prime example of that.

"At Troon you can't get away with things if you hit the ball short or in the wrong place. The first par-three, for example, the 210 yards fifth, if the pin is left, you can't miss left, or shouldn't, because there's nothing to hit off. Then when the pin is at the front, there's a big bunker right at the front, so he'd said, 'The one thing I mustn't be is short.' After saying that he came up short and hit into that bunker, leaving himself a 60-foot shot out of the sand. He hit it to six feet and made the putt. That was a case of getting away with it, but he didn't get away with it a couple of times in the second round or his score would have been better than 68.

"The result at the fifth rather summed up Mark's week. Even on the holes where he did what he said he shouldn't do he largely got away with it."

Light rain had calmed down the fiery Troon links and that certainly helped the man in plus-fours, Payne Stewart, who soared to a spectacular 65 to pick up the gauntlet held by Australia. The Australian in question, however, was not Greg Norman.

Wayne Grady had shown there were other sharks with sharp teeth from Down Under when the 31-year-old Queenslander brought off his maiden victory on the U.S. Tour, the Westchester Classic, not long before the week at Troon. A 67 in the second round earned Grady a two-shot lead on nine under par over the surging Stewart and a Tom Watson ready to win again— if he could control his unruly putter. The five-times Open champion said his putter felt like "a hissing snake" every time he put his hands around its grip. That snake was to subsequently bite its master once too often. Greg Norman was tracking the leaders ready to show his fangs, it seemed, lying five under par.

Calcavecchia's 68 had also taken him within four strokes of the lead and earned him a place in the top 20, thus among the later groups out in the Saturday third round. As yet neither the bookmakers nor the pundits were giving any hint that the big Nebraskan would be a threat to anyone's hopes, although at least two chief contenders, Nick Faldo and Seve Ballesteros, looked to have fallen by the wayside.

If the experts were not talking about Calcavecchia's winning chances then caddie Oddy might well have toyed with the idea of placing a bet on his man when he found day three to be calm and windless.

"There was no wind whatsoever on the third day. That meant we could really go for it. Any course where you can shoot straight at the pin is to Mark's advantage. We had made allowances for all kinds of conditions when we practiced and judging what it would be like with no wind was one of the things we considered.

"There were lots of things to take into consideration, like shooting straight at the pin when it was rock-hard. One of the things that worried him in practice was that when we played the first he hit a ball pin-high and it wound up 40 feet away at the back of the green. He'd said, 'We might have to change a couple things this week.' Luckily, when the tournament started they put enough water on the greens so that you could shoot at them if there was no wind. This was good because Mark's game is not the 'bump-and-run' sort. With no wind he could get to within 20 or 30 yards at the first and then go for the flag without worrying if he was going to run through the green.

"Without a breath of wind on the Saturday the par-fives were playing exceptionally easily, too, so we had to take advantage of those. We did. It helped him to another 68. It was another unspectacular round, though. The fireworks didn't start to go off until the last nine holes of day four."

Fireworks that were to be lit by not only Calcavecchia but also by Greg Norman. For the third round, though, the Shark had not really drawn his teeth. A 72 took him seven strokes off the lead and seemingly out of it at that stage. He did have the script in his pocket, however! His compatriot Wayne Grady was still carrying the torch for Australia. A 69 to be 12 under par kept his nose in front of Tom Watson. They would form the final group out. Ominously, the last time Watson had gone out in the final group on day four, seeking the elusive sixth Open title, it was with an unfancied Australian, Ian Baker-Finch, in 1984. It all ended in tears then. Would history repeat itself? The penultimate group out would include Payne Stewart, now lying third two shots off the pace. For Calcavecchia, his second 68 earned him a share of fourth at nine-under. He was moving up in the world but still few were even remotely considering him as the new champion. The fireworks were soon to go off, however.

Norman lit the fuse by capturing a remarkable six successive opening birdies, setting off nearly two hours before the last group out. The Great White, though, was confounded by the smallest hole on the course and his dropped shot at the infamous Postage Stamp was to prove a crucial mistake. His magnificent 64, though, set a 13-under-par target. The script was going to plan again.

Soon, however, the 12th hole at Troon, rather than the Postage Stamp eighth, was to cause the Claret Jug engraver to work overtime and wish he were on piece-work. Caddie Oddy was with the man who played the shot of destiny at the 12th hole.

"Going into the last day Mark sensed he had a chance to win, even if nobody was talking about him as a potential winner very much. It didn't go all that smoothly, though. He made a couple of birdies but then three-putted the seventh from only about 18 feet. At that point he got somewhat discouraged because Wayne Grady had gotten off to a good start. We were five behind Grady after eight holes then.

"Once you get on the back nine of a tournament's last day and you're not at least three or four shots off the lead, there's not much you're going to do about it normally. These are not bad players. They're not just going to lie down. We were beginning to wonder, 'Has it all gone now?'

"But then things started to happen. Boy did they happen! There were a couple of keys to winning the tournament and one of the really true keys was the 11th. It's a shortish par-five but Mark's drive went into the overgrowth to the right. He then tried to hit out on to the fairway, but the ground was so hard the ball just bounced and rolled and rolled. It ran under one of the thorny bushes on the left. He then only hit it about 60 yards.

"Mark was very discouraged but he hit the ball on the green. It didn't exactly cheer him up when it rolled about 50 feet from the flag still. He then ran in the putt and made par! At that point he said, 'At least something good's happening today.' There was much more to come.

"The 12th was just unbelievable. His second shot had sent his ball into real rough stuff. The chip out was going to go 20 or 30 feet by the hole. That green was as hard as rock. But the shot he tried to hit was the only shot he had to play. He just hoped to get lucky. He did. He hit the pin full-on and the ball dived into the cup. He hit it with an L-wedge and that's what the club's made for. You can hit it high and hit it soft. He hit the ball hard but he hit it with perfect accuracy!

"At that point I think he was four behind, 11 under par to Wayne Grady's 15-under. We looked at the scoreboard and knew that the rest of the holes were playing downwind. He figured if he could make two or three birdies now he could move up because no one else was playing all that well by now. All except Greg Norman, of course. While we were playing the 12th Norman was on 13 and at that point we couldn't worry too much about Wayne because if we didn't catch Greg it wouldn't matter. It did seem it was now him and

Wayne to worry about because Tom Watson looked as though he wasn't going to be the danger.

"At 13 we left it short at about 20 feet and made no impression on the leaderboard. Then at 14 we were short as well but here we were in the bunker at the par-three. But then I knew Mark was feeling confident because he was lining up the pitch out as if it was a putt, looking at the line as if it might slide out and roll on into the hole. It nearly did roll in, just lipped out. But at that point I knew he was in the groove, that he felt confident and wasn't just trying to get through or just go through the motions.

"When we played 16 he finally got his drive on the fairway after missing it all week. He could have laid up a three-wood because he was on a bare patch. He said, 'I'm not sure I can even get off this,' and then decided on a driver, which I agreed with. One reason we get along is because we think the same way. We always play an aggressive game. Our theory is 'Always get as close to your objective as possible. Don't worry about what the shot's going to be like around the green. Don't worry if it's in a bunker. It's still going to be an easier shot from 10 or 12 yards than it is from 100 yards.'

"At that point, though, there wasn't really any other choice for him. He was still three shots behind the lead and this is the last hole you can think about as a birdie chance. He hit the shot unbelievably to 30 feet and his putt really didn't miss by much for his eagle. He was glad of the birdie, though. He knew that every one he made now would take him closer to the lead.

"At the 17th he hit a three-iron tee shot with the pin tucked around to the right. This par-three seemed to play the toughest all week. You couldn't really go for the pin. The green was real hard and his ball ran towards the back left edge to about 40 feet. The putt broke six inches more to the right than we thought. But it turned out that went in our favor in the end. It was exactly where it went in the playoff. He missed both times, leaving it over the edge, but it was a much easier putt and a par in the playoff when it really mattered.

"By the time we got up on to the 18th tee, Norman was long done. We knew what we had to do, therefore: make birdie to join him. The hole, it's 425 yards, was playing short and Mark's drive ran through a very hard fairway only a few yards from the bunker Greg went in for the playoff. If Mark had hit straighter he would have been in the bunker as well, then it would have been all over for us. His drive had gone about 325 yards, so he only needed an eight-iron and he had a good lie. The scorching weather had meant the rough was not nearly so high as it could have been and it was quite easy to play out of it.

"Now people always talk about his five-iron from the right rough in the playoff here, but that was in fact a much easier shot to hit when you think it out. He knew he just had to make birdie this time or he wasn't going to be able to get up with Greg Norman. He pitched it to about ten feet. It took one hop and sort of juiced back to the right to about four feet. With out-of-bounds being only 20 feet past the pin, it was a fantastic shot under pressure. He just could not afford to be anything other than perfect with it.

"It was a perfectly straight putt but I'm not sure if it had any break, he would have played for break anyway. We think: if it's only got a little break then the best thing to do is to hit it a little firmer and straighter. Then you don't have to worry about the break. That's what he did. We were tied with Greg.

"It wasn't until we got off the 18th green that we knew Wayne had made bogey on 17. Then when we saw his ball go over the 18th green we knew it would be hard for him to make birdie. He didn't. We were in a playoff in 20 minutes' time."

Even now, the portents seemed to be in Greg Norman's favor. He had been finished for at least an hour and had had plenty of time to weigh up his options, plenty of time for practice. There is the disadvantage of possibly having too much time to think about things, however.

When the playoff got under way, by the time the second hole of the historic four-hole aggregate playoff had been completed, it looked as though Norman's 64 had earned him the Open Championship in extra time. Adrenalin and the awkward 17th, however, along with Nebraskan grit, would soon rewrite the 1989 Open Championship script.

"As soon as we knew what was happening Mark went straight off to chat to an ABC interviewer. Suddenly I realized I might not have enough golf balls. I had just three new balls left and the playoff was over four holes. You never know what might happen. We normally go through 12 or 13 balls a round on average because Titleist are so soft. Luckily, Tom Watson had plenty. He'd come off the last green with Wayne after a great bid for the title himself but he'd missed out on the playoff. He left us half a dozen balls. As it turned out we only needed our three.

"We still had 15 minutes left before the restart, so we just sat around the putting green with Greg and Wayne. It was all pretty friendly. They'd played a lot of golf together. The four-hole playoff was more relaxing. There wasn't so much tension on the first tee, knowing that it wasn't a case of bogey you're out, birdie you win. Mark was very wary, though, and still surprised it was over four holes. He kept asking the Royal and Ancient Golf Club guys, even on the tee, 'You're sure now? I mean, it's four holes, right? After one hole nothing changes, right?'

"It was a good job it was four holes, the first, second, 17th and 18th. Greg made birdie on the first. Mark made a really brave six-footer for par. He didn't want to be two down right at the start.

"At the second playoff hole, Mark hit a good drive but the second shot to the green bounced over into the back fringe. It was a good shot but the green was so firm. Sometimes, when we line up putts, Mark has a feeling, sometimes he doesn't. Sometimes he can picture a line better than others. Sometimes he says, 'This is in.' I would say he only does that 10 or 12 times a year. The putt goes in 80 percent of the time; I'm talking putts of 30 or 40 feet, which is what this one was. As he went over the putt he said to me, 'This one's in, I know.' It went right in the middle of the hole. But Greg got his from about 10 or 12 feet, so we were still one behind. At least we were keeping within range. Wayne parred again.

"On 17 we hit the same shot as earlier on, back left edge. Greg hit first, a three-iron that looked perfect, in the air it was right at the pin, but it finished over the back edge. Wayne hit his into the bunker. We were surprised when Greg decided to chip instead of putt. There didn't seem that much between his ball and the green that would cause him trouble. But you can only go with what you feel at the time. He ran it by the hole but he could still make the putt to save par. We'd played with David Feherty in the last round and he'd had the same putt, a good four-inch swing to the right on it, and missed it. We knew that Greg would have to read something in it that David didn't see. He didn't and we were level. Wayne bogeyed from the bunker so he was one-over. Mark and Greg were one-under, so we thought it was now Mark versus Greg.

"I'd thought I'd have to be calming Mark down by now but I was amazed to see how cool he was. Here we have the biggest tournament in the world, seen by the most people, and he looked pretty cool. Some players work better being excited. Not Mark. Four or five birdies in a row and the gallery's going crazy, even his wife is hopping about, but Mark feels the next hole is just as important as the previous one. That's what amazed me about the playoff. We had a laugh about something after we'd putted out on the 17th green. He'd be able to tell you what we were laughing about because I was so nervous I can't remember what it was! I do try to have a laugh most of the time; I try to get his mind off it when we're not actually playing. You have to have some kind of outlet.

"It was no laughing matter at the 18th. He hit an awful drive. It wasn't totally out of control but it was really going right. But it hit some of the photographers around the edge and came back. If there were no photographers and no gallery it would have been 25 yards further right of the fairway where the rough would have been just that bit higher. But you don't want to hit it left. There's a series of bunkers and if you get in one of those you can't get to the green. One day in practice we hit left of those bunkers and it was the only place where the grass was high. Left was no place to be, especially hitting first. You don't want to make it easy for the other guy. I don't think it was a matter of him letting up on the swing on the tee, just that he spun out more than normal.

"Then Greg hit his into the bunker. Wayne was safe. We had a good lie. But before we hit our second, we walked up to look at Greg's lie. We had to see the situation. At this point, Mark and Greg could make bogey and Wayne birdie, so it could finish in a tie. It was like matchplay now. We didn't think there was any way Greg would try to go for the green. It wasn't just because he was bunkered; the bunker face was hard-packed. If you were to catch any part of it you were more likely to hit yourself than the green. We felt the very best Greg could do was a four.

"We had 205 yards to the pin. We decided on a five-iron. All Mark was trying to do was land it on the front part of the green and let it roll. It took off and never ever wavered. It didn't fade an inch, didn't draw an inch. He could have hit a hard six but that may not have done the job and he could have finished short, even worse—in one of the bunkers.

"When it was in the air he said, 'It doesn't matter where the ball goes. I don't have any better than that.' If, while it was in mid-air, someone had said to him, 'Do you want to try that one again?' Mark would have told them, 'I'll take that one.' We knew it was inside ten feet, and so did Greg. He knew Mark had a good chance of birdie, so he had to go for it. He was unlucky in that it trickled into the bunker. Once he was there it was a hard shot.

"We walked up to the green. It's a great feeling to be on the last in a British Open the way things were. It's like being in a stadium. The crowd are excited but knowledgeable at the same time, appreciating what's going on. It was a fantastic atmosphere. We saw Mark's putt was about six or seven feet, but it wasn't quite the same as knowing you had a two or three-shot lead. We still had some work to do. If we'd known then that Greg was going to hit out of bounds it would have felt a lot easier.

"There was great confusion after Greg hit his third shot out of bounds at the back. Wayne was on the green. Greg was told by a man from the R and A that he must hit another shot. Greg just said 'Go ahead. I'm done. If you happen to four-putt from there, I'll go back and hit another one!'

"Mark just wanted to know where he stood. He didn't want to get in a position where he thought his opponent had taken a certain number of strokes and he'd counted wrong. That's part of my job—to keep track of where he is and where everybody else is.

"At that point, with Greg having blown out, Wayne was in with a chance of birdie. He'd hit a great second shot from the fairway which came close to going in, which would have meant Mark needing a birdie to win. As Wayne was getting set up for his putt, Mark said to me, 'If he makes this, how many putts do I have to win?' I said, 'If he makes it you've got two putts to win. If he misses it, you've got three.' Wayne missed the putt. Mark said, 'I got three from here? That I think I can hit.'

"He lined up the putt and I said, 'What are you lining up for?' He said, 'It would be nice to make it.' But then, as he walked towards the ball, he started worrying. He told me afterwards, all he could think of was, 'What can possibly go wrong now?' All he could think of was hitting the ball twice accidentally. 'Don't double-hit the ball,' he said to himself.

"He hit a great putt and that was the only way to win. He'd been right the first time. It was better than dribbling it up or lipping out. It would have been great to have made that putt if the competition was close. It just put the icing on the cake.

"As happy as Mark was, though, his first thought when it was all over was his family. We talked to the folks back home. We'd have loved to have been with them. Mark was worried about his wife because she was about to go into labor. He still had time to think about his mom and dad, because they'd sacrificed so much for him to be able to play golf. His father had died the year before Mark won his first tournament. He stopped to think just how his dad would have felt as he held on to the British Open trophy."

1990 ST. ANDREWS

Nick Faldo with Fanny Sunesson

Nick Faldo	England	67 65 67 71 270 (par 72)
Payne Stewart	USA	68 68 68 71 275
Mark McNulty	Zimbabwe	74 68 68 65 275
Jodie Mudd	USA	72 66 72 66 276
Ian Woosnam	Wales	68 69 70 69 276
Greg Norman	Australia	66 66 76 69 277
Ian Baker-Finch	Australia	68 72 64 73 277
David Graham	Australia	72 71 70 66 279
Steve Pate	USA	70 68 72 69 279
Donnie Hammond	USA	70 71 68 70 279
Corey Pavin	USA	71 69 68 71 279

"At the 18th I just thought, 'Hit a good drive now and let's finish really well.' After he hit a good drive I just stopped and thought to myself, 'This is really happening now.' Walking down the 18th was just unbelievable. Nothing's finished until the last putt is holed but Nick had such a big lead I just felt, 'This is it. Nick is going to win the Open now—at St. Andrews. And I'm caddying for him.'"

A woman in a man's world

In 1990 Nick Faldo, at 33, broke and equalled several records as he made his relentless way to eventually becoming arguably the best British and European player of all time. In 1990 his caddie Fanny Sunesson also made history. Sunesson, a one-time five-handicap player who could spot a swing or a putting-stroke fault nearly as quickly as her man's revered coach David Leadbetter—in fact she worked in harmony with Leadbetter on many occasions—set records herself in only her first year with Faldo.

At 22 years old, Sunesson became the first female caddie to accompany the winner of the U.S. Masters. Then she repeated the feat in the Open Championship. One year earlier, by the side of another Englishman, Howard Clark, Sunesson had also become the first female professional caddie in the Ryder Cup. In the '90s the partnership of Faldo and Sunesson became the best pairing in the world as they scooped five majors—two Opens and three Masters—and played four Ryder Cups, in which Faldo gleaned eight points.

At five feet six inches tall, Sunesson makes up for her height with great stature in the golfing business. She is famed not only for her acumen as a reader of swings, putts, yardages and awkward situations; her stentorian commands to fidgeting and chattering galleries have become legendary.

When Faldo and Andy Prodger, another caddie with great experience and his companion for major titles of 1987 and 1989, parted company, it was to Sunesson that the ambitious Briton turned as he sought to become the best golfer in the world. By the end of 1990, with success at Augusta and St. Andrews, Faldo had achieved his target. Although Greg Norman theoretically carried the world ranking number one title, Faldo was easily the best player worldwide, having left Norman in his wake in the Open Championship.

By Faldo's side was the girl with the bounce and the flounce who had decided in 1985, when watching the Scandinavian Enterprise Open, that the caddying life was for her. Imbued with a fearless spirit and Nordic phlegm, Sunesson broke into a male bastion to become not only the best-known female caddie in the world, but also probably the best-known caddie in the world. She began touring life sharing digs with the boys, but there was never any funny business. In fact, the young Swede found she had suddenly inherited dozens of minders and big brothers. Soon she was making her mark as a serious "rake-rat."

Sunesson came to Faldo by way of a string of players in her first full touring year of 1986—Brazilian Jaime Gonzalez was her first bag—before she caddied rather more long-term for Jose Rivero. After the Spaniard decided to take his brother on the bag at the 1987 Ryder Cup at Muirfield Village, however, Sunesson decamped to compatriot Anders Forsbrand for 1988. Her next long-term player was Howard Clark of England. With Clark, Sunesson achieved her dream of caddying in the Ryder Cup as she accompanied the Yorkshireman in the tie at The Belfry in 1989 that enabled Europe to retain the Cup.

The following year she was called to the Faldo ranks and within a few months Sunesson was marching with the big Englishman to victory at Augusta. Then, in June, the pair nearly pulled off the U.S. Open, Faldo having to settle for a share of third place behind the playoff pair, the winner Hale Irwin and runner-up Mike Donald. Faldo nearly won his second major of the year—and he was only a month or so away from doing that very thing.

First, though, it was a battling playoff victory against Ray Floyd in the twilight of Augusta, a particularly sweet success for Faldo. There was little love lost between the pair, their frostiness with each other stemming from an altercation three years earlier when Faldo clinched his first major, the 1987 Open at Muirfield. Sunesson knew little of the bad feeling between the two, however. It had been Andy Prodger on the bag when their original spat took place in the second round of the Open of 1987. Sunesson just enjoyed the euphoria of winning at Augusta with Faldo within weeks of starting as his caddie.

"Nick was playing really great golf, pretty well right from the start of the year. His confidence was high and I thought he was capable of winning any given week, right from when I first started out with him. That was at the start of 1990 at a skins game. It was my first year with him so I didn't know what to expect. It was a dream come true to just be carrying the bag at Augusta within a few weeks of starting with him. But it was beyond my wildest dreams, when I first started caddying, to be with the player who won the Masters. For me to come in as a new caddie with Nick and him to win a major so soon was amazing.

"I was on such a high at the end of the playoff. It was a fantastic win by Nick, doing what he did, especially hitting into the bunker at the 10th hole and getting up and down, then getting it to the 11th hole and winning there. That was magical, typical of Nick's character, his determination.

"Then it was really, really close in the U.S. Open. It was a breathtaking time. He could have won all the first three majors. On the last hole at Medinah he hit a putt of about 12 feet that looked certain that it was going in but then at the last second it veered off. If he'd holed it he'd have been in the playoff with Irwin and Donald. It's easy to say 'if' and 'but' over the outcome of any tournament, but we felt as though Nick could have won that week. That putt definitely looked as though it was going right in the middle of the hole. Then Nick had shown he was good at playoffs, of course! But he didn't hole it, so that was that. He was playing so well, though. You had to feel that he would do well at St. Andrews as well."

Faldo and Sunesson warmed up for St. Andrews and the 119th Open Championship at Gleneagles the week before the major, the testing Scottish Highland course just up the glens and braes from the "Old Grey Toon." It was a good week of preparation and it was a week where Sunesson's knack of reading a good line on the greens was well appreciated by her boss. Faldo asked his caddie to help him with the tricky borrows on the Gleneagles greens, something he had not done a great deal until that week before the Open.

"Fanny has unlocked the door to some putting mysteries that have been confounding me," said a delighted Faldo as he looked forward to tackling the yawning links greens of St. Andrews the following week. For a time he had wondered if his putting might spoil his chances. Sunesson's sharp eye for a line and a subtle borrow, however, left him brimming with confidence for the third major of the year.

His caddie was brimming with feeling, too—mainly nostalgia and delight at being at the Home of Golf.

"Arriving at St. Andrews that week was something really special. It's a magical place. I'd been before but this time it was different. I'm with the best player in the world. I've always loved the Open. It gives you such a buzz. It's an international field—and we had just about the best field ever for an Open at the time that week—and you meet so many different players and caddies from America and Australia and so on. I love the links, love it for being so tough when it's windy, just love that type of golf. It's so exciting being in an Open. You don't know what to expect for the week, but you feel you will be in the middle of everything that's going on.

"Early in the week a few of us caddies were sat around talking and we were saying that the Open was the ultimate tournament to win and to caddie for the winner at St. Andrews was the ultimate honor. While we were talking I couldn't help but hope that it was going to be me, winning at the Home of Golf.

"I'd had some experience of the Open because I did 1987 with Jose Rivero, 1988 with Anders Forsbrand and 1989 with Howard Clark, so I pretty well knew what to expect, with the crowds and the excitement. The atmosphere wasn't new to me, just the feeling. This was St. Andrews. And if you've got a player standing on the tee who's got a chance to win, it's very exciting.

"I enjoy the people at the Open, the crowds. They are very knowledgeable and they are definitely there for the golf, nothing else. A lot of the times it's not great weather and they are out there come whatever. St. Andrews galleries, particularly, are not fair-weather golfers!

"After the Scottish Open I went straight down to St. Andrews after play finished on the Saturday. It had been quite a memorable Scottish Open because before we started the third round, Nick said to me, 'Today you read the greens.' That had happened very seldom before, so I was pleased, of course. After the round a lot of journalists asked me questions and then I found out Nick had told them the day before that I'd be reading the greens with him. On the last hole we were studying a putt for a long time and someone in the crowd shouted out, 'Let Fanny do the putting!' Nick handed me the putter for a joke.

"I was staying at the Dunvegan Hotel, which is only a minute or so from the course. That was great because I go out early in the morning to check the pin placements. I think I went out on the Saturday night, even, to check on the course, because it didn't get dark until really, really late. Sunday morning I was out early to take in whatever I might have missed the day before. I can't remember if we played a practice round but we did practice. David Leadbetter, his coach, was there and Nick did a lot of work with him.

"The practice was enjoyable and it was good practice. Nick practiced on his own and with other players but because I was concentrating on the course and the job in hand I don't even remember who we practiced with. That's how I am. Certainly, in the tournament, I get so wrapped up in what's going on with our play that 24 hours later I might not remember who we went out with!

"St. Andrews is a course that is tough and you need to know where to hit it, so I was concentrating fully all the way to the first round, so I'm not surprised I can't remember our practice partners. I do remember huge crowds watching Nick on the practice ground. The work with Leadbetter was really good. Nick felt positive all week. It felt like I was with a potential winner walking on to the practice ground. Well, looking back on it that's how positive I felt about it.

"On the Thursday morning I was out by six o'clock to check the pin placements then went back for a quick breakfast. We were out later in the morning [10:50 A.M.], so I had to be fairly early, pick up the clubs and then pick up Nick at the hotel for our last practice before the first round. David Leadbetter joined us for what Nick calls 'fine-tuning.' That's all routine.

"We were playing with Scott Hoch for the first two rounds. I think Nick and Scott had a long talk. I think he went over what happened for the press. It was all about things Scott was supposed to have said about Nick after Nick beat Scott in the Masters the year before. But the press really built it all up bigtime, changed things around and made something out of nothing. They wanted a story and I'm sure it wasn't meant to be said the way it came out. It got out of hand. Anyway, there certainly was no bad feeling when Nick and Scott played together at St. Andrews.

"It's difficult to remember every crucial part of the first two rounds. It was the weekend that sticks most in the memory, of course. I know we were well up there after the first round and that Nick again asked me to help him read the putts.

"Nothing much happened on the first nine but Nick really got going after the ninth and he made three birdies in four holes, which got us into contention. The Road Hole, the 17th, was the only hole where we dropped a shot, but then we did a couple of days there. It was playing like a par-five, anyway. Most of the time you're happy to walk off with a five. Even if you do make five it doesn't really feel like a bogey. We played down the left because that way there's not such a chance of going on the road. The second shot went left and from there it was difficult to make par. He missed about an eight-footer for the four.

"The 18th does stand out vividly in my memory—an eagle-two to finish with. He went with the two-wood off the tee again and it was a great drive because he was just over the Valley of Sin. He decided on the eight-iron himself because he wanted to play a pitch-and-run shot. There was no need for me to talk about the club with him because it was a 'feel' shot for him and he knows which club will work best. I did help with the club selection all the time, but this was one where my opinion was not needed.

"He struck it perfectly, just amazing, because it bounced a few times and ran straight into the hole. It was just a fantastic feeling. The crowd were going wild. It was such a shock. But it was a great finish—and a great start to the tournament."

Faldo had typically worked to a set regime, using the two-wood he'd placed in the bag for St. Andrews as often as possible "to get penetration through the wind." But even he was surprised to hit it as far as he had on the last hole. He was left with little option then but to chip and run. The eagle finish then provided him with a telling bonus. He had taken a sideways glance at the leaderboard when he played the 18th and saw that he was three shots behind his arch foe, Greg Norman, for the right to be pronounced world number one. The two at the last hole for a five-under-par 67 meant Faldo pulled back to within just a stroke of the Great White Shark.

With Norman at 66 was an unsung American, upstaging his more illustrious brethren—Michael Allen. Faldo was in third place on his own and there were eight players who recorded rounds of 68, among them Ian Baker-Finch of Australia, making a second bid to clinch an Open at St. Andrews after his disappointment of 1984. American Payne Stewart was also making another bid to put the Open title on his curriculum vitae. Stewart and Baker-Finch would be chief adversaries for Faldo but it was the Great White who first had to be caught and then hopefully netted. That was not going to be an easy task right away.

"It was very exciting for the crowds and the newspapers to have the best two golfers in the world at the top of the leaderboard and, of course, I was conscious of Greg Norman being the big danger. I suppose it was understandable that they would be locked together and finish up playing together on the Saturday. Nick had a really good second round and it let him catch Greg. This time I seem to remember Nick played well on both nines. He holed some really good putts, two or three around the 15- to 18-foot mark, but his irons were great, too.

"One of the most enjoyable holes for us—I know Nick enjoyed it very much—was the 17th this time. We parred it. We were in the left rough again and the ball finished up a long way from the flag but Nick managed to get down in two putts. It was great for Nick to shoot a 65 and really something not to make a bogey."

A card containing seven birdies without any blemishes enabled Faldo to match Norman, who shot another 66. That really did leave the top golfers of the time out on their own. At 12 under par they were four shots clear of the field as they equalled Henry Cotton's fifty-six-year-old record for two rounds.

Their nearest rivals were Payne Stewart, a player who stayed to dog Faldo right to the very closing stretch on Sunday, and another Australian, Craig Parry, who had temporarily taken up the mantle of Ian Baker-Finch.

It was the Faldo–Norman show part two, however. Part three was about to unfold. This is what Faldo thought about their potential showdown at the time: "We are sailing along. Greg and I are holing putts and seizing opportunities. It's great stuff. But there is a long way to go and the guys behind now know what they have to do. The pressure is off them and they can go for it and catch us up."

The clement weather contributed to a blaze of fine scoring which produced a record low cut-off of one under par, thus putting out such luminaries as the defending champion Mark Calcavecchia, Tom Watson and Severiano Ballesteros. Faldo had been astonished at that record-equalling 12 under par leading after two rounds until he surmised that the wind had hardly bothered anyone yet. "When it blows at St. Andrews the seagulls don't bother trying to fly, they walk," quipped Faldo.

There were to be no obstructive gusts all week. And it was not to be any ill-wind which blew Greg Norman no good at all in the third round. When Norman began Saturday afternoon, playing alongside Faldo, with a rush of three-putts, great black storm clouds began to gather for the Great White, as Fanny Sunesson noticed.

"I was conscious that there had been a big build-up by the press and tele-vision about the third round. It was going to be a golfing battle between Nick Faldo and Greg Norman. For me it was a case of going out there and con-centrating on what I was supposed to do. I had to do my stuff no matter what excitement was going on with Nick and Greg being head to head.

"It was going to be vital to get off to a good start bearing in mind that the two were playing together, and we got it. Nick's shot in with his sand-wedge wasn't that brilliant, to about 18 feet, maybe just a bit less. Greg got inside Nick by at least four feet or so. Nick ran the putt in and Greg missed his. That set the scene for the day.

"Greg then bogeyed the second with a three-putt, so that was a two-shot swing in two holes. Nick's putting was great again. He had four putts for birdies that must have been 18 feet or so, from what I remember. It was just the opposite for Greg. His putting really let him down. But even though Nick's putting was good, it wasn't just that. The greens are big at St. Andrews, some of them double-greens, of course, so you can have some very long putts if you don't hit them in the right place. If you hit a wayward shot or get a bad bounce you can have a putt of 60 yards and then it's difficult to get down in two. Nick hit at the pin all week and we didn't have too many bad bounces. Just one bad bounce at St. Andrews and, wham, you can be really unlucky.

"We did get a bit lucky on the 12th. We were in the gorse but Nick could get a swing at it and the ball was lying reasonably so he could chip out okay. Then he made a great recovery pitch, it didn't cost bogey. The bogey didn't come until the Road Hole. By the time we reached the 17th, Greg had fallen well behind. He made a lot of three-putts that day. The putting just killed him.

"We finished up one shot worse than perhaps Nick deserved and it was the Road Hole again. This time we were short with the three-iron, not unusual. The pitch-and-run was not a bad one, but the putt didn't drop, so that's a five again. As I've said, though, you take a five there. When you think of the sort of tragedies there, you take five. It could be seven, eight, even worse.

"Anyway, he came straight back and birdied the 18th. That was a nice finish, a lovely little wedge to about two feet and another 67. Bearing in mind what had happened to Greg, that was a great round."

The battle between Nick Faldo and Greg Norman was over, with the Great White Shark the loser. That battle had largely been fought on the ample greens, won by Faldo and Fanny Sunesson, while the arch enemy floundered in a tide of three-putts.

Modest Sunesson refuses to take any great credit for her part. Her adage is always, "It's the player who plays the shots and hits the putts." But Faldo had this to say after a round which had seen him vanquish his most serious rival: "With Fanny helping me on the greens, as long as we are both on the same train of thought, things have gone really well. It is just to confirm what I'm seeing and that's really important. Looking at it from both sides, I can see this, she may see something else, and I really believe that this week two heads are better than one. You get the odd one wrong, but, obviously, it's working well. It started at the Bell's Scottish Open last week, when I was not reading the greens at all well."

Faldo was now five strokes clear of the field at 17-under-par 199, the Open record for three rounds and the first score under 200. He had an Australian for a final-day playing partner. This was not Greg Norman, however, but Ian Baker-Finch, who had moved up to second place by equalling the Championship record for nine holes by reaching the turn in just 29 shots. That man Payne Stewart tagged along determinedly, also at 12-under, to share second spot. Yet another Australian, Craig Parry, was a further stroke behind. England's Paul Broadhurst equalled two records to lie yet another shot off the lead. He was out in 29 and carded a 63 to equal the best 18-hole score.

The Australian who was supposed to be Faldo's chief challenger, however, had crashed nine strokes adrift of the lead. A 76 was not heralded by trombones for Greg Norman as yet another major championship and yet another Open slipped from his grasp.

A second major of the year was on the cards for Nick Faldo and his diligent Swedish caddie. Their chief challenger was about to be the man dressed in plus-four trousers with a Stars and Stripes shirt, the irrepressible Payne Stewart.

"Five strokes ahead of the field, but the final round was a lot of pressure. I thought, 'Well, you can only do your best. Just go out there and do your normal work. It will happen if it's meant to happen but, whatever the final round brings, you have to concentrate and do your job regardless.' The trouble is, when you have a five-stroke lead you are expected to win and people think you should win easily. That's why there's so much pressure. It's not fun. It's not like you're leading by one. But if you play half-decent then you should win— unless someone shoots ten-under, or something.

"Nick got off to a great start again and that made me think that everything was going to be all right. He stiffed it at the first this time. It was a two-iron off the tee and pitch over the Swilcan Burn to about three feet. It was a great start to the day.

"But everything went quiet for us then, just nothing much happened. Nick wasn't in any great trouble anywhere but you wondered if people were catching up. I remember getting to the 11th and the pressure was really on then.

Payne was playing just in front of us and after he'd played the 12th he had got to within two shots of us. Mark McNulty was up there too. He'd come right through the field. Payne was really chasing us, though.

"I had to keep calm myself and I remember thinking that I must keep Nick calm as well. He was obviously tense, well aware that he had someone running as hot as he could to try and catch him. I just tried to take his mind off the tournament, tried to switch off a little bit from hitting shots. Nick's great for chat, he tells some great jokes all the time, but this was the last day. My turn. I felt I had to relax him a bit, so I talked about dogs, wallpaper, how many bedrooms he was going to have in his new house, anything I could think of.

"Nick did seem to relax, especially when we realized that Payne had dropped a shot. A birdie on the 15th really took off a lot of pressure. That was a great shot by Nick at that stage, a six-iron to about eight feet. When I saw the scoreboard Nick was well clear again, so it looked as though it could be over.

"But then it was my turn to need to relax. I remember at the 16th helping to read the putt and thinking, 'It is important that we get this one right because we've got 17 to play.' I can't remember now whether the putt was for birdie or whether we made it or not. I know we didn't drop a shot and that was important with the Road Hole coming up. It looked good on the leaderboard but anything can happen at the 17th and you can't relax until you've played it.

"We hit it short and the ball was then short of the bunker, short right. All I remember thinking was, 'Don't put it in the bunker.' He was either going to chip it or putt it, that's the way the ball was lying. There have been plenty of people putted into the bunker. It's nasty. You can do a lot of damage there. Nick was looking long and hard at the line, so I knew he was thinking the same as me. So we discussed it. It was a tricky shot, especially in the circumstances. And there was the other way round. You could stick it on the road from there if you got it too sharp. Well, he didn't do any of those things and the danger passed.

"At the 18th I just thought, 'Hit a good drive now and let's finish really well.' After he hit a good drive I just stopped and thought to myself, 'This is really happening now.' Walking down the 18th was just unbelievable. Nothing's finished until the last putt is holed but Nick had such a big lead I just felt, 'This is it. Nick is going to win the Open now—at St. Andrews. And I'm caddying for him.'

"It was just unbelievable, walking over the Swilcan Bridge, walking up the fairway, the crowd was going mad in the big stand. It's such a special place. The crowd was shouting my name and Nick just turned round and said, 'Enjoy this moment.'

"We walked up, I was in a bit of a dream almost, and as soon as we hit the second shot the crowd just started running. They use a rope now to hold them back, but not then. We had to run to try and stay ahead of the crowd. It was frantic. But I'm glad that did happen because it's a special moment. Just having to struggle through the crowd and work my way to the green was just—magic, unreal. And then when he holed the putt, two-putted I guess—I can't remember. It was so emotional. Such a high. I don't think I shed a tear. I've no idea why not."

Faldo had won by five strokes after Stewart's attack fizzled out, leaving the American sharing second place with Zimbabwean Mark McNulty, who had scorched through the field with a 65. The new Open champion's 18-under-par score was a record in a year when he set and equalled many. Caddie Sunesson had played her part. Faldo and the gallery were not about to let anyone forget it.

"The Open Championship prize-giving is something I'll treasure all my life. Nick said some nice things about me and the crowd shouted for me to go up there with him. The presentation was by the first fairway and they were shouting, 'Get Fanny here.' That was really neat. They wanted me to hold up the trophy. I wasn't going to go up but then Nick asked me to hold the trophy. That really was a dream come true."

1991 ROYAL BIRKDALE

Ian Baker-Finch with Pete Bender

Ian Baker-Finch	Australia	71 71 64 66 272 (par 70)
Mike Harwood	Australia	68 70 69 67 274
Mark O'Meara	USA	71 68 67 69 275
Fred Couples	USA	72 69 70 64 275
Jodie Mudd	USA	72 70 72 63 277
Eamonn Darcy	Ireland	73 68 66 70 277
Bob Tway	USA	75 66 70 66 277
Craig Parry	Australia	71 70 69 68 278
Greg Norman	Australia	74 68 71 66 279
Bernhard Langer	Germany	71 71 70 67 279
Severiano Ballesteros	Spain	66 73 69 71 279

"On the driving range on Sunday Ian was hitting the ball so well. As a caddie you kind of look at your player before the round's started, to gauge how he's hitting the ball. If he's not connecting well it starts you thinking. Every drive was perfect, every three-wood. He was nervous and said, 'Man, let's get this thing on the road.' I knew he was going to play well by the way he'd warmed up."

Nice guys sometimes win

Ian Baker-Finch came to Royal Birkdale in 1991 as a man in form and a man who felt the Open Championship might just owe him a favor. The quiet, much-liked Australian had had the 1984 Championship in the palm of his hand going into the final round, but an agonizing spin back by his ball at the first, which left it trickling into the Swilcan Burn, wrested Baker-Finch's grip from the Claret Jug handle. He had made a couple of brief forays for the major title since then, only for his hopes to be dashed once again. The previous year, for instance, he was again out in the final group at St. Andrews, only to take a back seat to an irresistible display by Nick Faldo.

However, Baker-Finch's determination to hold the oldest major title was undimmed by the time he teed off in a cold, stiff breeze at the Lancashire course. This time he had on his bag a caddie who had won once, the man who accompanied Greg Norman to Open victory in 1986, Pete Bender.

One of the most respected caddies in America, Bender had twice carried for Jack Nicklaus before making his second Australian connection with Ian Baker-Finch. The highly experienced American bagman from California, 30 years on the fairways by the time the millennium ended, first found Open success at Turnberry with Norman. Norman heaped praise on Bender, mainly for being such a calming influence, after collecting his first major. When they parted company in 1987, Bender did not have to wait long for a top bag. The following year he was accompanying Nicklaus for a second time.

However, Bender loved touring Down Under and when he returned to Australia with Nicklaus for a "skins" game that year he got talking to Baker-

Finch. Their friendship continued the next year when Baker-Finch came to America. "I knew he was a nice guy, a down-to-earth kinda guy," says Bender. Baker-Finch approached Bender at the Los Angeles Open and asked if he would like to work for him one day. That was 1989. By the following year they were together and the pairing lasted three years.

It was 1991 that proved the value of similar spirits working together as Baker-Finch rose to fifth on the world money list with a win in America and five second places on the U.S. Tour, as well as his triumph at Birkdale. The week before the Open Championship, Baker-Finch lost in a sudden-death playoff to Bruce Fleisher in the New England Classic at Pleasant Valley, Massachusetts. It was no ordinary shootout, either. It took seven holes of sudden death to decide it.

"Fleisher holed a real long putt to beat us and he'd had to shoot a 64 in the last round to get into the playoff with Ian. Ian played so well that week. Rounds of 66, 68, 66, 68 showed just how well. We left directly after the playoff to take our flight to the British Open and he was a little bit down, as you might imagine. I said to him, 'Try and forget it. You're playing good. This one is the one we want to win.' I reminded him of that on the next Sunday night. 'Bruce won that one and we got the British Open. I think that's a fair trade!'

"We got to Birkdale and in the morning I went out and walked the course, mapped it out and did my yardages like I do at every tournament. Then I met Ian in the afternoon and we went to get our locker organized in the locker-room. He knew my lucky number was 19 and he said to me, 'Try and get locker number 19.' I first of all had to find out if they had a locker numbered 19 and they said the did, back in the corner, so Ian requested it and they said we could have it. I felt at ease with Royal Birkdale right away.

"When we went to practice, naturally he teamed up with his mates from home. We played with Wayne Grady and Greg Turner. There wasn't any talk about Wayne's playoff miss a couple of years before at Troon. I was glad about that. I tried to put positive thoughts in Ian's mind. When we'd lost the Boston tournament on the Sunday I'd said to him, 'That's over now. You would have won that tournament if just one putt had dropped that didn't, but it's over.' For this week I just reminded him we're coming into the British Open now; just remember that you're swinging real good. But I knew he hadn't lost anything in the swing. When he went out to the range with David Leadbetter, I knew he was going to be tough to beat that week. He didn't miss one shot on the range. Some guys don't warm up very well but when Ian's hitting every shot really solid like he was on the range, I knew it was going to be a good week.

"When we began the first round I guessed he was going to need to be in good shape, too, because it was windy and a little bit on the cold side for the time of year. We needed sweaters and a wind-breaker. Ian played pretty solidly, shot a 71, one-over, to be in the top 20 or so, but no one took a lot of notice of us. They were too busy talking to Seve, who'd shot a 66 to lead. We played with Fuzzy Zoeller and an Englishman, Andrew Sherborne. They were real different characters. Fuzzy's full of fun and pretty loose on the course, always wants to chat. That kept Ian loose as well. Some players don't like playing with Fuzzy because he does talk so much, but Ian likes to go with the flow. He's pretty mellow. Andrew wasn't very talkative at all. That was his thing. I think Fuzzy probably helped Ian relax, though."

Seve Ballesteros mastered the awkward conditions and perplexing greens the best on the first day. The charismatic Spaniard went in search of his fourth Open title with gusto, carding a four-under-par 66 to lead three outsiders by a stroke. They were the young Englishman Martin Gates, a player who survived being struck by lightning in Italy that year, Santiago Luna of Spain, the son of the Puerto de Hierro odd-job man, and American Chip Beck, who was to go on and play in America's Ryder Cup team at Kiawah Island. Another Open specialist, the winner the previous year at St. Andrews, Nick Faldo, lurked a further shot back. However, Australians were to the fore. Mike Harwood was just two strokes away from Ballesteros's lead, the veteran Graham Marsh and Wayne Grady were only three behind.

There was plenty to talk about at dinner that night. Two of Baker-Finch's practice partners were on the leaderboard. Baker-Finch was not quite there, but his caddie felt it would not be too long before he either joined his fellow countrymen to challenge Ballesteros and Faldo—or before he overtook the lot of them. It just needed patience from both player and caddie. Something was going to happen.

By the end of round two, however, Baker-Finch had slipped a little further behind, although it was still only four strokes. The new joint leaders were his friend Harwood, the latest American challenger, Gary Hallberg (of the Fedora) and the Scots-speaking Englishman Andrew Oldcorn, who came in with his score at around twilight to cause the journalists a large headache as they rewrote their stories. In fact, Oldcorn was so late coming in that several missed the fact that a Briton shared the lead. The trio were two under par, a stroke better than a group containing Ballesteros and two more Australians—Grady, still, and now Steve Elkington.

Before the third round on Saturday could be started there was something of a cavalry charge to be sorted out. Perhaps because of the inhibiting nature of the course, no less than 113 qualifiers lined up for the third round, the "ten-shot rule" providing the Royal and Ancient with an extra £100,000 bill for reserve money to pay for all those sharing the cut-off mark. It also took the total prize-money up to nearly a million—the richest Open ever.

The greens continued to try everyone's patience and some were not looking forward to a weekend duelling with the embroideries of Birkdale's putting surfaces. But this was where Bender would come into his own.

"It was a case of hanging in for the first two days, not losing it because of the greens, for instance. They seemed very spongy and a lot of players complained about them. We got good and bad breaks and a second 71 was about right for the way Ian was playing. It kept us well up there because we were only four shots off the lead. Ian was pretty pleased at who was leading. His good friend Mike Harwood was up there, so they had plenty to talk about after the second round. I didn't hang around after practice, though. I was pretty content where we were because we were in a position to make a move. We were still in contention. That's how you want to be. Make your move at the weekend. He certainly made his move on Saturday.

"He got off to a great start, birdieing the second hole. He sank a great putt, about 20 feet, and that was encouraging. The greens were pretty poor in places. In fact, Ian thought they looked more like Wimbledon when the grass has been scarred. Everybody was finding them difficult, but not Ian on the Saturday. Ian just got it into his head that he was going to try to make as many birdies as he could. He went for it and the policy worked. It wasn't just the putting. Agreed, he sank two or three big ones, but he also hit the ball real close to the flag most of the round. He wasn't all that happy with reading the lines on the greens, so he did use my help a lot. If I have a strong point in caddying it's reading greens. I read greens for Nicklaus and Norman. I'm one caddie who likes to be put in every situation there is out there during the round. I love the pressure. I don't like to caddie for a player that's not going to ask me for my advice. That's being a 'yes' caddie. You know the sort: the player will say to him, 'Is it a four-iron?' and he'll say, 'Yes.' 'Is it downwind?'—'Yes.'—'Is it right edge?'—'Yes.' The caddie's afraid to give an opinion, so he agrees with everything the player says to cover all bases. That doesn't work. Those sort of caddies never prove themselves. I'm not afraid to make a mistake. I'd say, 'No, no, it's not a six-iron, it's a seven-iron,' or, 'No, I don't think it's right lip, just straight.' I'm very aggressive with my caddying.

"So I got involved and it was great fun on the third day. We picked up more birdies, on the third and fifth. The fifth was another 20-footer and we're really on a roll now. But then just after I looked up at the leaderboard and saw we had the lead and nobody else was making a run, we bogeyed the par-three seventh with a three-putt. I'd been thinking 'this is fun,' but then Ian missed a four-footer for the second putt. It had been another birdie chance from about 25 feet, so that kind of pulled him up and made him think. I tried to keep him relaxed, talked to him to try to stop him looking at the leaderboard, keep him focused. I told him to just be patient, that the greens are difficult to read and that everyone was going to be missing short putts. I told him that good things will happen because I didn't think anyone was swinging any better than he was. I said, 'Be patient Ian. The cream will come to the top.'

"I guess he took the advice because he could have got the shot back straight-away on the next but missed about a seven-foot birdie putt, and he didn't show any sign of frustration, well hardly at all. Sure enough, one of about that length did go in at the tenth and he was really flying. He hit a great shot at the tenth against the wind, a five-iron, I think. We discussed the club; we discussed every club. Ian didn't just pull a club and go. We talked about it as usual. I told him whether it was a big five-iron, which is hit 100 percent, or a smooth five-iron, which is 70 or 80 percent.

"He made my job so much easier because he was playing so good. For instance, his next birdie, at the 13th, was with a shot in to less than two feet. He missed another short one and bogeyed the 14th with another three-putt, but then Ian really got at the course over the last two holes. He hit a great second shot in on the par-five 17th, about 200 yards with a five-iron, and then ran in his third putt of around 20 feet. At the last it could have been big trouble because his ball bounced into a divot but he hit another great shot to six or seven feet and made that one as well. I knew that his swing would never let him down that week, no matter what he came up against. As I said in *Golf World* magazine that week, 'Ian was playing so well it was like riding a winner, like being on the great Secretariat. It was like being on a fine stallion. I wasn't going to pull back—just let him go!' "

Gregarious Englishman Richard Boxall nearly captured the major headlines in the third round when he broke his leg on the tee in a bizarre accident. Boxall just went to swing and his leg gave way, broken by a stress fracture. But there was still plenty of room for the headline writers to wax lyrical about the formidable Birkdale course being taken apart.

Baker-Finch's 64 was the course record for the revamped Open course in a week when that kind of scoring seemed impossible. There was a touch of *déjà vu* about the 64 because, a year to the round, Baker-Finch had also shot 64 at St. Andrews to provide opposition to Nick Faldo. There was no Faldo to play with this time, though; it brought him alongside Mark O'Meara who had added a 67. That left them sharing a one-shot lead over pal Harwood and Eamonn Darcy, the Irishman with the unorthodox swing but the deadly short-game and determined temperament. Ballesteros still lurked, too, and the Spaniard was still sure he was going to win. It was a case of waiting for his opponents to fall, Ballesteros was reported as saying in the newspapers. Baker-Finch and his caddie had other ideas, however, and Ballesteros's over-confidence did indeed serve to spur on the Australian and the American caddie.

"I remember Ian had read the newspaper and there was a quote from Seve, saying, 'Well, I feel I have a real good chance of winning this Open because none of the guys up there have ever won, and I don't think they are a threat.' Ian told me that motivated him. He wanted to prove that he wasn't a fluke all the times he'd been up there. I guess it reminded him a bit of the times he'd come so close and all. Ian felt he was certainly capable of winning this British Open. It kind of motivated both of us. I felt Ian was perfectly capable of winning.

"On the driving range on Sunday Ian was hitting the ball so well. As a caddie you kind of look at your player before the round's started to gauge how he's hitting the ball. If he's not connecting well it starts you thinking. But I had so much confidence in him. I never saw him mis-hit a shot. Every drive was perfect, every three-wood. He warmed up really well and looked relaxed, ready to go. He was nervous and said, 'Man, let's get this thing on the road.' I knew he was going to play well by the way he'd warmed up.

"He was real loose that day, lost his nervousness very early on. He wasn't choking on me. I've seen a lot of players lose major championships because they couldn't handle it on the final day, but not Ian. We played with Mark O'Meara in the final round. That was good for Ian because they were close friends. They lived near each other in Florida and I knew Ian would be pretty relaxed with Mark. I felt good about the day. But whereas we got off to another good start, Mark didn't. He had some catching up to do later on. He played the last five or six holes four- or five-under, but by then it was too late to catch us.

"We were going to take some catching after birdieing three of the first four holes. Ian seemed to have the ball on a piece of string, drove it perfectly, hit some great iron shots and holed some wonderful putts. He birdied the second with about a 12-footer and it was the same at the third, about half that at the fourth. It was all relaxed off the tee as well and he hit a great drive at the sixth, which is like a par-five; birdied that. He then sank another big putt on the seventh, about 15 feet this time. We were five under after seven and everyone else was playing catch-up by the time we reached the turn. Ian played fantastically for the front nine, five under for a 29 [an Open nine-hole record for the final round at that time]. But, believe it or not, he played even better on the back nine, hit the ball even closer, but didn't get all the rewards because he didn't make a lot of putts."

Baker-Finch looked to have the Open at his mercy. With O'Meara falling away, the American Jodie Mudd, with a breathtaking 63, and Greg Norman set the target of three-under-par 277—but Baker-Finch was already six strokes better than that. He lay four ahead of the field, with Darcy, Fred Couples and Mike Harwood as his only real challengers out on the course. Nerves jangled, however, as soon as the leader began the back nine.

"We bogeyed the tenth, I guess through trying to protect what he had—a four-stroke lead. He cut the drive into a bunker, steered it really. I didn't like the thought of him trying to protect his lead and told him so: 'Don't hold yourself back; you know you can trust your swing, so just play the same game you've been playing all week.' I could see by the leaderboard that Freddie Couples had been making a charge. He looked dangerous, so it was important for Ian to keep focused. He soon got the tenth out of his mind and from then on didn't try to protect anything.

"At the par-five, the 15th, he was really getting into his swing. I pulled the head cover off the driver and he said, 'You like a driver?' I said, 'Sure, I like a driver.' I remember watching the video afterwards and Jack Nicklaus had said at the time, 'I can't believe he's hitting a driver. There's so much trouble. He could drive it in the bunkers, he could drive it right in those bushes. It's the wrong play. I can't believe he's doing it.' As a caddie I knew the strong points of my player and Ian's strength was his driving. I wasn't going to let him hit a three-wood and show him that I didn't have confidence in him hitting that driver. He striped that drive and Mark O'Meara said, 'That's pretty impressive.' Ian turned round to me and said, 'How do you like that one, Petey?' I could feel the confidence oozing from him. When we got down there Ian said, 'Do you want to go for it?' I said, 'Definitely. If you hit your best shot you can run it on to the green.' I knew he was swinging good; there was no way I was going to back him off. I told him he could hit three-wood and he wondered if he could carry the bunkers. I told him 'sure you will.' When I got home and watched the recording, Nicklaus was going nuts again on the video. This time it was, 'I can't believe he's hitting a three-wood. He could make a big number here.' I just thought, 'I wasn't caddying for Nicklaus, I was caddying for Baker-Finch.' He was swinging good and it was the right decision. He hit that three-wood maybe ten yards short of the green. Being aggressive was right. He didn't make a good chip and we parred the hole but I patted him on the back and said, 'That's the way to play the hole.' He said, 'Just keep pointing me in the right direction!'

"I felt we were going to be difficult to catch now. It was the only time I had any worries. That was because it was the only time we'd had to wait. We were quite a few minutes on the tee. One of the reasons why I think it was all so relaxed in the final round for Ian was the pace of play. We kept up a nice steady pace all day. Ian couldn't stop and think about what was going on. We just kept a good rhythm going, hit our shots, walked to the ball, discussed our clubs, hit it again, walked up, weighed the putt and hit it. We had no slow play where it meant he was sitting about thinking of what was going on. It wasn't like '86 with Greg. He wasn't hyper, didn't start running. I didn't have to slow him down. He was a lot more relaxed than Greg. Then when we birdied 17 I knew we'd got it. We had a three-shot lead.

"There was a bit of a shock for us at the 18th, though. As he went to hit his tee-shot at 18 there was a terrific commotion. There were some guys climbing the tree next to the tee and one guy slipped and started to fall and shouted out right when Ian was swinging. It made Ian flinch a little bit and he pulled his ball into the left rough. Not many people know why he hit a bad drive on the last hole. It was because this guy was out of his tree! The guy finished up falling right out of it. I don't know whether he'd had too much to drink, or what. It's a good job the last drive wasn't crucial. Well, we laid up out of the left rough and he pitched on about 12 feet behind the hole.

"It was amazing at the end. There was a real stampede. Spectators were trying to grab my towel, the head-covers, anything they could get their hands on as they swamped us. Ian kind of got away from me because I had the crowd running in front of me and he'd got two cops escorting him. I didn't, so I never got chance to walk alongside him up the last to the green. Anyway, he lagged the putt up for bogey to win by two with a 66 instead of three with a 65 to follow on from a 64. It didn't matter. He'd got rid of his 1984 ghost. I told him I was really proud of the way he handled himself.

"After they gave him the Jug he ran over to me. He handed the Jug over to me and made me carry it. That made me feel part of the team. Some players don't do that, but Ian is that way, very thoughtful. He had a copy of the Jug made up for me by Tiffany's in New York. Greg did the same in '86, so I now have two copies of the Auld Claret Jug. It was nice to be a part of it. In all my 30 years caddying Ian's been the nicest person I've ever met. It's been so sad the way things have gone for him since.

"We went back to the house he'd been staying in all week for a little party and as we drive up to the door I happened to look up at the number on the mailbox. I said, 'Ian, have you seen what the number is on the door?' He stood back and looked and said, 'Can you believe that? Number 19. I hadn't noticed that all week.' Locker 19 and house 19. It was meant to be."

1992 MUIRFIELD

Nick Faldo with Fanny Sunesson

Nick Faldo	England	66 64 69 73 272 (par 71)
John Cook	USA	66 67 70 70 273
Jose Maria Olazabal	Spain	70 67 69 68 274
Steve Pate	USA	64 70 69 73 276
Donnie Hammond	USA	70 65 70 74 279
Andrew Magee	USA	67 72 70 70 279
Ernie Els	South Africa	66 69 70 74 279
Ian Woosnam	Wales	65 73 70 71 279
Gordon Brand Jnr	Scotland	65 68 72 74 279
Malcolm Mackenzie	England	71 67 70 71 279
Robert Karlsson	Sweden	70 68 70 71 279

"John Cook had gone in front. We saw that on the leaderboard. I don't think Nick could believe what was suddenly happening. He said to me, 'Well, I'd better do something special now.' He told me afterwards that he said to himself, 'I'd better play the best four holes of my life now,' and he needed to."

Somebody did read the script

There was a sentimental return for Nick Faldo in 1992 to the Muirfield links. It was the venue that had set him on the road to being the world's best golfer, a point he was to achieve in a year when he again became number one in Europe and then rose to the top of the world rankings.

Faldo had achieved his maiden major success with Andy Prodger by his side in 1987 but the English professional returned to the Honourable Company of Edinburgh Golfers this time with the lady who had accompanied him to victory at St. Andrews in 1990. The success story of Fanny Sunesson with Nick Faldo was about to add another chapter to the girl's own story.

Between winning at Augusta and St. Andrews in 1990, Faldo and Sunesson had a moderate year, but by the time they came to Muirfield, the partnership looked capable of once again mastering the rest in a major. The only blot on the landscape was Faldo's sudden penchant for snatching defeat from the jaws of victory, or trying to. He rode high in Europe by the summer and he had performed well in both majors, tied 13th at the U.S. Masters and then even better in the U.S. Open, where he just again fell short of clinching that major, having to settle for a share of fourth place. He was also second in the tournament everyone was touting as the "fifth major," the U.S. Tournament Players Championship.

However, twice Faldo showed an unusual chink in his armor as he warmed up for the third major of the year. It first manifested itself in the Irish Open at Killarney, a tournament Faldo was fast making his own property. There he allowed a mammoth lead to melt away with a closing 75 and he was hard-pushed to win after a playoff with the South African Wayne Westner. That was not the only blemish on Faldo's finishing, for two weeks later his closing 74 in the French Open at the National course in Paris did cost him this title, when he seemed to have it won easily, having built up a big lead. That was until out-of-character mistakes in the final round left him only sharing third place behind Spaniard Miguel Angel Martin.

That kind of behavior was decidedly alien to the Faldo psyche. Normally, his very presence near the top of the leaderboard was enough to put the frighteners on his opponents. Faldo just did not crumble like that. In the 1992 Open Championship Faldo showed, though, that the sudden fault in his normally rock-solid approach had not gone away.

As usual, caddie Sunesson was getting on with the job, terrifying unthinking, fidgeting spectators with her bark and looking as though she could bite, too, if any inexperienced photographer even allowed his or her finger to hover near the shutter when Faldo's putt or swing was imminent.

Sunesson had been able to bask in the triumph of three major successes before coming to Muirfield and life was very much different to when she had stayed near the Edinburgh course for her previous visit to the Open Championship. That had been in 1987 when she was on the bag of Spaniard Jose Rivero, just a year after she had joined the caddying cadre.

"I stayed with a friend in a caravan at a family's home during the week of the 1987 Open and it was horrendous. It was cold and there was water running down the walls inside. They didn't have sheets. We were sleeping in curtains! It was my first full year on tour and things were very different for me then. I couldn't afford anything better. I made my mind up there and then that I'd have somewhere better to stay the next time. When I came back five years later, things had changed dramatically for me. I would be staying somewhere much nicer. It was nice to have a proper room and bed for the week. I stayed at the same hotel as Squeeky, Nick Price's caddie. There's a very, very nice restaurant in Gullane where they do a fantastic five-course dinner, and I loved eating there. I thought back to how it was five years before!

"It was obviously very memorable for Nick coming back there—even more than for me, of course—and I didn't have too many good memories of the tournament in 1987 because the player I was with, Jose Rivero, missed the cut that week in the Open. Coming into the Open, Nick was in really good form, even if things didn't go completely his way at a couple of tournaments. When I saw the rough at Muirfield, I thought he'd need to be in good form—everybody would. The rough was so high. I couldn't believe how thick it was when I went out and walked the course for the first time. I could see right from my inspection of the first hole that the course was going to be tough to play that week."

Rough or not, it was hardly surprising that Sunesson's player began favorite for the 121st Open Championship. Although he had not achieved all his glory by her side—two of his majors were fashioned with English bagman Andy Prodger—the Faldo–Sunesson combination was, to use the ebullient Swedish caddie's own favorite superlative, "awesome."

Faldo himself had the best record of the world's top players for that era. He had overcome Paul Azinger in 1987 to clinch his maiden major title, lost a U.S. Open playoff to Curtis Strange in 1988, won the U.S. Masters in 1989 and 1990 and taken the 1990 Open Championship. Faldo had also only twice finished out of the top 20 in 21 majors since his last Muirfield triumph. Couple that with his current form and it was not surprising that the bookmakers installed him favorite to extend that magnificent record.

Matched against Faldo in one of the strongest Open fields were the U.S. Masters champion Fred Couples, the U.S. Open champion at Pebble Beach, Tom Kite, and a whole string of U.S. and European Tour players who were perfectly capable of clinching their first major titles: Ray Floyd, Paul Azinger, Lee Janzen and Steve Pate from America; Colin Montgomerie, Jose Maria Olazabal and Ian Woosnam from Europe were just some of the names being touted as potential winners.

One name certainly not tripping off the pundits' tongues, though, was that of John Cook. It would become a name as synonymous with Muirfield, the Open and Nick Faldo, as that of Paul Azinger's. The pundits were soon to be booking the Cook for his first major success—but just like in 1987, Faldo would be the one to have the last word.

When Faldo stood on the tee for a 9:45 A.M. start on Thursday, curiously he had none of the illustrious names in the field—no Couples, Kite, Floyd, Ballesteros, Norman, Watson, Nicklaus, for instance—ready to do battle alongside. His partners were English journeyman Peter Mitchell, admittedly the Austrian Open winner that year, and the Australian they called "Popeye" because of his brawny forearms, Craig Parry, a tough, but fairly anonymous, contender in Opens. Parry, who led the Masters that year after three rounds, until allowing the Augusta gallery to upset him on the final day, was a possible winner, but it seemed a strange draw.

That fact never crossed caddie Sunesson's mind. As usual she was far too intent on bringing out the best in herself and her player to ponder over playing partners. She was more interested in how the Royal and Ancient Golf Club had grown up the rough and narrowed the fairways than how it had arranged the draw-sheet. And then there was the weather to worry about.

"The rough caused us problems straightaway in the first round because he hit his first shot into it and the ball finished up in the bunker. Just as we set off it started to rain. That meant having to get the umbrella out. There wasn't much wind but it was miserable, rainy and gray. Well, the drive cost a bogey five, not a very good start. But after that he played some awesome stuff.

"At the fifth we got quite a break, although it was a fantastic chip back. We were through the green with the second shot, a two-iron if I remember correctly, then Nick got the return chip just perfect and the ball just ran in nicely. Later, everybody was talking about Nick's chip-and-run in the first round in 1990 at St. Andrews on the last. It does make you think. He went on to win after chipping in then and people were speculating that history might be repeating itself. That certainly got back at the bogey on the first, anyway.

"Then there was a really good run from Nick which put him right into contention. It seemed to coincide with the weather getting a bit better. In fact, the middle of the round was brilliant because he played it six under par. We picked up birdies at the eighth, ninth and tenth and then there was another soon after, at the 13th, I think. We only just missed a couple of other really good chances and I thought Nick would share the lead because we still had a par-five to come. He hit a pretty good drive at the 17th but then found the sand again. There was no chance of getting close from the bunker and that was the birdie chance gone.

"After the bad start, though, I was very happy with the 66. Nick played some great golf after the first. I don't think the weather helped at the start but then he really buckled down. It was crucial because the scoring was fantastic in the first round."

With benign conditions after the rain flurry in mid-morning, the players took the formidable course apart and Faldo could include himself in that category because, given the rub of the green, he fully deserved to be at least sharing the lead. In front were his old adversary Ray Floyd and the promising Steve Pate, forming a twin-pronged attack of autumn and summer. Floyd was nearly 50 years old but still showing he had major titles left in him, and Pate had been to the fore for about three years. Both shot 64s to hold a one-stroke lead over

Welshman Ian Woosnam, one of the fancied British contenders that week, one year after winning the Masters, and Scot Gordon Brand Junior, well into a successful European career.

Floyd, just pipped for the Masters title by Fred Couples in April, was an intriguing co-leader. Despite his veteran status and three years after captaining the USA to an honorable half against Europe in the Ryder Cup, there was every reason to expect he could contend strongly for his first Open title. Those in the know were already relishing another showdown between Floyd and Faldo, knowing there was little love lost between the pair. Faldo had been rankled by Floyd when they played together as long ago as 1987, when the American upset the Englishman in the second round at Muirfield with a comment about his slow play. Faldo had, of course, gone on to Open glory that year. Then, three years later, Faldo fought tooth and nail against his old foe to defeat him in extra time at Augusta. Add to that a defeat of Floyd by Faldo in their 1991 Ryder Cup singles and the double-looped 18-hole arena of the Honourable Company of Edinburgh Golfers could be preparing for the arch foes to cross swords once more.

Pate was interesting, too. He was the man who had to withdraw from the singles at Kiawah Island the previous year because of injury, so the gallery as well as the pundits were intrigued by his appearance at the top of the leaderboard. He would continue to intrigue them throughout the tournament and only lose his chance very late on, playing alongside Faldo in the final round.

Faldo's faithful carrier Sunesson had again been far too busy considering any of the implications of the leaderboard—apart from the fact that her player had shot a 66 which left them just two strokes off the lead. Sunesson did not even look twice at the name of John Cook—who had claimed a significant eagle at the 17th—alongside Faldo's name on the 66 mark. It was a case of wake up, go through the early-morning routine of checking pin placements, snatch breakfast, pick up the clubs and then Faldo, perform diligently on the range while her player honed himself for action, and then try to help him improve on the previous day's score. Her efforts were certainly not in vain.

"Nick practiced really well and you could just feel the confidence building in him. It was very windy at times for the second round but we got off to a much better start and he had birdie chances at pretty well all the early holes. There was no trouble at the first. This time he hit a good drive and a good second shot and we could have started by picking up a shot instead of dropping one like the first round.

"It was the ninth which really got him going, though. It was one of the best shots I saw him hit all the time I was with him. We'd dropped a shot at the par-three, the seventh, after going into the bunker, and then had a bit of a struggle with the eighth. He needed a big putt there to save his par. Then it all came right. Nick hit a good drive and that left about 230 yards still to the front of the green, perhaps just a bit less if I remember correctly, because the hole's over 500 yards long. We were hitting into the wind as well, but he really caught it beautifully and it was covering the flag all the way. We could see it take the bounce and skip on to the green and we knew it was really, really close, even though you obviously can't see just how close from where we were. We had a pretty good idea how close as we walked down because the crowd were going wild. He'd hit it to four feet. The putt went in for eagle and Nick was really pumped up. We could see that Steve Pate had gone to ten-under but we were now only two behind him.

"Nick said afterwards that it was one of the best three-woods of his career. I think it had a lot of bearing on the 1992 Open Championship, that shot. It certainly seemed to spur him on and he hit another shot in to about four feet on the tenth. Then the putting just got better and better. He made three more birdies with pretty good putts, all between 15 and 20 feet. He'd done a lot of work with David Leadbetter on the putting so that seemed all worth while.

"The wind got even trickier on the back nine but the only bad hole was the 17th. It wasn't the drive but the second shot which caused the trouble. Craig [Parry] had hit his second through the green, so we went with a five-iron and the ball came up short, left. That cost the birdie and we had to settle for par. But it was a round of 64 and Nick was very pleased with that. So was I."

Faldo was more than pleased. He told his press conference that the seven-under-par return, with the eagle and six birdies on a troublesome day of capricious, strong crosswinds, "That was my best round in an Open Championship."

The 64 took Faldo to 12-under-par 130 and that enabled him to achieve a record he had come close to breaking the last time he won the Open. In 1990, his two-round aggregate of 132, shared with Greg Norman, only equalled Henry Cotton's record of 1934. This time Faldo had broken it by two strokes.

That earned him a three-stroke lead over the player who was to become the man who stood in the way of triumph, John Cook, and over another contender who was arguably even more popular with the gallery, the home favorite Gordon Brand Junior. Steve Pate, who had faded towards the end of his back nine, was a further stroke behind Faldo and Ray Floyd stayed at seven under par to share fifth place.

As well as his magical three-wood shot, Faldo was delighted with his putting form. It was a confident 15-footer on the 12th which had wrested the lead from Pate in the second round and Faldo's performance on the greens on Friday was significant. In 1990 he had praised Fanny Sunesson for "unlocking" some of putting's mysteries for him. Well, Sunesson was still helping with the reading but the stroke was the key. This time it was his coach David Leadbetter to whom Faldo paid tribute. The second-round leader jokingly called his new method taught by his teacher "codename Basil" and would not reveal its technique. But those watching on the practice green, including caddie Sunesson, knew the secret. Leadbetter had advised Faldo to "watch it then brush it." Soon he was sweeping all before him and nothing looked as though it could go wrong.

Saturday dawned. As usual at the Open, the week provided Faldo with a birthday. This time he celebrated his thirty-fifth. Faldo and his caddie would save the big celebration for Sunday night, when, they hoped, they might have even more reason to remember July 1992.

First came the chance to gauge the mettle of John Cook as they played with the American—who looked for a little help from his friend when it came to yardages.

"John Cook had a friend on the bag that week, least I think he was a friend. He was not a professional caddie, anyway, not that it made any difference, and I just remember thinking that was a bit unusual for a major championship.

"Nick played really well again because the wind was even trickier than the day before. It was always the crosswind which caused the biggest problems with getting the clubs right. The putting wasn't as successful as the day before, not bad putting, just that the putts didn't drop so well. It could have been a better front nine. We missed good birdie chances on both the par-fives, the fifth and the ninth.

"The hole I remember most on the Saturday, though, was the tenth. We bogeyed it totally from nowhere. It was such a good drive that we only needed the eight-iron and it's 475 yards long, the longest par-four. Somehow, the second shot left us in the bunker and even then it should have been par because he played a good, solid pitch out to three feet. He was very annoyed with himself when he missed the putt and he said: 'Forget the other two [at the fifth and ninth]. That was the really silly one.'

"It was a very tricky day, though, and, really, that was the only bad mistake of the day. He played really great from the 11th on. At the 12th, for instance, he hit a great shot in, very brave, because he took the tougher way close to the bunkers. He deserved the birdie there. If the putter had worked anything like the day before his score would have been much better than a 69."

Faldo could enjoy a quiet evening celebrating his birthday and then sleeping on a four-shot lead to take into the final round. His advantage had been five strokes the last time he held an Open Championship lead after three rounds. In 1990 it had proved too much for anyone to overcome. Would it be the same this time?

His main rivals were Steve Pate, with whom he would feature on the tee for the last round, and John Cook, sharing second place. Ernie Els at eight under par and Jose Maria Olazabal, seven-under, had a mountain to climb to catch Faldo, who had equalled his 1990 three-round Open Championship record. Really it should have been a one-man procession, unless, that is, you cast your mind back to Killarney and Paris a few weeks before the Open. Fanny Sunesson was not harping back, rather she was looking at omens.

"When I went to pick Nick up that morning after collecting the clubs, we found we were wearing exactly the same color shirts—blue. It was pure coincidence, but in 1990 we'd both decided to wear blue without telling each other we were going to. Now it had happened again. I thought, 'This is a good omen.'

"I did wonder, though, if we were going to be literally blue, because he hit into the bunker again off the first tee. I thought, 'Well. we started the week like this and it all came right, so don't worry.' He could only chip out and he was a long way from the flag with his third shot, so that was bogey. It wasn't a good start to the final round.

"Things didn't get better, either. It started raining and so that meant sorting out all the rain gear. That happened as we were playing the second. We finally made par after all the stopping and starting and that was a good result, really. But we couldn't hole anything and absolutely nothing happened. Nick and I did check the leaderboards now and then and we could see that John Cook was going well just in front of us. There was a lot of pressure building, waiting for the first birdie that wouldn't come.

"The fifth, the first of the three par-fives, was a bit of a struggle. We found the sand and Nick had to stand half out of the bunker to play the shot from nearly under the lip. He did well to par. After the ninth hole, things started looking pretty good again, though. We had missed picking up shots at both the par-fives and for a time it was very tight on top of the leaderboard. John Cook got to within a stroke at one time, and then Steve Pate, who was playing with us, chipped in, I think to be only two behind, and so he looked like a big threat, too. Nick hit some good shots but the putts wouldn't drop and so the field came back to him. But then the others dropped shots at the ninth and that gave us a bit of breathing space."

Cook had gone out of bounds at the ninth to drop back to four strokes behind Faldo and a bogey by playing partner Pate left him three behind. Well ahead, Jose Maria Olazabal continued to charge, but the Spaniard was also four strokes behind as Faldo embarked on the closing nine holes.

"By the time we got to the back nine, Nick was back in front by three, but he needed to settle himself with a birdie. He said afterwards that the last day of 1987 kept flashing back, how he couldn't make birdie then and shot 18 pars in the fourth round. If the ten-footer on the tenth had gone in, things might have been different from then on. But it was another birdie chance missed and there was a lot worse to come over the next few holes. The 11th was so unlike Nick, it was incredible. He found the bunker with a wedge shot in and bogeyed it. About the same time, John Cook birdied the 12th so we're in trouble now, only one ahead.

"The 13th, the par-three, was a terrible moment. I could hardly dare look at the leaderboard after it. The shot in was fine, a nine-iron, but there was still a three-footer left after the first putt and I wasn't the only one willing it in. The crowd let out a terrific groan when it didn't go in. Nick was so upset with himself. I was a bit shocked. Then at the 14th we found the bunker with the drive and that was another shot gone. It hardly seemed possible.

"John Cook had gone in front. We saw that on the leaderboard. I don't think Nick could believe what was suddenly happening. He said to me, 'Well, I'd better do something special now.' He told me afterwards that he said to himself, 'I'd better play the best four holes of my life now,' and he needed to.

"It was really windy. When we got to the 15th tee there was a terrific crosswind, a real tough tee-shot. There wasn't much I could say. I just reminded him to keep his head still. Nick hit a great drive, then an unbelievable second shot. It was with a five-iron, I suppose his favorite club at the time. We discussed the club as usual, and it fitted the distance perfectly. But there was the wind. He hit the ball to three feet. That was the point when he at last turned it round on the last day. Up to then nothing seemed to be going right. He was really lifted when he holed the putt, a birdie at last.

"At the next hole, 16, we hit it over the green with the five-iron. He made a great save, though, chipped back stone-dead. That was so important, not to drop a shot. At that stage we were feeling we might even need to make four birdies to win, so he just couldn't afford any dropped shots.

"It was really tense. We heard a cheer that was a sort of groan first, then a cheer, when we were leaving the 16th green. I thought, 'Wow, that doesn't sound good for him, but maybe it is for us.' We knew something really vital had happened up ahead."

John Cook had completed a three-putt on the 17th, having set himself up for first a possible eagle chance and then the birdie. His missed short putt on the par-five that left him with only par, allowing Faldo a glimmer of hope.

"We were still a stroke behind when we played the 17th but Nick was awesome. He hit a great drive and then controlled a lovely four-iron into the green to about 20 feet. The first one missed but it was only a tap-in for the birdie. The scores were level then and the crowd noise told us that perhaps Cook was having another problem on the 18th. It was incredible, the atmosphere.

"When we walked up 18 we could see what Cook had done on 17 from the scoreboard, that he'd missed the putt. We knew he'd got on to the green, but we couldn't tell what had happened after that, just heard the crowd noise. It was a case of, 'Do it now. We've got our chance back.'"

Cook, who had surged in front with three birdies from the 12th to the 16th, had been caught. He then pushed a two-iron second shot right and into the gallery at the last green after being in prime position on the fairway, fazed by the strong wind in his face. He failed to get up and down and bogeyed. Faldo then had the destiny of the Claret Jug in his own hands.

"Nick hit a great second shot on the 18th, a three-iron, but it just ran through the green. He knew by now he had only to make par to win. He decided to putt up from off the green and ran the ball up to a couple of feet, maybe a bit less. He holed the putt. That meant there was no playoff. He then just collapsed with emotion. It was more relief than joy. He burst into tears. I did, too. I suddenly realized, as well, that I'd got a pounding headache. I'd been so wrapped up in the tournament I hadn't even realized. But then it hit me. Maybe it was the relief of it all with me, too.

"Then Nick made his speech—it got him into a bit of trouble with the press [whom Faldo thanked 'from the heart of my bottom' following several spats with the fourth estate]—and he also sang 'I did it my way'! It was quite a presentation that year, different, that's for sure.

"But the final round was certainly different to 1990, and quite an experience. I'll never forget how he got it back after making all those bogeys and going through such a shaky time. It showed tremendous strength of character. He got the chance because John Cook missed that putt on 17 and he had the determination to take advantage of it.

"The five-iron at 15 was the key, though. That started the late, late charge. In all my time with him it was one of the most crucial shots he played. It was now or never. The five-iron said it was now."

1994 TURNBERRY

Nick Price with Jeff "Squeeky" Medlen

Nick Price	Zimbabwe	69 66 67 66 268 (par 70)
Jesper Parnevik	Sweden	68 66 68 67 269
Fuzzy Zoeller	USA	71 66 64 70 271
Anders Forsbrand	Sweden	72 71 66 64 273
Mark James	England	72 67 66 68 273
David Feherty	N. Ireland	68 69 66 70 273
Brad Faxon	USA	69 65 67 73 274
Colin Montgomerie	Scotland	72 69 65 69 275
Tom Kite	USA	71 69 66 69 275
Nick Faldo	England	75 66 70 64 275

"I marched off and I was about 60 or 70 yards from the 18th green. I looked around and I can't find Squeek. He's 20 yards behind, so I said, 'What's the matter?' He said, 'Go and enjoy it.' I said, 'No, I'm not walking down there on my own. You're coming with me.' Squeeky looked so delighted. He came scurrying up in his own inimitable fashion and we walked up together. This will sound a bit Churchillian, but that was our finest moment."

Nice guys don't always come in second

The 1994 Open Championship finally laid to rest the bogeys of 1982 at Troon and 1988 at Lytham and St. Anne's for Nick Price, as the Zimbabwean, born in South Africa to English parents, finally got both hands on the famous Auld Claret Jug. In 1982 he had looked certain to win at the tender age of 25 when he stood three shots in front of the field in the final round with just six holes to go, but blew his chances and let in Tom Watson. In 1984 he could do nothing about Seve Ballesteros's charge with a 65 in the final round to snatch the golden prize from his hands.

When in 1982 the callow Price turned to his caddie and suggested, "We've got it now," as he pulled three strokes clear, his confidence of youth was soon shattered. Price reckoned that his crushing disappointment was the making of him. Then, when Ballesteros usurped his crown in 1988, it served to strengthen Price's character and resolve.

One thing is likely: if he had had Jeff "Squeeky" Medlen on the bag in '82 when he made his observation that the Championship was as good as his with six holes to go, the American would surely have quickly reminded his master that "It ain't over 'til it's over."

Price teamed up with perennial joker Medlen (he insisted on his nickname being spelled "Squeeky" and not "Squeaky") in 1990. They soon fashioned one of the most endearing partnerships in the business, collecting the 1992 U.S. PGA Championship title together, then finally erasing the memories of defeat for Price in 1982 and 1988 in spectacular fashion at Turnberry. Then, a few months after Price prevailed in the Open, he and Medlen were triumphant in a second U.S. PGA Championship.

Tragically, that was to be their final major victory together. In 1996 Medlen was diagnosed as suffering from leukemia. He died a year later.

That jubilant week at Turnberry and the caddie–player relationship is not lost with the passing of Squeeky Medlen, however. Nick Price kindly agreed to relate this chapter and talk on behalf of his late assistant and friend. As ever with the erudite Price, this chapter is a whole lot more than simply anecdotal about the 1994 Open Championship; the friendly Zimbabwean gives an insight into just what a solid working relationship with a caddie is all about, a story about the mutual respect of two men.

"David McNeilly caddied for me for seven years in America and, towards the end of 1990, he said he wanted to go back to Ireland. I asked him not to tell any of the caddies about it and suggested he and I draw up a kind of short-list of who he thought should come and caddie for me. He and I sat down to dinner one night and went through all the caddies who were available; I wasn't going to pinch one from someone else: it was purely caddies who didn't have bags. Squeeky was on that list. So over the course of the next three months I surreptitiously spoke to all the guys on the list, just got them on the putting green and chatted away without any of them knowing I was giving them an interview, just testing the water with them. I didn't know any of them very well. I'd seen them caddying for other players but I'd had no first-hand experience of what any of them was capable of.

"I knew that Squeeky had caddied for Fred Couples, Jeff Sluman, Billy Andrade; he'd been a bit of a journeyman out there, not latching on to any-one's bag for any great length of time. Anyway, the conversation I had with Squeek on the putting green was memorable. It was humorous, insightful and he impressed me more than anyone else with his knowledge of the game and the players involved. So, three weeks later, I approached him to work for me. This was towards the end of 1990. He looked at me and said: 'Tom Watson asked me to work for him full-time two days ago! I've told him I'd give him an answer in the next week.' I told Squeek, 'Well I've looked hard around the caddying circuit and talked to a lot of caddies and I've come to the conclusion that you and I would do well together.' So he said, 'Well, look, I'll give you a call within a week. It will only be fair to Tom.' I agreed. He phoned me two days later and said, 'I've made my decision. I'm going to come and caddie for you.'

"This made me feel pretty good. At that stage in my career I hadn't won anything, no major championships, nothing really significant. Tom Watson had done everything and he was still only 41 years old and plenty of winning left in him. Squeek took a bit of a punt there by choosing me. That's just one of the things I'll always remember him for. He took a big chance with me.

"We began working at the start of 1991 and within four months or so I won—the Byron Nelson Classic in Dallas. The chemistry was right and we had ironed out a few of the little idiosyncrasies that irritated both of us. We worked very hard on improving how he caddied and how I played. It tied in with what I'd been working on with Bob Rotella, a sports psychologist, the year before. One of the things Bob had told me was to always talk in positives. Never, for instance, let your caddie say anything negative to you. We spent about three weeks out on the course practicing the philosophy: 'Oops, caught you; you said something negative. I can't . . . oops, that won't do; no such thing as can't.' It could be coming from either of us. We were determined to cut it all out. No negatives, only positives. It was a lot of fun and Squeek had an incredibly sharp mind. He reacted brilliantly. He'd been paying attention when he went out with other players before me and when it came to caddying and knowing about golf he was phenomenal. He hadn't been going out swanning, waving to the girls in the gallery. He'd already picked up an awful lot about the game before he met me. He was a pretty good golfer in his own right, too. He'd been a college golfer and even with all his caddie duties still played to about seven-handicap when he met me.

"But after we won the Byron Nelson we went through a bit of a lean patch. I wasn't at my best and I slipped back to the previous year's type of form, back to the previous few years. Before the Byron Nelson my previous win had been the World Series in '83 in America. Squeeky was indignant. He told me: 'I'm not going to sit back and let you carry on like this and finish up having the Byron Nelson as our only win this year.' I said, 'What do you mean?' He said, 'Well, you're playing like you've achieved everything you want to achieve this year. It's only July. You've still got a full year left.' He'd noticed that little spark had gone out my game. I could get a little upset if I missed a green, for instance, all the kind of things that make you know you're trying your best. It wasn't happening for me—and Squeek had spotted it.

"Well, his comments were a real wake-up call to me. I said to myself, 'He's absolutely right. I'm just cruising and I should be more focused.' I pulled myself together and, sure enough, I won again in '91, this time the Canadian Open. I really have to give Squeeky credit for that. He was the one who kicked my backside and stopped me resting on my laurels.

"Then 1992 came along and this time I struggled with my game, not lacking motivation but just struggling with my game. We worked hard but things weren't really happening until July when I changed some clubs in my bag. I have to give Squeek credit for that, too. I'd been tinkering around with the new clubs but felt apprehensive about changing. He said to me, 'You hit the new clubs well so put them in the bag.' I did for the week after the British Open and they did the trick. I came in second in Hartford and then the following week I won the U.S. PGA Championship. I'd got over the hurdle or whatever it was that was holding me back. It all clicked. Everything we'd worked on in '91 came back into place and I left all the frustration by the wayside.

"What ensued was a remarkable period of my career. I never looked back from July of 1992. I won the PGA, then the Texas Open, New Zealand Open, the Grand Slam . . . everywhere I was playing I had a chance to win. Then when '93 started, I won the TPC [Tournament Players Championship] and took four titles that year. My life had changed and so had Squeek's.

"When '94 came along everything was going just great. It was such a wonderful time because we'd win a tournament, have a lovely party, have a great time and then the following day we'd be on the practice tee saying, 'Right. We've got to win this week.' It wasn't like we'd sit back. Squeeky would never let me do that, sit back and just cruise for a week. He'd say to me, 'If you want to cruise for a week, take the week off and go home. Don't be out here on the golf course cruising. You've got to be out here with a sense of purpose.'

"He knew me so well and I knew him so well, too. There was a lot of motivation he gave me. I always said to him, 'Constructive criticism I will never hold against you and I hope you'll never hold it against me, too. If you think I'm doing something wrong on the golf course, it's up to you to tell me. No one is going to run up to me and tell me I'm doing something wrong. And the longer you leave it, then the harder it's going to be to tell me, so don't hold back. If you see me do something and screw up—whether it's bad attitude, not trying hard enough, not looking at a putt from a certain direction—you tell me. I'm going to do the same. If I see you screwing up, I'm going to jump down on you straightaway.' It's not a question of hitting an eight-iron, hitting a bad shot, coming over the top of it or something and then blaming your caddie for wrong club selection or yardage. You both know when you've hit a bad shot. I never once questioned his club selection because I was always the one who pulled the club out of the bag. You should never let your caddie pull the club out of the bag. Always do it yourself because that lets them off the hook. We could talk about it and may be indecisive about a club—he'll say he thinks it's a little seven, I think it's an eight. Then if you're that unsure about the shot and you hit over the green with a seven-iron, you're the fool and not the caddie because you should have gone with what your instinct told you in the beginning. Anyway, if you both accept the blame and say 'maybe it was an eight-iron,' the next shot you hit you will hit with a clear mind. But if you hold it against your caddie and you don't tell him, you're hitting the next shot, the chip, in an angry frame of mind. If that's on the second hole of the day, then you've got 16 holes to play and it's only going to get worse between you.

"We always said what we felt. That was what was brilliant about Squeek: not manipulating me but understanding me completely. And I understood him so well. We could sit at a table and eat dinner for four hours and never exhaust our conversation. He was one of the few people, besides my wife, who I could do that with. There was always something for us to talk about and he was a wonderful companion. All the hours I spent on the golf course with him makes it hard to not have him with me any more. He was with me for such a golden period in my life. Even though my wife was always around, she wasn't right there when all the pressure was on me on the golf course. It's left a big hole in my life. There were shots I hit under pressure alongside him that proved so important in my career, not necessarily the ones you might have seen on the television, like a crucial three-iron to the last to make a cut in a tournament. It could have been a particularly difficult line, you'd have to maneuver the ball, but you'd hit it perfectly. He'd remember that shot. Squeeky could remember them all. He had a photographic memory and he'd remind me of them when he felt it was needed. He'd say: 'Remember that shot to the 18th at Hartford? Well, try to hit this one like that.' I think every caddie-player has that recall of shots but Squeeky's recall was something else. He'd remember how I drove into the water in the Canadian Open but then produced a perfect chip and chipped in for three. There were so many memories he brought back. I don't have the perfect memory by any means and he'd do the recalling for me. That part of my life has gone now. It's like bitter-sweet. I love to remember how we used to be but it hurts to remember at the same time.

"A lot of people got the wrong impression of him with his squeaky voice but behind that façade there was a very caring, intelligent person and I miss him enormously. Even if he were still around and had retired from caddying I'd still call him to talk each week and meet up to reminisce."

Nick Price's greatest reminiscence, of course, would be their triumph at Turnberry in 1994. Price's most precious major success, the one which at last saw him put both hands on the Claret Jug, came in the middle of his most golden career period. It was a much-deserved success but, ironically, it came when a young opponent to his aspirations made similar errors of judgment to the ones he made 12 years previously at Troon.

Coming into the third major of 1994, Price was in superb form, clinching the Western Open just before Turnberry, one of no less than six U.S. Tour titles he captured in the year. Squeeky's philosophy of never resting on his laurels was never more in evidence.

"I did something unusual before the British Open in that I had a week off between the Western Open and the British Open. I practiced the whole week at home in Florida and I was hitting the ball so well still. But then on the Monday, for my first day of practice, I was like a totally different person. It seemed like somewhere over the Atlantic my golf brain had left me. I was pathetic. I told David Leadbetter [his coach] about it and Squeek was there. I was shellshocked. 'What's going on here?' David suggested I was just all out of sequence, jet lag or something, but deep down inside I was panicking a little. I hadn't come all this way to play badly for a week in a wonderful season. I wanted to contest.

"Squeek put things into perspective, though. He said to me: 'You've played so well all year. How can one bad practice round destroy your whole year?' That's how depressed I was feeling, so upset with the way I was hitting the ball. He said, 'I can't believe you. You've played unbelievable golf all year, won a tournament two weeks ago and you're worried about one bad round. You haven't played like that in two years.' I said, 'Well, that's why I'm worried.' Squeeky said, 'It just proves it's something that's passing. It'll be gone before you know it.' That was the kind of positive thing Squeeky would say. He always looked at a much bigger picture. He was sometimes hilarious, though. He'd impart these words of wisdom, really shake me down, and then three fairways later he'd be pulling himself down over something and I'd say, 'Hey, hang on a minute. You've just had your say at me and now you're talking about yourself the same way! Practice what you preach.' We were always trying to catch each other out, particularly over negative thoughts. To give an example: there are bunkers in front of a green and the pin's cut in the front of the green. Squeek would say, 'The pin's five yards "over" the bunker,' instead of saying, 'The pin's five yards "from" the bunker.' Or, when checking a club he'd say,

'There's plenty of green behind the pin,' or, if there was water on the left-hand side, he'd say, 'There's lots of room on the right.' He became much better at the positive thinking than I was. Obviously, I was focusing on trying to play, thinking about my swing, thinking about my putting stroke. He was more concerned about the strategy we were playing so that when we got to the shot, he would be aware of how it was to be played. Once he had planted the seed, we would go from there.

"Sure enough, as the week progressed, I got better and better and I think it was Squeek's attitude and David Leadbetter's attitude that pushed me along. I don't have any reason or excuse for the game suddenly vanishing but Tuesday I started playing a little better, Wednesday much better and by Thursday I started playing really well again. I began the first round really well. We played with Corey Pavin, who, of course, I knew pretty well on the U.S. Tour, and Peter Mitchell from England, a nice mid-morning draw. We picked up a couple of early birdies, at the second and third, and the front nine was pretty satisfactory. I could feel Squeeky thinking, 'There, just as I expected.' The back nine was much tougher and I was happy with a 69 (one under par) in the finish. The wind was very strong and I couldn't believe I'd hit a three-wood 315 yards against it, nor could Squeek. We saved par there and that was important for the morale. It was an unusual wind for Turnberry. You expect the first hole to have a right-to-left wind, the prevailing wind, and you budget for that over the rest of the course. This time it was at the back so you knew you were in for a tough time on the back nine. It was a case of making your score on the front nine and then hanging on. We needed a lot of long irons into the wind on the back nine—plenty of chance for Squeek to trawl his memory banks over where we'd played some good ones in the past. At the best of times you don't want to be hitting long irons into the last five holes. We played them fairly well and one-over for the back nine wasn't too bad. I thought the course was very fair and Squeeky and I felt that, whatever happened with us, it was going to be a very good championship that week."

Price's 69 left him four shots away from the leader, Greg Turner from New Zealand. Turner's brother Glenn had caused the sporting headlines up until then—the brilliant opening bat had served a notable term as New Zealand's Test captain while also breaking numerous records in English county cricket. This time it was younger brother Greg, carding a 65, grabbing the space in the newsprint as he led the field by a stroke. A young English surprise package took up second place, Jonathan Lomas. Andrew Magee from America was a further stroke back and then came a pack of 11 lying two under par, one shot better than Price. Among them was Tom Watson, the man whom Squeeky Medlen had spurned in favor of his current master. Before long, Watson would remind Medlen even more forcibly that he was by no means a spent force, when the second round completed. Thoughts like that were kept locked in Medlen's mind, however, and his positive attitude was shared by Price.

"The second-round 66 was probably the best I played all week. It gave me the confidence to feel that if I just carried on doing what I was doing, I was going to have a shot at winning. I was getting better and better and the thoughts I'd had on Monday were in the distant past. Squeeky had been absolutely right. I needed to be on top of my game as well because the course played completely differently to the first round. This time the wind made it toughest going out. It was left-to-right this time instead of downwind. That's the toughest for the first nine at Turnberry, I think. I couldn't wait to get to the downward side on the back nine. It was a good start, though, birdies at two of the first three holes and two more by the turn to make up for the bogeys. The difficult holes on the back nine were the 12th and 14th and we decided if we could par them then we were on for a good score. Of course, Squeek was in no doubt we'd make par at the very least. It was a shame we made bogey on the last this time but two halves of 33 was pretty good. The main thing about the round was that the putting was very good again. I'd really found my touch during the Western Open and it stayed with me that week. The ball stayed pretty close to the fairway all the time. There wasn't much chance of getting it close on the greens even from the short rough because the ball came out flying all the time."

Price was deadly off the tee, too. He missed only one fairway going out, causing him a second bogey of the outward nine at the eighth, having missed the green at the short fourth to drop another shot. The final-hole bogey for his 66 denied him a share of second place, only a stroke behind that man Tom Watson, who shot a 65. The young Swede Jesper Parnevik, the man who was to help fashion Price's destiny in the coming weekend, tied for second place with another American, Brad Faxon. Price held fourth at five-under.

It was no surprise to Price to see Watson up there. He had predicted that Watson, with a supreme long game which reduced the chances of problems on and around the greens, would once again be a thorn in his side. Hopefully not the thorn he proved to be in 1982. Price and his caddie were very aware of his presence, despite Watson being in his mid-forties.

"I don't think Squeek was wondering if he'd backed the wrong horse when he saw Tom Watson on top of the leaderboard. We'd won so much since I asked him to decide between Tom and me, six in America and another six around the world. Tom may have won once during that time. No, I think Squeek was comfortable with who he was with. But it was great to see Tom up there.

"We were drawn with Brad Faxon for the third round, though. I'd played a lot of golf with Brad over the past few years, a lot of practice rounds together. He's a real easy-going guy and it's always great fun playing with a person you know so well, especially in a major. Squeeky and I knew that with things going so well for nearly two years, and the form currently so good, now that we were in a contending position we could have a really good shot at it this time. Personally, I felt my game had gone up another notch at least in the last two years. There was no reason why I couldn't take it up another notch by winning my first British Open.

"I felt very much up for the third round. It was a lovely sunny day and there was a great atmosphere with a really big crowd. For a change, there was little wind and it proved to be a ball-striking game. You could get away with a few mis-hit shots. While you thought Tom Watson was going to be your chief threat because he was dying to add that sixth British Open title, I was aware Brad was playing well enough to chalk up his first major. He was in great shape for the third round and I just couldn't quite get in front of him. Mind you, I would have at least been tied with him—and Fuzzy [Zoeller] if I hadn't fallen foul of the 18th yet again.

"Both of us were pretty fed up with the last hole by the time we came in. Squeek didn't say anything but I could tell he was really disappointed at the finish. We had 175 yards to the front and we agreed it was a seven-iron to hit the front of the green and then let the ball do the work. We were both shocked to see it pitch pin-high but then take an almighty kick through the green. We'd decided on the two-iron off the tee to make sure we hit the fairway because it's a difficult shot if you aren't in the middle of the fairway. I was just trying to get it into the throat of the green and I couldn't believe it could have bounced on. Well, the chip back was to about nine feet and I missed the putt and missed the chance of sharing the lead."

Birdies on the 2nd, 7th, 15th and 17th beforehand, however, took Price to third place at eight under par, only a stroke behind the joint leaders, his playing partner Faxon and the veteran Fuzzy Zoeller, who stormed into contention with a third-round 64. Tom Watson was still well in the thick of things, sharing third place, and so was Jesper Parnevik, also tied for third. A fourth player shared second place, Northern Ireland's Ronan Rafferty. Another Ulsterman was a further stroke back at seven-under, David Feherty. It would be the two Irishmen, but particularly Parnevik, who were to stand in Price's way on the Sunday until the affable Zimbabwean finally lifted the Auld Claret Jug, to the delight of his faithful bagman.

"Before the final round, particularly on the night before, you think about what score is going to be needed to win. You feel if you shoot 63, 64, no one's going to touch you. But to shoot that kind of score you have to take some chances, you have to gamble a little bit. I'd learned in all the previous victories that I'd had that it's going to come down to the last nine holes. That was a point that Squeek and I were adamant about. Play your 63 holes, play yourself into a position and then when you have to take chances or whatever, then it's in the lap of the gods. That was about all we said to each other as far as the final round strategy was concerned. You don't really want to say too much in case you put your foot in it. You don't want to be saying something like, 'Tomorrow we're going to play well, Squeek,' and then you go out and bogey the first hole. Then you're done. It's almost an unwritten rule among caddies and players that you don't do a lot of forecasting!

"But when I got on the practice tee on Sunday morning Squeek was fired up. I could tell. And I was, too. I don't want to say I had a bone to pick with the Open, or even a score to settle, but perhaps it did owe me a third chance after '82 and '88. I certainly had something to prove. I was going out there as a man on a mission with something to prove—to myself: that I could win the Open Championship.

"Well, we did just as we talked about, Squeek and I—to be in some kind of position by the time we turned for home. I was one behind the lead. I couldn't even tell you who it was. It could even have been Ronan Rafferty, who I played with in the final round. He certainly did go ahead. Jesper Parnevik was up there, Fuzzy Zoeller, and so was Brad Faxon, as I'd expected, but Tom Watson looked out of it. No one was actually doing anything stunning, everybody around one-under for the day, perhaps two-under, a lot level for the day, so no serious moves by the time we got to the tenth. I look at leaderboards a lot.

"It wasn't a tough day, either, not the kind of day you'd expect to keep the scoring down. It was like everyone was kind of waiting for someone else to do something. But then when I got off the par-three, the 11th, Jesper had obviously made some birdies because he was on top by three strokes. He'd birdied 11, 12 and 13. I said to Squeek, 'That's the man we're going to have to beat today. He's the man.' Squeek immediately came right back and said, 'Well, let's go and beat him then!' That was his kind of attitude.

"I birdied the 12th with a 15-foot putt, the second pretty big putt since the turn because I'd saved par from that length on the tenth. The 13th was a big hole, though, a really good up-and-down. The pin was cut in the back left-hand corner and the green dropped off. I drove it in the fairway and I was in between clubs but I felt we had to play aggressively now. This is where taking chances and taking gambles comes into play. We could play an eight-iron short and try to hole up the green from 25 to 35 feet or try and attack the flag. I went for the latter and Squeek was with me. I pushed it. The ball went down the bank. It was a really tough chip with a 60-degree wedge, but I chipped it up to about three feet and made it.

"The next hole I attacked again, I went for the flag with a five-iron. I pulled it a little bit, it pitched on the edge of the green and ran all the way over by the television stand in wiry stuff again. I had to pitch up with a seven-iron this time, low, and again made it to about three or four feet and sank the putt. Those two were very key holes in the way things turned out. Miss one and you're finished. I'd tried to play them aggressively to make birdies and finished up having to work desperately hard to save pars, but save we did.

"Every hole was going to be crucial, though, and the 16th was no exception. People don't very often think about 16. Making a par as we did on 13 and 14 when you need to is one thing, but making a birdie when you have to is another, especially in that situation. That was the case on 16. When I got on 15, the par-three, I hit a really good five-iron to about 15 feet. Now I had to make a birdie or there'd be no chance of catching Jesper Parnevik. Once again the gambling tactic—go for it. I had to find birdie soon because Jesper was still three ahead. Squeeky and I both knew this. We were at the point where we assessed the situation every few seconds, it seemed. I can't recall exactly what we said but we were of one mind and that was to pick up shots before it was too late. I knew I had to find two birdies in the last four holes to make a playoff or three birdies to win.

"I missed the putt on 15, it wasn't a particularly easy one, so things are getting pretty desperate now. There's birdie chance on 17 but he's three ahead. At 16, downwind and where I'd been hitting one-iron most of the week, I said to Squeek: 'Where's the pin?' He explained and I knew exactly where it was.

I just pulled the driver without even asking his advice. He didn't even question it. Squeek knew that was the right play. I hit the driver down there and left myself 89 yards, which was perfect for my 60-degree sand-wedge. It's a club with which I can put the maximum amount of spin on the ball. The hole was cut just over the burn and I said to Squeek: 'I'm going to hit this a little left of the flag and back it up off that slope on the left.' This was because if you just miss your shot marginally when you go for the pin, you're in the burn. It was what we called conservative aggression. I'm playing away from the pin but playing positively and aggressively because I'm going to try to bring the ball back to the hole. Squeek knew exactly the shot I had in mind.

"I hit the shot, one bounce just past pin-high, ran up the slope and sucked back down 12, maybe 14 feet from the hole. I made that putt. That was what gave me the momentum to go to the next hole and make the eagle, because now I pulled within two of Jesper. I knew I still had a chance to do it. The 17th was a birdie chance and anything could happen on the last—to Jesper or to me.

"The eagle at the 17th was just a huge bonus. If I'd made birdie on 17 then I would probably have made birdie on 18, that was my mentality by then. But to sink the putt from 50 feet was a huge, huge bonus. It was an unbelievable feeling."

Price's mammoth putt at the penultimate hole proved the killer blow for Parnevik, who had refused to check the leaderboard to find out what the situation was. The Swede, up ahead, had heard the cheers for Price's birdie on 16 and was sure he needed to birdie the last to have any chance of winning, maybe even needing to make a three just to get into a playoff. He attacked the green, only to miss it and bogey. That took Price within a stroke of the lead. The eagle gave the Zimbabwean the lead for the first and final time. When Price's putt raced in, the bogeys of 1982 and 1988 had well and truly been laid to rest.

"After I holed the putt on 17 it was pandemonium. We're running around, Squeek and I. It's high-fives, absolute bedlam. Well, I went to walk off the green and Squeek said breathlessly, 'Parnevik's just bogeyed 18. You know what we've got to do now. A four and that's it.'

"Well we hadn't played 18 very well all week—a scrambled par and two bogeys to be precise—but I was so pumped up at this stage that as long as I put the ball in the the fairway I'd have a really good chance to make birdie. As Squeek said, though, four was enough. The 18th will stay with me for the rest of my life. There's a big 'D' in the middle of the green, a shadow caused by one of the stands and the pin was cut left of it. The D was 25 feet right of the pin. We were thinking about the club for the second shot and Squeek said to me, 'I think it's just a perfect seven-iron.' I said, 'I think so, too. I'm going to hit it at the D.' He said, 'Split it in half.' I don't know how you split a D in half, but I did. I hit this seven-iron right in the middle of the green, 25 feet from the flag. Two putts and it's over.

"I marched off and I was about 60 or 70 yards from the 18th green. I looked around and I can't find Squeek. He's 20 yards behind, so I said, 'What's the matter?' He said, 'Go and enjoy it.' I said, 'No, I'm not walking down there on my own. You're coming with me.' Squeeky looked so delighted. He came scurrying up in his own inimitable fashion and we walked up together. This will sound a bit Churchillian, but that was our finest moment. He knew what it meant to me, how much I loved the British Open, how much I'd relished the prospect of winning it. It was a moment for both of us to savor. Of all the times he'd caddied for me, he knew that was the most meaningful day, even if it had been the most pressure-packed of my golfing life. It's much easier to win a tournament that doesn't mean that much to you. When you love a tournament so much, it makes it harder for you to win. But now we'd done it.

"We had a very special relationship, Squeek and I. He took ill in June 1996 and he died in June 1997. I remember the week of the U.S. Open at Oakland Hills. I was sick with a sinus infection and couldn't play. I was at home feeling sorry for myself and Squeek phoned me and told me he had leukemia. We flew from Washington to Columbus, Ohio, the Monday after the Congressional the following year, the U.S. Open that Ernie Els won, and spent the whole morning with him, stayed until 2 P.M. He died about 7 P.M. that night."

1995 ST. ANDREWS

John Daly with Greg Rita

John Daly	USA	67 71 73 71 282 (par 72)
Costantino Rocca	Italy	69 70 70 73 282
(Daly won after four-hole playoff)		
Michael Campbell	New Zealand	71 71 65 76 283
Mark Brooks	USA	70 69 73 71 283
Steven Bottomley	England	70 72 72 69 283
Vijay Singh	Fiji	68 72 73 71 284
Steve Elkington	Australia	72 69 69 74 284
Corey Pavin	USA	69 70 72 74 285
Mark James	England	72 75 68 70 285
Bob Estes	USA	72 70 71 72 285

"He was totally unafraid about using the driver all week. That was his strength and he knew that he would live and die by the driver. He proclaimed to me, 'I'm really going for it this week. I'm going to win this thing.' I said, 'You've got as good a chance as anybody, in fact better than anybody. This course is tailor-made for you.'"

Sweet drives and chocolate chips

Notorious rather than famous was the best way to describe John Daly in the couple of years prior to his dramatic playoff success against Italian Costantino Rocca at St. Andrews. Daly had not earned the sobriquet "Wild Thing" lightly. His extravagances in the bar and in the casino had been well documented by the time he came to the Home of Golf. He was already well over halfway through the millions of dollars fortune he gambled and drank away in less than a decade since winning his first major, the 1991 U.S. PGA Championship.

However, that wild nature was to be tamed four years later, by Daly himself. Instead of a thirst for alcohol, it was for further major success. Wild Thing had a hunger, too, for steaks, ice-cream—and chocolate chip muffins. The 1995 Open could perhaps go down in history as the Chocolate Chip Championship. Daly cleaned out Scotland of his favorite cakes on his way to savoring a second major success.

His caddie for the 1995 Open Championship, the highly experienced Greg Rita, had plenty to do with the Daly wild nature being harnessed, if never the driving power of the man. Rita met Daly three months after the extrovert player's victory in the 1991 major at Crooked Stick, probably when the burly, blond American was spending, drinking and gambling most as he celebrated a memorable and totally unexpected maiden U.S. Tour success. Rita saw something in Daly that was removed from the Wild Thing image. He was to be proven right at the most hallowed golf course in the world.

Rita knew a thing or two about players' capabilities. The bagman from Jacksonville, Florida, had been by the side of Curtis Strange at Brookline in 1988 when the 2001 Ryder Cup captain squeezed the last-gasp playoff with Nick Faldo and then overcame the big Englishman the next day in a 72-hole shootout. And Rita was again by Strange's side as he clinched back-to-back U.S. Open successes by winning at Oak Hill the following year.

It was at a 1991 skins game near Thanksgiving Day when Rita and Daly first met up. Rita made the overture, asking Daly if he could work for him in 1992, having no definite bag for that year. They began working together in the Tournament of Champions in San Diego and soon Daly chalked up his second U.S. Tour success, the BC Open title. Never a prolific winner of titles, Daly to date has collected only one other U.S. Tour title, the Bell South Classic of 1994. He and Rita had briefly parted company for that one, so Rita had to rely on major success and the occasional top finish on tour to earn his corn with Daly.

He was with Daly, however, when Daly teamed up with Fred Couples and Payne Stewart to take the 1993 Alfred Dunhill Cup—at St. Andrews. And there lies the rub. Daly played well at the Home of Golf. Rita knew he would relish the legendary links when the Open returned there in 1995 for its second visit in six years.

The pair parted company after the 1993 season but Daly asked Rita if he would like to work for him again in May 1995 and the bagman agreed. For both it proved an inspired decision. Daly had told the world that he was off the booze and had stopped gambling. He had married and it looked as though, at last, he was settling down. His game was getting back into shape and there was one significant fact that made Rita sure it would be a good idea to return to Daly.

"I was very happy to get the opportunity to work for John again because I knew St. Andrews was coming up and I'd seen how well he'd played in the 1993 Dunhill Cup. He won four of his five matches and was a major factor in the U.S. team's win. I felt St. Andrews suited his game and so I snapped up the chance of working for him again. I'd worked a couple of Dunhill Cups with Curtis Strange and then the Open in 1990, so I had plenty of experience of the place and knew what suited it and what it suited. He'd said all along that if he was going to win a British Open it was going to be St. Andrews. I've been to nearly all the Open venues and I definitely agreed with him.

146

"In the short time before going to the Open I became even more excited about John's chances. He had stopped drinking and a sober Daly was an entirely different prospect to the other character. It wasn't because of his form that I was enthusiastic about his chances because we took three or four weeks off before St. Andrews to recharge his batteries and get himself ready for the fray. We'd had a moderate U.S. Open at Shinnecock Hills, made the cut but didn't finish that high up [45th tied], and his actual playing form was not that stunning in May and June since I took over the bag. What was good, though, was his attitude and temperament—and his health, it seemed.

"You really can't stop John gambling, though, and I remember on the Wednesday in practice with Phil Mickelson they wagered substantial amounts against each other in a big-money match. One of his main practice partners is normally Fuzzy Zoeller, but Fuzzy missed the 1995 Open with a bad back. Maybe the stakes would have been even higher had Fuzzy been at St. Andrews!

"John might have been gambling in practice but he was also being very sharp with his course knowledge, taking everything in, especially with the bunkering. His attitude to the week was attack. After all, as everyone knew, he was a big hitter and, provided he could stay out of trouble, hitting the ball a long way to give yourself easier shots in to the green is a major factor at St. Andrews. A lot of people during the tournament, especially on the last day, thought he was taking too much of a gamble always pulling out the driver from the bag, but that was what John decided right from the word go and he was always going to stick by that. He knew he had a real feel for the course and he was going to stick to his game plan—that was to attack the hole and worry about what happened when he got to it.

"He was totally unafraid about using the driver all week. That was his strength and he knew that he would live and die by the driver. He proclaimed to me, 'I'm really going for it this week. I'm going to win this thing.' I said, 'You've got as good a chance as anybody, in fact better than anybody. This course is tailor-made for you.'

"For instance, at holes like number nine [356 yards] and number 12 [316 yards] and even 17 [the infamous Road Hole with the Old Course Hotel in view and little room for error] he was going to hit a driver at them as much as he could, even though not many other players were thinking that way. There's always a bunker that's going to come into play at pretty well any hole at St. Andrews, so it was, I guess, a pretty brave tactic. The bunkers are so strategically placed, no matter what the wind's doing, one is going to come into play on every tee-shot, but I wasn't going to dispute his strategy. Hitting a driver as much as possible was in my way of thinking, too. He had to go for it. Anything else was so out of character, he would not have got the best out of a great opportunity.

"The days leading up to the first round went well. John was staying at the 'big house' (the Old Course Hotel) and I was staying at a fantastic house with a whole bunch of us—I remember Payne Stewart's caddie was with me for one—rented for about £10,000 for the week, through an ex-caddie. It was a castle, turrets and all. It was about twenty minutes from the course, so that kept us all out of mischief! I like meeting up with the guys in the Dunvegan Hotel normally, for a few beers.

"I needed a clear head because it was going to be quite a week. For a start we were playing with two great champions. Larry Mize had won the Masters [in 1987] and John respected him, but he really got a great buzz out of playing with Seve Ballesteros for two days. That definitely lifted John. Seve didn't play that well but John was really impressed with the way he handled the crowds. He said to me that he hoped one day they'd get behind him the same way as they did all the way round with Seve. It was something else. Seve had had the great win there in 1984, of course, and they loved him for that alone. John took a back seat—even though he shot a 67 with seven birdies to share the lead after the first round. He didn't mind that

"It was a bit ironic that John played the whole of the first round with a migraine. He's been off the drink for two years and he has a headache! But he didn't let that hold him back. His driving was long and pretty straight. He'd used a new driver with an eight-degree loft at the U.S. Open and brought it with him to St. Andrews, kept the ball a lot lower than normal and he got a lot more penetration. And he was far more accurate. That was the key for the week: distance and accuracy. That's why Tiger Woods [was] the man to beat at St. Andrews in 2000.

"For instance, he birdied the fourth, which is a really long par-four [463 yards], purely because of the drive. It's not quite as fearless as you might think because he could hit it virtually as far left as he liked there, except the wind blew pretty hard for the first nine holes and then it went flat calm. We got the best of the day in the later afternoon, but John played well early on, hitting the driver and birdieing three holes in a row from the second. We dropped shots on the sixth and the eighth which could have been avoided. The sixth was a three-putt and we got the club wrong on the eighth because of the wind. It was one of the holes with the right-to-left prevailing wind and we misread it. We decided on the six-iron and went through the green. I don't think we got the club right until the last day.

"But then we birdied the ninth where he nearly drove the green, as planned. His greatest strength was either driving or nearly driving holes like the 9th, 10th [342 yards] and 12th, which he played well all week. He birdied it for the first three days and nearly drove it on the last day and three-putted from just off the green. On the first day he could have eagled the 12th, drove the green to 20 feet and just missed the putt. That was birdie and he made another at the long 14th. On the 18th he was right up there. He wasn't worried about the Valley of Sin and he had a chip very close for birdie. In fact, I only recall two driving holes where he didn't take the driver on the first day, the 13th and 15th.

"It wasn't just the driving, though. At St. Andrews, with such huge undulating greens, a lot of them double-greens, you're going to get a whole lot of 50-feet, 80-feet, 90-feet putts and his lag-putting was just phenomenal all week. With his length and the wind blowing, as it did most of the week, he probably had more long putts than most people. On the 12th in the second round, for instance, he drove the green pin-high some 75 to 80 feet and two-putted that for birdie. The sixth on the first day was an exception, when he three-putted from 40 feet or so."

If Daly had not three-putted the sixth, he would have led the first day on his own. As it was, he shared the honors with two more Americans, the inevitable Tom Watson and Ben Crenshaw, and Zimbabwean Mark McNulty.

Watson was still seeking that elusive sixth Open title which had eluded him several times since his fifth win—no more so than in 1984 when Ballesteros snatched it from his grasp at St. Andrews. Crenshaw was trying for his second major title in the year, having secured his second Masters months earlier. McNulty was bidding to be the second successive player from Zimbabwe to hold aloft the Auld Claret Jug after compatriot Nick Price's triumph the previous year at Turnberry.

When he had played so successfully in 1993 at St. Andrews, Daly had sprayed the ball around a great deal. It led Irishman David Feherty, the master of the one-liner, to say, "Don't worry, John, there are five courses out there—you're bound to hit one of them!" But this time Daly was not spraying it quite so far and he had defied the odds. Those odds came in the shape of the infamous bunkers of St. Andrews, such as Deacon Sime, the Principal's Nose, Cockle, Hell Bunker, where the mighty Golden Bear Jack Nicklaus had taken five to extricate himself on the 14th and run up a ten. Daly's smash-and-grab tactics, or "grip it and rip it," as he preferred to term it, had somehow seen him avoid them all.

For the second round, the leaderboard showed formidable opposition for Daly, but his confidence was high and by now he had the gallery firmly ensconcing him as the man to watch, even if he was playing with their hero Ballesteros.

Daly wanted victory badly. His hunger was plain to see, not least when it came to chocolate chip muffins, as caddie Greg Rita found out.

"We didn't have time for a whole lot of practice on Thursday because we finished in early evening, but John had not lost any of his will to win. He seemed really fired up when we met up for the morning round. When these guys get up there they are raring to go. Golf's a confidence game and he'd done better already than he would have taken early on—to get himself into position for the last nine holes on Sunday, when it really all happens.

"The wind got a little bit worse every day and a very stiff breeze greeted us on the second morning. John refused to change tactic, though, even when he really ran into trouble on the fifth. His drive did find a bunker this time and his bravado more than anything got him into trouble. Instead of playing it conservatively, as you nearly always have to do when you get in a fairway bunker at St. Andrews, he tried to play forward. He learned a quick lesson because his ball hit the lip and went back into the sand. I didn't want to say 'told you so.' He knew that I was thinking more about getting it in play from the bunker rather than trying for distance. Those bunkers need respect, you just can't be too ambitious; discretion has to be the better part of valor. I was mighty glad when he didn't try it again and he chipped out sideways. When St. Andrews decides it's going to grab you there's nothing you can do about it, though, and he missed the green and missed the putt when he chipped back, so that meant double-bogey going on the card.

"But John was really up for it and he wasn't going to let the course do all the dictating. He got the two shots back and another besides after we went through the turn. We missed a chance on nine but then he came back with a bang, birdieing three in a row. We had the wind with us when we turned and it just needed a flop shot from the fringe on ten to very close. Then his putting powers really came into their own. His putting was every bit as good as his driving all week and he coaxed in a 30-footer or so on the 11th. Then he proved just how good his lag-putting was because I even thought his feat on the 12th was something extra special. We decided on a one-iron off the tee because the wind had really got up and he carried it all the way to the green but the ball got hurt on the way and finished up, I guess almost a couple hundred feet away from the flag. The green is so huge. Well, when he rolled it up to only three or four feet I thought it was one of the best demonstrations of lag-putting I'd ever seen. The gallery were already on John's side and they were really appreciative of that kind of art. The crowd at St. Andrews is always knowledgeable; they knew what a fantastic piece of judgment that was. He could have used up at least twice the amount of putts on that one.

"Just goes to show, though, that the Old Lady doesn't take kindly to being mastered. He then went and three-putted the next from about a quarter of the distance, to drop a shot! John was mad at that but he didn't let it unsettle him and got it straight back. The 14th can give plenty of problems if you let one go on the right but his strategy all week was not even to mess with the wall and the road on the right. He preferred hitting close to the fifth fairway and worrying about that old Hell Bunker when the time came. In fact, we worked out that if you're hitting driver there as far as John was that week, you have no problem with Hell Bunker. With a drive of about 300 or so yards it's only just over 200 yards to get over Hell.

"Things went well up to the last hole and then he was disappointed again, but not with bogey—with not making eagle and having to settle for par. He hit a mighty drive again and found the edge of the green, about 50 feet from the flag. He wanted the eagle badly but that cost him. He can be over-aggressive at times and this time he ran the ball six feet past. Then he missed the one back. That was not a good note to finish on.

"He soon got over it, though. Another chocolate chip muffin took care of that. I guess his supply of muffins was replacing other urges. Tracking down chocolate chip muffins became a major task for me. I had to seek them out about every other hole. There was a big supply particularly behind the tenth. John sure ate a whole lot of chocolate chip muffins that week."

With one American golfing hero taking his final bow, the St. Andrews gallery were ready to pin their allegiances this week on another player from the States, and Daly was ready to fit the bill. Arnold Palmer, who years before had successfully urged his fellow countrymen to travel across the Atlantic and play the oldest major, had his Open swan-song as he bade farewell to an adoring crowd. So the gallery needed a replacement and Daly was it.

Once again, however, a three-putt had cost Daly the chance of the lead on his own, despite his mastery of the greens. On the 12th, for instance, he could have been excused chipping on the putting surface but Daly immediately put that idea out of his head. He had the gallery on his side and he did not want to alienate them by digging out a divot on their hallowed Scottish turf. One past Open champion had done that very thing when playing a Dunhill Cup match at St. Andrews and nearly found himself in the stocks at the "Old Toon's" market place!

Daly settled for a 71 and share of a one-shot lead at six under par with two others this time—Brad Faxon, again making a bid for Open honors, and a Japanese outsider, Katsuyoshi Tomori. Tomori's compatriot Tommy Nakajima had gone looking for the Auld Claret Jug a decade or so earlier but then came to grief at the Road Hole bunker, allowing one astute headline writer to talk about the "Sands of Nakajima" when the Japanese failed in numerous attempts to extricate his ball from the trap. Ironically, it was an Italian who would suffer similar cruel fate at the same hole on the final day in a playoff, to see his Open chance disappear in the sands of time. Costantino Rocca was in the group at five-under, tracking the leading trio.

It was another American with whom Daly played in the third round, however, an American looking for his second major success of the year, an American whom Daly respected greatly—the U.S. Masters champion Ben Crenshaw, also only one off the joint lead.

"John was excited about his pairing with Ben. John considered him an all-time great sportsman and gentleman and looked up to to him. John was pretty pleased with his placing because his intention had been to be up there in contention for the weekend and he had exceeded that expectation. But he was wary at the start. It's an old golfing cliché that you can't win the tournament in the third round—but you can lose it. John was aware it was going to be a big day. That's why he was pleased to be playing with Ben because I think that settled him down right away.

"Not that it was a great start, though. We went through the green on the first with the second shot, always awkward judging the distance over the Swilcan Burn on how much the ball is going to run. It ran and ran and he decided to putt back but knocked it eight feet past, missed the one back for bogey. Nice start.

"The wind didn't seem quite as strong but it did seem trickier to judge and we got the par-three eighth wrong again, hit over the back and even though the pitch back was a good one, we bogeyed it for a second time. I was determined to get it right next time, darn it! He did drive the green on nine this time and two putts from about between 20 and 25 feet knocked out one of the bogeys at least. We let the 10th off lightly but not the 12th. It had been a putt of between 180 and 200 feet the day before and this time it was about 120 feet. We chose the two-iron off the tee this time, so the wind was stronger, and he again lag-putted brilliantly, again to three feet or so, for the birdie. For any of those really long putts, John did hold himself in check. We could have run up eight putts in two days on the 12th but both times he birdied and took only four putts for the two rounds. That was going to be crucial—the lag-putting again.

"All the real dramatics came right at the end. On 17, because of the swirling wind coming across, he was forced to go conservative and we chose the one-iron off the tee. You need to keep it left in that case and he caught it a little bit too much left and found the left rough, definitely not where you want to be because it then makes the second a very difficult shot. He'd hit it pretty pure and it was only a wedge out, but it was from a bad lie. He was trying to get a little more out of it than the lie dictated and with the wind knocking it down from the right, his ball went into the bunker [Scholars] about 100 yards from the green. There was very little chance of getting on. It was a typical British Open bunker. You might get 20 yards, maybe 30 yards, out of it, and that's all. He was still left with a pitch to the green. He pitched to about 20 feet and missed the putt, so that was a tough deal. It nullified all our good holes around the turn.

"After that we could do with some luck and on the 18th John had the kind of luck that wins majors. He hit a drive which was hooking low downwind and his ball ran on and on by the side of the green on the left, through everything, Valley of Sin, the lot. It scuttled up the path and the upslope and tried to get up the steps to the clubhouse. In fact, it did get up two or three steps. It came within six inches of going out of bounds. When you're talking about a golf ball going 360 yards, as John's ball had done, and less than a yard more and the ball's out of bounds, that's scary—scary for the caddie as well. He nearly paid for choosing the driver and I hadn't done anything about persuading him differently. Remember, it was driver week. Anyway, it didn't go out and the ball then ran back down that upslope into a perfect lie, so perfect he could get the putter on it. Putter was always the best play from just off the green, always is in links golf. He rolled it up to eight feet and made it for birdie. It could have been the end of his Open chances. Instead, there he was, signing for a three. If he had had to reload it could have been double that. Mentally it was a big, big hole for him.

"We couldn't get off the course quick enough. I think I was even more relieved than John. I didn't see much of him after his press conference. Most of the tournaments we do in Europe we stay together but, with his wife being with him, we went our separate ways each night. Best not to dwell on things. I know that John was looking forward to a big dinner. He was talking about eating two steaks and several dishes of chocolate ice-cream. That was about his diet for the week. We'd been hunting chocolate chip muffins during the round again. He was looking to take a few back to the hotel but he needn't have worried. The muffin man had heard about his liking for chocolate chips and a boxful had already gone to the hotel!"

After a medium-rare and a few scoops, what the pair might have dwelt on was the fact that Daly had now slipped four strokes off the lead and did not even hold third place after sharing top spot for the previous two days. That was down to a remarkable third round by the young Maori Michael Campbell. Campbell was a mere rookie on the European Tour but he had not let that worry him as a stunning 65 in the capricious winds saw him command a two-stroke lead. This was over Costantino Rocca, with the Australian Steve Elkington coming between the Italian and a group of four which contained Daly, fellow American Corey Pavin, the giant South African 1994 U.S. Open winner Ernie Els, and the dogged Katsuyoshi Tomori of Japan. Campbell's 65 had in the end relied on one of the most accomplished bunker shots played from the Road Hole bunker in St. Andrews' Open Championship history. Caught right underneath the towering front wall, Campbell somehow defied the odds to splash and coax his ball just over the multiple ribs of sand to save par. The next day, that very spot would see the hopes of two players alternatively wither and bloom.

The 17th was a long way from Daly's mind when he rose to take on the St. Andrews links for the last time in the 124th Open Championship. All week he had found inspiration in his playing partners and his fourth round companion Els, as tall as Daly was broad, would not be an exception to the rule. They provided the final day's most laid-back pairing. Most of the reason for them being so laid-back, however, came through being buffeted by winds which whistled over 50 m.p.h. at times as the links found extra protection.

"Two things worried me about the final round. First there were no chocolate chip muffins. I think John must have had the last batch the night before! Secondly, the wind was howling. I'd say it was the strongest wind I'd ever experienced. I wasn't sure how John was going to cope. It was not as if he'd grown up with these type of conditions, like the guys from Texas who hit the low ball. He's always been a high-ball hitter [sic]. I just didn't know what was going to happen. He was about to surprise me, though. John played some marvelous 'knock-down' shots during the last day in all that wind. He played as if he grew up in Texas.

"I was looking for something positive to draw on before we went out and I cast his mind back to the 18th the night before. I said, 'We got a big break there, so we've got to capitalize on it. You could look back today and say that was the break that meant the difference between winning and losing this thing. But only if you capitalize on it.'

"He started to on the fourth. Driver again—didn't matter it was blowing people off their feet. He only needed a little nine-iron in and the hole's nearly 470 yards with plenty of trouble on the way. It needed a good putt from about 15 feet to birdie it, though.

"His big move came at the seventh and eighth. He drove it so far on seven that he had just a little flick from about 80 yards. Ernie Els gave us a clue what to do when his ball hit the green and released all the way through it. We decided we had to hit the apron—it's like a kind of false front to the green—instead of hitting on and seeing the ball go through. He hit a beautiful shot over the ridge and it just trickled nicely to about six feet. He holed a real crucial putt which put him back high on the leaderboard. Then on the eighth, we finally pulled the right club. Glory be! We went for the eight-iron and that was just perfect. The putt was straight back into the wind, though, so not easy, it was howling. He made it, about ten feet and he's three-under for the day.

"If you're going to win a major, though, you need breaks. The 18th the day before was a prime example. We got another huge break at the tenth. He would not waver from using a driver but this time he pulled his drive into the big bushes, real thick stuff. It could have been the end. First of all we thought the ball was lost but then we found it, just clear of the heavy stuff and on shells and dirt on a small path. That was a huge break because the provisional he hit would have been in bad shape. The wedge shot off the patch finished up 50 feet short of the hole, so it needed a solid approach putt to avoid giving anything away. The ninth was a huge break. I thought about capitalizing again. We had to use that luck. We're back up there. All we have to do is—hold on. The wind's terrible by now.

"We were both scanning the leaderboard constantly. Young Campbell was not having a good final round early on and he lost his lead to us. I remember Mark Brooks coming up after us but he fell away and it was just as well because the 16th and 17th cost two shots. The 17th had not been played well all week and that was no surprise to make bogey there, almost regulation, but to drop a shot on 16 was a blow and I guess that stopped John getting things done without needing the playoff. In fact, it could have been a four-putt there, double-bogey. The wind was affecting everybody on that green and John had to sink a five-footer to only three-putt it. He was about 60 feet from the flag with just a nine-iron, to show how strong the wind was at that stage. It was ten feet away for the second and then five feet past. I thought the Championship could slip away there and then. We just could not afford to go to the 17th off a double-bogey. But he holed the third putt.

"At the 17th he hit his driver in the left rough. We know the wind's coming hard from the right and the one place you don't want to go is the Road Bunker. He was in it. Once again, though, he got a bit of a break. Ernie Els was in the same bunker, about a foot away from John. John told me he wasn't even sure he could get the ball out. Ernie played first and got his ball out kind of sideways and then he's got a difficult pitch on anyway. I think that made John's mind up for him. He told me he was going to give it a go at getting over the lip. I could hardly dare look. But he did it, splashed out to 30 feet or so and almost made par. I guess that could have been double as well.

"John worked so hard for that he wasn't going to give anything further away now and he knew he had a similar wind at the back of him and coming across, as the day before, so this time the driver stayed in the bag. He hit a one-iron off the tee on 18. He had a great chance to birdie still, but the putt stayed out from about 12 feet. His was the target, though."

That target, after a closing 71, was six under par. England's surprise package, Steven Bottomley, had set the earlier target of one worse. Mark Brooks matched Bottomley. Only two players were left out on the course; one of them was the third-round leader Michael Campbell. He could not get on terms with Daly and would have to settle for a share of third place with Brooks and Bottomley. The other was Italian Ryder Cup player Costantino Rocca, and it was with Rocca that the destiny of the Auld Claret Jug lay.

Rocca, after a magical save on 17 by fashioning a shot off the Road with his putter, came to the last lying five under par, still one behind Daly's target, but the likeable, cuddly man from Bergamo launched an enormous drive to the left of the 18th green. The tension on Rocca's face was visible even to the spectators outside the fence down below Grannie Clark's Wynd. It was all too much for the emotional Rocca. He produced a nerve-jangled chip which would have been disowned by a 28-handicapper, fluffed still 60 feet from the hole. But then, almost as if it were hit with nothing now to lose, the tension all gone, Rocca's subsequent putt provided the lasting memory of the 1995 Open Championship. Unerringly it set off on a course for the cup which could have been pre-set by sonar. Up and over the Valley of Sin it accelerated, slowed and then accelerated again, slaloming on its way, only giving doubt about its chosen mission towards the end of its journey as it threatened to career on and betray its master right at the death. As the ball, still nowhere near the nadir of its flight, made its final adjustment to do the honorable thing and dive into history, the roly-poly Rocca also went to ground. And he stayed to ground, flat out, flailing his arms up and down, thumping his fists into the turf like a cartoon cat that has lost its prey. It was not frustration for Rocca, however, but uncontrollable relief. His outrageous putt, on a par with champion Nick Price's at the penultimate hole at Turnberry the year before, had drawn the Italian level with Daly. Thus it brought the man who loved chocolate chip muffins to a four-hole showdown with the man who loved pasta. The denouement, though, would hardly prove a feast, but it left Daly the satisfied of the two protagonists.

"John disappeared after the round, into the recording caravan with his wife, to watch the last group finish on the television monitor. I stood watching behind the 18th green and after Rocca 'chilly-dipped' his chip, one of John's managers walked by and said joyfully, 'We won.' I said, 'It's not over yet,' even though I perhaps thought it was. It was unbelievable. I just saw the guy lying there thrashing his arms and thought, 'I'd better find John.'

"By the time I got to him there were American players all round him. They were saying things like, 'Go get him. Bring home the Jug.' John was very pensive. He told me afterwards that his heart had sunk when the putt went in but all he said to me when I got back to him to prepare for the playoff was, 'We've got some more work to do now.'

"It was pretty chaotic but we got ourselves organized and somehow I managed to blot out all that had gone on since finishing, just talked about yardages and things like a normal round, even though you churn inside. Rocca helped settle us a bit because he bogeyed the first, got a huge gust of wind as he putted and ran the ball well past the hole. John seemed very composed and made par to give us the advantage.

"Then at the second I thought we were going to pay for the lucky break we'd had at the ninth in the round proper. He hit into the mounds on the second, the Himalayas, and that stopped his ball. Without hitting the bank he'd have run down real close. John was first to putt, though, from a long way off, about 45 feet. It went in. Rocca had opened the door by three-putting the first and now John had walked in. If we could only play 17 a bit better than we had done all week, we had it. If we could hold Rocca there then it would be good to go to 18 with a two-shot lead. It wouldn't matter then if Rocca made birdie and we made only par, which was about the worst you could imagine from that kind of finish.

"John hit a beautiful drive on 17. I had very few worries then. Rocca was the first to play the second and he hit into the Road Bunker. We knew exactly what we had to do now. I wanted John to now pull off the shot that should win the tournament. He needed to hit the shot that the hole tells you to do, hit it short right. Whatever you do, don't hit in the bunker left and don't hit too long right. He hit the most beautiful punched nine-iron, maybe 160 yards or so to around 20 feet. Rocca was in the bunker in just about the same spot as John had found in the final round. I knew Rocca would have to go for it. He had no other choice. Bogey was no good. It was a very dangerous shot.

"Well, it didn't come off for him. He left the ball in and it was all over. John had five shots to play with going into the last and it was all a bit of an anticlimax.

"But that didn't mean we felt flat. It was a fantastic feeling for me, so I've no idea just how good John must have been feeling. It was very emotional, his family and all. After all the formalities and company pictures, John asked me if I'd like a picture taken with him and the Claret Jug. We had it taken sitting on the Swilcan Bridge. It's my most prized possession in golf.

"I was ready for a few drinks after that and I went to my old haunt, the Dunvegan Hotel, and had quite a few lagers. John went back to his hotel and if he somehow managed to avoid the drink to celebrate, I guess he went looking for chocolate chip muffins!"

1996 ROYAL LYTHAM AND ST. ANNE'S

Tom Lehman with Andrew Martinez

Tom Lehman	USA	67 67 64 73 271 (par 71)
Mark McCumber	USA	67 69 71 66 273
Ernie Els	South Africa	68 67 71 67 273
Nick Faldo	England	68 68 68 70 274
Jeff Maggert	USA	69 70 72 65 276
Mark Brooks	USA	67 70 68 71 276
Peter Hedblom	Sweden	70 65 75 67 277
Greg Norman	Australia	71 68 71 67 277
Greg Turner	New Zealand	72 69 68 68 277
Fred Couples	USA	67 70 69 71 277

"Losing the U.S. Open was a bitter pill to swallow, but I felt again I had a player who is playing the best golf in a major. I could feel it. I felt it in practice, which went so well. Maybe it hadn't been our time last month at Oakland Hills. Now I felt like it was our time. So I said that to him. 'Go out and prove it.' I told him I wouldn't say that if I didn't believe it."

Flying with the Eagles

Veteran American caddie Andrew Martinez had seen it all and done it all when he met Tom Lehman in 1992 at a U.S. PGA Tour Bible study meeting, held every Wednesday before tour events. Martinez was the man who walked beside the great Johnny Miller in Miller's glory years. However, glory had faded to a mere memory for Martinez by 1992. That year, Lehman asked Martinez, who had just been fired by John Cook, to carry his bag at the Open Championship at Muirfield. But because Lehman dropped out of the top 50 to 52nd in the world rankings, he decided not to try to qualify for the Open, so the relationship was put on hold until after Muirfield. At the Western Open soon after, Lehman finished only three shots away from victory and decided to hire Martinez in August 1992. They have been together ever since.

Before Lehman and Martinez teamed up, it had proven to be a checkered career for Lehman, on and off the U.S. Tour. He admitted at Lytham that he had been "down to my last few bucks" when ends were not being met as he travelled the world to play his golf, unable to make a full U.S. Tour card. But he has not looked back since joining up with Martinez, a man who shares his religious beliefs and who still attends Bible study meetings with him at tour events.

They had won two U.S. Tour events leading up to the 1996 Open and in 1994 Lehman earned over a million dollars and finished fourth on the American money list. The year before that, Lehman came close to clinching his first major when he finished third in the U.S. Masters—with Martinez by his side, of course. Losing out at Augusta proved to be Lehman's most disappointing career point. In 1995 Lehman finished 15th on the money list but by the time the Open came round the following year, he already threatened to finish much higher than that. The partnership of Lehman and Martinez had chalked up two runner-up spots in the three weeks leading up to Lytham and in the 1996 season they had earned no less than eight top-ten places, including a third and fourth to go with the two second places.

Best of all, one of those runner-up spots was in the U.S. Open, where Lehman lost the second major of the year by just a stroke to compatriot Steve Jones. Lehman was on a roll and his caddie knew it. Martinez, too, was determined, if he could help it, that his man would not let another major slip from his grasp if he got into contention again.

"The build-up to the 1996 Open was kind of a dream experience, the whole thing. We decided—Tom, myself, his father Jim—to fly into England early. We got into London on the Friday before the Open and almost off the plane we went off to play one of the world's great courses, Sunningdale. The next day we played Swinley Forest and then played Sunningdale again on Sunday and then drove over to Lytham. I felt that was an important lead-up to the Open, not only to get acclimatized but to begin the build-up in a relaxed mood. Rather vital in the whole experience and what made it seem like a dream was what happened on the Saturday night. We attended an Eagles concert at Wembley Stadium and if what happened there wasn't some kind of an omen, then I don't know what would be. There was kind of a 'raiding party' over from the States for the week, a kind of bachelors' party—Jim Lehman, a real good friend, Ken Kendrick and two British friends, Jamie Birkmyer and Roy Edwards. We all teamed up to play some relaxed golf before the Open. Glenn Frey of the Eagles was one of the friends Tom played with on the Sunday. But before we played golf with Glenn, all of us in the raiding party went to watch the Eagles play at Wembley.

"One of the funniest things happened at the concert. Glenn Frey introduced Tom to the audience—there were 70,000 people at Wembley Stadium—and said, 'I'd like to introduce a special friend of mine from the professional golf tour and who will be competing in the British Open Championship next week at Royal Lytham and St. Anne's.' Well, among the 70,000 people we'd spotted Nick Faldo, and you could see Nick getting ready to stand up to take the acclaim of the crowd. But then Glenn said, 'I give you American golfer Tom Lehman'—and Nick Faldo was thunderstruck! I don't know what went through Nick's mind, but I can tell you it did Tom a power of good. It's my perception that Tom has never had much confidence in his own playing ability. I always felt if his confidence level reached his playing skill then there'd be no stopping him, so to be acknowledged at such a spectacle as an Eagles concert, filled him so full of elation and pride. When Glenn Frey said, 'Go get the Jug, Tom,' he looked as though he'd burst with sheer pleasure. What a great start to Open week.

"Well, we went backstage between sets, talked to Glenn for a while and the other Eagles. Tom mentioned about Nick Faldo being there. I don't think Glenn knew Nick was in the audience. So when Glenn came on for the second set, he introduced Nick. Nick got up and really milked the crowd, posing a little I guess. Glenn said, 'Okay Nick, that's enough now. We have to get on with the concert.' It was all in jest, of course, but you could see that Glenn was getting one over on Nick for the sake of one of his buddies. It was really ironic that it was just how the tournament was going to go the next week—Tom getting the accolade first and then Nick getting applause after for a good try!

"It wasn't just fate, or omens, that helped Tom Lehman win the 1996 Open, though. It was the relaxed way we went about things—and some hard practice beforehand to back everything up. Monday and Tuesday we had 27 holes of practice before anyone got there. It was great. We got out there early when no one was out there, and late in the day when no one was out there. An Open Championship was a daunting task—for me personally—because I hadn't seen all of the Open venues. It was my first time here, so that meant a lot of work for me. I spent a lot of hours working on yardages and noting the course's various foibles. For a start, there were a lot of bunkers out there! At one time I came off the 18th and looked up at the big clock near the stand and it was 10:05 P.M. Another time it was 10:15 P.M. So there were really long days for me before the Open even began, but really good, useful days, to get that course fully mapped out.

"We played with Mark O'Meara and Anders Forsbrand for the first two days. Conditions were perfect for us. Tom likes a course that plays hard and fast with the ball running and that's how it was. I remember him saying it reminded him of Scottsdale in the spring. I like it better, too, because you have to do more thinking off the tee. You don't just pull the same club off the tee, hit the driver all the time. You had to go point to point at Lytham that year, really have to figure out where you want to hit the ball and keep out of all those bunkers. You can't fly the ball to the hole, so I think it brought some brains into the equation. Conditions were mild and we didn't have that much in the way of wind. In fact, I guess it was a heatwave by UK standards! We saw a lot of guys who'd obviously had a lot to drink, stripped right down, so they must have found it hot.

"Tom started off playing flawless golf, pretty much textbook from tee to green. He had three successive birdies early on and hit a lot of shots close, could have been better than three under par after 12 holes. That was the worst he could have been. Mark O'Meara was about the same and we knew we were both in pretty good shape. Then we came to the 13th hole and just mis-hit the tee-shot, a one-iron, out to the right. There are a lot of bunkers out there you have to carry, even with an iron, and he hit into one of them. He then hit out of that into another bunker. Then he put it into yet another bunker, this one greenside. Three shots, three bunkers. Finally he was out of the sand but missed the putt; double-bogey. Devastated. Here he was, having been play-ing flawless golf, the worst he could have been was three-under, and now we've missed one shot, the tee ball, and we're back to one under par. He was really upset.

"I could feel it emanating from inside Tom, but I didn't say anything, he was so angry inside. At the 14th tee he was so angry he really cracked one, way down there, just a great drive. I felt it was time to say something, some-thing to calm him down, something for him to focus on, so I said to him, 'Tom, do you mind if I say something, speak frankly to you?' He looked at me kind of strange and said, 'Go ahead.' I looked him in the eye and said, 'I feel like I'm caddying for the best golfer in this tournament.' I kept looking him in the eye and let that statement settle. Then I added, 'It's just a question of going out and proving it.' When I said it, I meant it. This wasn't some kind of contrived pep talk kind of thing. I meant it because I'd watched him play the U.S. Open a month earlier and thought he was the best player there then. We should have won the tournament but somehow let that tournament get away. We lost by a stroke to Tom's good friend Steve Jones. Losing the U.S. Open was a bitter pill to swallow, but I felt again I had a player who was playing the best golf in a major. I could feel it. I felt it in practice, which went so well. Maybe it hadn't been our time last month at Oakland Hills; now I felt like it was our time, so I said that to him. 'Go out and prove it,' I said. I told him I wouldn't say that if I didn't believe it.

"So we walked down the 14th to our second shot. He hit a nine-iron to ten or twelve feet and knocked the putt in for a birdie and then followed up with two more, on the 16th and 17th. The 14th through 18 at Lytham and St. Anne's are known as the most difficult holes, but Tom got his act back together to finish three-under for the last five holes for a 67."

According to the history books, no American had ever won an Open at Royal Lytham, but the portents this time were good for a victory from the other side of the Atlantic. There was little wind on the first day, the ball was running long and the course parched, all the ingredients for the big-hitters from America. Right away, those portents proved accurate as U.S. Tour players mounted a breathtaking opening charge. No less than seven of them were on the leaderboard, all in second place, however. It was a Briton showing the way—Englishman Paul Broadhurst, the player who carded the exhilarating 63 at St. Andrews to break records in Nick Faldo's 1990 Open success. He led the field by two strokes after a six-under-par 65. The 1991 Kiawah Island Ryder Cup player led by two over Japan's Hidemichi Tanaka and the American big guns of Fred Couples, Mark McCumber, Brad Faxon, Mark O'Meara, Loren Roberts—and Tom Lehman. They all shot 67s and Lehman already had another one over on Nick Faldo. Faldo had to settle for a 68 to be three strokes off Broadhurst's lead. But there was a remarkable first day return from top American players. Jack Nicklaus, for instance, shot 69 and there were 70s for Payne Stewart, Fuzzy Zoeller and John Daly. Faldo, and nearly all the U.S. players, would stay the course.

Lehman still could not get out of his mind how he had blown his chance of a major success only a few weeks beforehand and was still digressing on his demise going into the second round at Lytham. But by now he was becoming philosophical that if your name was written on the trophy, like Steve Jones's had been at Oakland Hills, then that was that. What Lehman had decided, however, was that it was high time an American won an Open at Royal Lytham and St. Anne's. Caddie Andrew Martinez was, by now, confident his man would live up to his estimation on the 14th tee in the first round, that he was simply the best in the field.

"The second round was another sunny day, not much wind, and it went pretty well the same as the first . . . except that the disappointment came straightaway when we bogeyed the first, the par-three, we made one birdie less. On the up side, we didn't have a double-bogey this time. The result was the same, a 67. Tom hit just about all the fairways, hit most of the greens, made a few putts, nothing spectacular apart from a real big one—about 25 or 27 feet—on the second. That one was timely after the bogey. It can be tough starting at a par-three. We just missed the green and the bunker shot to about 20 feet was a difficult one.

"It was a difficult day the way the ball was rolling. Sometimes it could roll into trouble through no fault of your own, but by the time we got to the turn we'd picked up another two birdies and then when we added another on the 13th, it was pretty satisfying. This time, with the wind helping, we went with the three-iron and missed the bunkers, which just goes to show how one bad shot can have such an effect. This time it only took a sand-iron in and a putt of about 12 feet for the birdie, three shots better than the day before. Another 12-footer went in on 17 and Tom holed a tricky six-footer on the last for another 67. Tom told me he felt his swing was getting better and better and I know the save on the last helped him mentally. He let out quite a relieved blow on the last.

"Another thing that helped Tom, I think, was the way the crowd appreciated him. He got a lot of encouragement from the Lytham gallery. It helped because they knew him from the Ryder Cup, I guess, and Tom felt relaxed with the gallery."

Lehman was once again in contention in a major. His eight-under-par figures were matched by Irishman Paul McGinley, who chalked up a hole-in-one on his way to a 65. The pair led by a stroke over a trio containing two formidable names—Jack Nicklaus, looking for yet another major title, despite now featuring on the American Seniors tour, and the giant South African Ernie Els, who had already clinched a U.S. Open title two years earlier. Sweden's Peter Hedblom in that trio was, like McGinley, an outsider expected to fall away. Players like Nick Faldo, Corey Pavin, Mark McCumber, Mark O'Meara and Loren Roberts, two strokes off the pace, were not expected to fade.

The odds by now were definitely on a début victory for America. Lehman and his caddie, if they were not to win this time, knew who they favored.

"All the clubhouse to-do was Jack Nicklaus being only one stroke off the lead. As an American, and being one of Nicklaus's greatest fans, it was pretty exciting. It was pretty exciting for Tom, too. I don't think he would have minded playing with Jack but we went out with Paul McGinley and mentally I think that may have been better for Tom. It was a great pairing. Paul is one of the best guys I know, a great sportsman and somebody with whom Tom's very comfortable. Our conversation was not just about golf; we talked about American football and Paul's first sport before he got injured, Gaelic football. I definitely have fond memories of that third round.

"The fondest memory is that one of Tom's greatest rounds was played with Paul McGinley. Tom had it eight under par until he bogeyed the 18th. He missed the fairway and put the ball into one of those bunkers and could only splash out. Bogey was always on then. He missed a save from about 20 feet but a 64 was the course record then. That staked him to a rather large lead.

"We were out in 30, five under par, with some great putts especially. It seemed every time he set the ball off it finished up in the center of the cup. Four of the five birdies came from big putts, all around the 15-foot mark, and there were a couple of good saves going out. We had to take the rough with the smooth on the back nine when for some reason a couple didn't drop. He made three more birdies but, really, he could have shot anything that day. It was mostly down to the putting. Tom really got the pace of the greens that day. Every putt slid in dead-weight. There was none of this aggressive putting; I'm not keen on that kind of putting. It was all silky smooth. We play on fast greens every week and he really enjoyed his putting that day. He told me he thought it was his best. I thought it was pretty fantastic. Tom told me—and, I understand, also told the press—that I encouraged him. When he got to five-under I said, 'Now the target is six.' When he got to six, then I said, 'Why not get to seven now?' and Tom responded to that. In the end there was a bit of a disappointment, but six strokes in front of the field was pretty good to sleep on that night."

The player who was six strokes behind Lehman's 15-under-par aggregate 198, a 54-hole Open record, however, was not Jack Nicklaus but another major winner who could strike similar fear into the heart of a player making his bid to take a maiden major title. It was that man Nick Faldo. And hadn't he gone into the final round at Augusta earlier that year six strokes behind Greg Norman? Faldo's third 68 left him a stroke ahead of three players—another American, Mark Brooks, and the formidable Fijian Vijay Singh. A stroke further adrift were Ernie Els and Fred Couples, with two more U.S. Tour players, Mark McCumber and Steve Stricker, at six-under to back up the challenge from over the Atlantic.

While Els, Singh, and the Americans were never far from Lehman's thoughts, he could not blot out the specter of Faldo—largely because the press had not let him. It had been suggested that Faldo's intimidation factor might be able to surmount the large deficit between first and second place, just like it had with Norman. And then there was the crowd. The gallery would be rooting for Faldo every step of the way. If Lehman had to fight to shut out any fears from Faldo, however, his caddie appeared to have the utmost confidence in his master's ability to clinch his first major.

"I'm pretty experienced. I've been caddying for 30 years. I caddied for Johnny Miller in his heyday. I worked for him one year when he won eight tournaments and then the next year in 1975 I was with him when he shot 24-under and 25-under in consecutive weeks to win by 14 shots and nine shots respectively. To me, I felt the tournament was over. I would never say that to anybody, the reasons being: for one—a six-shot lead; two—I'd been watching Tom Lehman play golf for a few years and seen him consistently play the game at the highest level. I decided not to think about his nervousness trying to win his first major. Myself, I was not nervous. I felt the winning of the Open was a process. You have a six-shot lead and you go on to win because you have a good tee-shot at the first hole. Then you pick the right club for the next shot, then you get the putt right. You go from point to point and do what you're supposed to do. No one can have a six-shot lead in a major championship without having played the game at the highest level. It's just not possible, especially when you have all the best players in the world at the tournament.

"I did my usual thing, which I do at all Opens, that is, to go out and check all the pin placements. I look at every single one very carefully and take it down in my yardage book. That's a very important part of my preparation, but I wasn't prepared for what happened out on the course.

"I'd been doing some running during the week. We were staying on the beach at St. Anne's, about a mile and half away from Lytham. I used to run a lot. I'm not as young as I used to be, 46 at the time, and as I was finishing off the pin placements, I felt a calf muscle go, probably because of the running during the week and then straining it. I thought, 'Man, here I am, I still have to get back to the house, it's still very early—we had a two o'clock tee time— and this calf is really acting up on me. What am I going to do if it prevents me doing my job, if I'm not fit to go out caddying this afternoon?' I was really worried. I certainly couldn't hurry back off the course and it took me quite a while to get to the clubhouse.

"When I got there, Tom was up. What was I going to say to him? Well, I didn't get chance to say anything, and it was just as well. He said to me, 'Come on. We need to talk.' I could see concern in his eyes and I wasn't going to add to it. He confessed to me that he was really nervous. I almost forgot my leg.

I thought to myself, 'Maybe this isn't going to be the victory parade I'd anticipated.'

"I asked him why he was nervous and he said, 'Well, I haven't won one of these things before. I have the big lead and it's possible I could lose the big lead. If I do that, what are people going to think?' I could see he was respecting my experience and he was asking me to put these things into perspective. So I told him, 'The other guys are the guys that should be nervous. We're the ones with the six-shot lead. They have to catch us. Our pursuers, whoever they may be, cannot afford to make a mistake. We can. The position we are in, we can mess up a couple of holes and still win this thing. They can't afford to do that. They have no margin for error.' Then I went on with how well he was playing, told him that I had confidence in him, how he was playing fantastic golf. I told him that, frankly, I wasn't very worried about it at all.

"Of course, there was the specter of the Masters. Faldo had made a late birdie on Saturday night to make the pairing with his to be six strokes behind, just as he had been with Greg Norman. As a matter of fact, when he went in to see the press on Saturday, that was the first thing they asked Tom: 'How do you feel about being paired with Faldo in light of what happened at the Masters?' They didn't ask him about his fantastic round of golf on Saturday, went straight for the Faldo angle. It was very negative when the guy had just played the round of his life and I guess it could have got to Tom. It was a shame to take that kind of line but as far as the press is concerned, I guess that's the nature of the beast.

"So we're paired with Faldo. He has a psych on a lot of people but I can tell you frankly that there is no golfer in the world that has any psych on me. That includes Jack Nicklaus, all of them. I started butting heads with golfers in the early '70s and I've seen the greatest players in the world hit some of the worst shots. They are all fallible. I can remember Nick Faldo when he was a skinny young guy, eating at a fast-food place with him down in Florida. I know Nick's a really great player and I really respect him, but he held no fears for me. We're not playing Nick Faldo anyway. We're playing Lytham and St. Anne's.

"I guess Tom and I expected to hear some raucousness from the crowds—and we did. Tom got the works. I didn't hear all the comments but someone referred to Tom as Greg, implying he was going to fold the way Greg Norman did. Well that kind of stuff doesn't really bother me and I hoped it didn't Tom.

You kind of expect it, especially when you are playing in Great Britain and playing with Nick Faldo, one of the best in the world and Great Britain's finest. So, hey, no big deal. It goes with the territory.

"But, as I said, we weren't playing against Nick Faldo. I felt that every par we made we were just eating up the ground, 'chewing up the clock,' to use an American football metaphor. When it gets late in the game, in the fourth quarter, and you have the lead, run the clock, keep the clock running; that's just what we needed to do.

"Well, first of all, I had to get my calf muscle in shape. It was not good and I just hoped Tom didn't notice me limping. It seemed to ease and by the time we got out there I was hardly noticing it. We got off to a shaky start and Faldo got off to a great start but he didn't take all his chances. He could have really closed the gap because we made a bogey before we made a birdie. It wasn't what I was looking for at all. I feel that the start is the key when you're in contention or when you have a lead like we did. Make a birdie before you make a bogey and it's half the battle. We bogeyed the third after finding one of the bunkers with the drive.

"It could have been worse. Faldo could have made up lots of ground and we made a great escape on the first par-five, the sixth. We pulled our tee ball after choosing a real courageous line, found the bushes in a spot which could have been a disaster. Faldo had a perfect tee shot and was more than likely going to make a birdie. If we make a six or a seven it's just about an even game between us and Faldo. Somehow Tom was able to hit an incredible shot, extricate himself from the bush and roll the ball out 60 yards and he ended up making a par. Meanwhile, Nick hit over the back of the green, didn't get it up and down and he made a par. That was some escape and I guess that really had a lot of impact on the outcome of the Open. That had to be a back-breaker to Faldo, had to be a crusher. I'm sure he expected to gain two shots minimum and instead it was even. I think that really took it out of Faldo and he never looked as though he would catch us after that.

"There were a couple of players still not done and they came right at us. Fred Couples and Ernie Els then became the dangermen. Frankly, though, I didn't pay much attention to it. It's one of my rules not to look at the leaderboard. I think Tom likes to look at them but I think it's detrimental and can affect you emotionally. If you see yourself way in the lead you think 'shoot' and it gets you hyped up. If you see somebody coming after you and you're not playing as good as you think you ought to be, then it can take you down, affect you the other way. So, especially with the lead we had, I thought it was best to just go about our business. From what I understood later, Couples had a tremendous front nine but then had disasters on the back nine, and Ernie had his chances later on. I was unaware of this and just stuck at the task of keeping Tom on the straight and narrow—and it did seem narrow on the last day."

Fred Couples, in fact, drew to within two strokes of Lehman as Faldo found the cup getting narrower than the fairways and it was his American compatriot who threatened to deny him his maiden major title. However, after going out in 30, Couples came back in 41 to throw away his chance of a first Claret Jug, the classic case of going out in a Rolls-Royce and coming back in an ambulance.

Ernie Els put himself in line for his first British Open title and kept in contention right until the death. The South African's four birdies in five holes from the tenth might have put the squeeze on Lehman if the American had not been more intent on playing the course and not the man. In the end, bogeys on the 15th and 18th put paid to Els's chances and it was yet another American who threatened. Mark McCumber began the round nine strokes adrift of Lehman and closed the gap to just two shots. But McCumber was in with a 66 to set a 273, 11-under-par target. Els eventually matched that. With Faldo always behind, the closing holes and that stretch from 14 to 18 were the only opponents to Lehman—that and Lehman's temperament. His caddie would not let it stand in Lehman's way if he could help it.

"When Tom finally made a birdie it was a burden off both our shoulders. He'd had all pars apart from the bogey on the third but still didn't lose his lead. With a six-shot start, of course, he had the great cushion. But when he at last made the birdie, it took all pressure off. It came at the really tough par-three, the 12th. He hit a fantastic shot, 200 yards with a four-iron to about 12 feet and got the putt. That ended a lot of qualms for him, I guess. His final round was really shaky, particularly with the putter. On Saturday he'd had the pace of the greens, got the speed perfectly and made a ton of putts. He didn't seem to have that on the Sunday, which made the job of winning that much more difficult.

"After making that birdie on 12, though, that's when I could feel it was going to be his day, but there was still some holding on to do. We parred 13 but then gave one away with a three-putt from about 50 feet on 14 and then he started hitting it left. He was by the path at the 15th. We heard he hit a spectator and got a better lie, so that was a break. He found a bunker but then made a brilliant recovery from the sand to about four or five feet, made the putt for par. Crucial.

"Our last crisis came at the 17th where we got into trouble off the tee. The ball settled at the back of the bunker under the lip and he could only pitch out. But Tom then played the shot that won him the Open. It was still a long shot, an eight-iron. There was a right pin placement, not the most comfortable for Tom Lehman. He would always prefer to bring the ball in from right-to-left most times. It was an approach shot that could have been very troublesome. If the shot had been missed to the right it was big trouble. But he hit a beautiful shot just to the left of the hole, cut it just a hair, and his ball ended up about ten or twelve feet from the flag. I felt he had the tournament then, even though he missed the putt.

"Tom ended up with a fairly safe par on the last and it was all over. I was kinda hoping we were going to win by quite a few, so that I could enjoy the last few holes, more or less relax a little bit. But I wasn't given that luxury. Nonetheless, coming up that 18th hole I was thinking what this tournament meant to Tom Lehman—and to me, I guess. It was my first major championship with a male player. I'd had a win on the ladies' tour with Sally Little but this was my first major on the men's tour. I had my thoughts shattered, though. There was one of these streaker guys grabbed everyone's attention and it was a bit chaotic. They soon bundled him away and we could bask in Tom's victory. It was by two shots and it was only a 73, not exactly the most memorable of finishes in a British Open, but it felt good.

"It was all a bit of an anticlimax in the end, though, something of a disappointment because I missed out on Tom's presentation speech when they gave him the Claret Jug, something I really wanted to see. That was because a radio reporter grabbed me for a live interview back to the States. He was plying me with all these questions. I was trying to hear what Tom was saying with one ear and listening to what I was being asked with another. I couldn't really hear what Tom was saying and that rather spoiled things a little.

"Tom is a great friend. We are brothers in the Lord and I wanted to hear him specifically praise God, thank God for his success. That always makes the hairs stand up on my neck when I hear people praising God, because I've heard so many people cursing God. So it was a great disappointment that I didn't get to hear Tom praising the Lord. Afterwards we hugged and we celebrated.

"There was quite a party at the little Italian restaurant we'd been using and I remember Sergio Garcia and his family coming in and joining in. Tom went outside and had pictures taken with Sergio and the Claret Jug. He told Sergio, 'One of these days you're going to be holding this for yourself.'

"Tom made my day when he went on the air to talk to the States because he wished my wife a happy birthday. It was her birthday on the day he won the Open. Wasn't that special? That's typical of Tom Lehman. He's won the British Open and he still remembers to wish my wife a happy birthday."

1997 ROYAL TROON

Justin Leonard with Bob Riefke

Justin Leonard	USA	69 66 72 65 272 (par 71)
Darren Clarke	N. Ireland	67 66 71 71 275
Jesper Parnevik	Sweden	70 66 66 73 275
Jim Furyk	USA	67 72 70 70 279
Stephen Ames	Trinidad & Tob.	74 69 66 71 280
Padraig Harrington	Ireland	75 69 69 67 280
Fred Couples	USA	69 68 70 74 281
Eduardo Romero	Argentina	74 68 67 72 281
Peter O'Malley	Australia	73 70 70 68 281

"He then hit a stock six-iron to the 18th green. We don't know what's going on with Jesper on 17 as Justin hits his first putt, maybe from 40 feet, a little past the hole. At that point, as he's standing over his second putt, they changed the scoreboard to reflect what Jesper did on 17. At that point I knew what had happened—that we'd just won. He'd no idea."

For the folks back home

It was the Open where the winner yearned for the folks back home to be with him. While Justin Leonard did not go into the 1997 Championship thinking he had no chance of clinching his first Open title at only his fourth attempt, he made the trip to Scotland with just his caddie as his companion. When he was handed the Auld Claret Jug after a pulsating finale at Royal Troon, it was his caddie, Bob Riefke, who found himself with another job—that of providing a shoulder to cry on. Riefke was the only one there who could share the tears of joy at a maiden major success against all odds.

Justin Leonard had been an aspiring 16-year-old the last time Royal Troon had been on the Open rota and he knew all about fellow country-man Mark Calcavecchia's dramatic success in 1989. In fact the Open had been something of a *cause célèbre* for Leonard after his first visit to the Open in 1993 at Royal St. George's. When Leonard missed the cut that year, after gaining his place as the 1992 U.S. Amateur champion, the man from Dallas vowed one day he would find glory in the oldest major.

It was not long coming. After twice qualifying, in 1995 at St. Andrews, where he finished tied 56th, and the following year at Royal Lytham, where he missed the cut, Leonard earned the right to an exemption to Royal Troon. Two victories on the U.S. Tour, the Buick Open of 1996 and the Kemper Open in '97, saw Leonard ride high on the world rankings. By the time he had putted his way to a memorable victory over Jesper Parnevik and Darren Clarke at Troon, Leonard would be able to command eleventh place in the world, seventh on the world money list.

His caddie during the steady climb up in the world of golf was a fellow Texan, Bob Riefke. Both men had Austin connections: Leonard studied at the University of Texas in Austin; Riefke lived there. The caddie had been on tour for four years, U.S. Tour player Rick Fehr being his main bag during that time. In 1994 Riefke decided to try his luck and wrote to Leonard asking if he could caddie for him. Leonard had already used two caddies when he turned pro in 1994. He hoped it would be third time lucky when Riefke got his wish at the end of that year.

It was a steady, formative year for their first season together as Leonard finished twenty-second on the U.S. money list without a victory in 1995. Then, in 1996 at Michigan, they found their first success together, the Buick Open, a runaway victory for Leonard. He had announced to the golfing world that he had made the transition from top amateur.

The following year the golfing world was at Leonard's feet. It all happened in a remarkable three months of summer. He had finished tied seventh behind the all-conquering Tiger Woods at Augusta but then moved into top gear in June, July and August. Victory in the Kemper Open was followed by a solid U.S. Open thirty-sixth spot—and then came triumph at Troon. The following month he finished second in the final major, the U.S. PGA Championship, behind Davis Love III. The Leonard–Riefke partnership was in full bloom.

There was a similarity between Leonard's second U.S. Tour win and his heady Open triumph at Troon. Both times he came from five strokes in arrears going into the final round. At Troon, at that time, it equalled the record catch-up—to be shattered, of course, by Paul Lawrie, who doubled that two years later, and it provided an entirely different finale to Calcavecchia's never-say-die success the last time the Open stopped off at the long and winding links. Caddie Bob Riefke was unsurprised at his man's powers of concentration when it came to catching up.

"We had a pretty good June and July before coming to Scotland and I knew Justin was at the top of his game. He made up five strokes to win the Kemper Open, just like he did in the British Open. He just was not prepared to accept second best. Then, after the U.S. Open, he came good again, finishing fifth and third in consecutive weeks. After his third place in the Western Open he decided it was time to practice for the British Open and he found some wind to practice in. It can blow a bit in Texas. He knew he'd have to get in shape for playing in a gale if necessary.

"After some pretty keen practice at home we came to Scotland early and arrived on the Saturday. We were out on the links on Sunday and we got in at least four rounds before the tournament started. He played with a couple of guys who are his normal practice partners, Mark Brooks, who had had at least two very good attempts at winning prior to this British Open, and Davis Love.

"We were very keen to make something of this week because the year before had been something of a great disappointment for both of us. I'd thought Justin was going to have a really good week at Royal Lytham and St. Anne's when he qualified at ten under par, but he missed the cut. This was the first time we had not had to qualify since Justin turned pro and we were determined that wasn't going to happen this week.

"It was a quiet time off the course and away from practice because there were only the two of us. Justin stayed at the Marine Hotel near the course and he's not much of a one for going crazy the week of a tournament. He was there by himself because this time his parents hadn't come to the tournament—they very often did—and I was there by myself. Our main source of entertainment was the Italian restaurant at the Marine. We ate there every night together and we got through a lot of pizzas! It was just long, long days on the course and practice and then a meal at night before bed.

"It was just as well we got plenty of sleep before the first round because it was going to be tough going. The wind was really blowing, a 40-miles-an-hour wind. Well, we'd practiced for that, back home in Texas and for four days in Scotland. We hadn't experienced wind quite so bad since arriving at Troon but we knew the course would be kinder to us on the front nine, the way the wind was blowing. It was a case of pick up as many shots as you could on the front side and then hang on when we got to the back side.

"Things went according to plan and we got off to a good start as far as the putting was concerned. Justin has a great eye and is one of the best long putters in the business. His first significant putt in the 1997 British Open was at the second, which he birdied from 25 feet. It was a one-iron off the tee to stay in play. We'd get plenty of chance to use the driver. For Justin, who at that time was not a real long hitter, Troon was a very long course. We'd soon find that out into the wind on the incoming nine holes.

"He holed another big putt on the sixth for eagle and it was a satisfying first nine even with a bogey on the card, two-under. The real hard work was coming now. On the 11th, for instance, it's a really long par-four, we needed a driver, a one-iron and still didn't quite make it on. Justin really did have to work hard on the back part of the course because he just couldn't hit long enough. It was a great display of hanging in. He never hit one green on the back nine holes because of hitting against the wind all the time, but he somehow came out of it even-par. When he did drop a shot he got that one back with another long putt for birdie. But it was a real test. We used the one-iron so much that it became a bit of a laughing matter between us. He'd never used the one-iron so much. He said he'd have to take it out of the bag and put in a four-wood just to give it a rest.

"The thing I remember most about the first round was the par he made on 18. It was straight into the wind and in '97 he was probably 20 yards shorter than he is now. Even though he hit it with everything he'd got he was still 15 yards short of the fairway. I couldn't believe he was going to survive the week if it was going to be the same tomorrow. He needed to chop out of the hay from a bad lie with an eight-iron and still had something like 158 yards left to the green, so we decided on a 'knock-down' four-iron.

"He hit it pin-high to about eight feet. It was one of the best golf shots I've seen in my life. Thankfully he made the putt. He was more than a little disgusted at not even being able to reach a fairway, but it had been an incredible back nine. He got up and down from absolutely everywhere. His putter was his savior, or he might have been heading home after the next round."

Riefke also played his part on those trying back nine holes. As a nine-handicap golfer the bagman had a fair idea how to play the often treacherous incoming holes and Riefke earned his tournament fee with his assistance with the irons on the back nine alone. With Leonard constantly coming up short, it meant consultation on every move between player and caddie. In that testing two hours or so the conditions proved the value of a good man on the bag. The quiet-spoken caddie also played a vital part with help in reading the lines on the greens, as Leonard produced—as he would again in the final round—the putting round of the day.

Following rounds of 67, another American, Jim Furyk, soon to be Nick Faldo's tormentor in the Ryder Cup, and a Northern Irishman, Darren Clarke, led the way after round one, two strokes ahead of a group of three which included Leonard. With Leonard after 69s were Greg Norman and

Fred Couples. Illustrious company indeed for the Texan. Another notable score was the 70 by Swede Jesper Parnevik, to place the 1994 Open runner-up three off the lead and one behind Leonard.

In the second round the weather took a turn for the better. Leonard's putting certainly did not deteriorate either as he came roaring into contention. Once again. his round was fashioned by his playing of the opening nine holes, with caddie Riefke continuing to provide input with his phenomenal reading of the often tricky Troon greens.

"The putter didn't go cold overnight and it was a wonderful start to the round. We sank some big putts early on, birdied the second and then he made two eagles. The wind wasn't so strong but again it was playing kind of down and left-to-right. Justin had been worried about his lack of length the day before and so he put a new driver in the bag. It worked well for him, although I think the less windy conditions helped a lot. He hit both the par-fives in two and knocked in good length putts, around 20 feet each time.

"It was exciting choosing the irons. We were really guessing some of the time on how much the ball was going to bounce up, but both the eagles were with five-irons, pretty short irons considering, so perhaps the new driver did help.

"He absolutely loved playing links golf and adapted very quickly that week, playing all the 'bump-and-run' shots we'd heard about so much from people like Nicklaus and Norman, shots that you need at a place like Troon. He could hit a bump-and-run with the best of them. We talked about the British Open when we first started working together and we considered the British Open the most important major to have, purely because of the shot-making you need.

"Well, the two eagles really fired him up. He had to think hard the last time he'd had two eagles in a round. It was back in his college golf days, so that was a pretty big deal for him. Because he wasn't such a big hitter, making the greens at par-fives in two was pretty special. Apart from flushing a one-iron 250 yards, nothing made him more satisfied. He'd have a special little saying whenever he did it: 'That's why we play the game, Bobby,' he'd say. He doesn't say it quite so much now because he's got a lot longer and reaches them in two much more often.

"Those two eagles were definitely a key to Justin winning that week. They were definitely the key to a second-round 66. We again had to hang on for the back nine holes after going out in 31 [five under par] because it was tough from the tenth again, even though the wind wasn't as strong. We still hit a lot of long irons on the back side. The 13th sticks in my mind because it was another great shot with a longish iron. He got it on to about 20 feet and he told me it felt like the third time he'd hit a long hole in two, so I was expecting his little saying again. It was a tough hole, the 13th, over 460 yards into the wind, so when he sank the 20-footer he was really pleased.

"It was an unsatisfying end to the round, though. This time there was no save on the 18th. He didn't make the fairway again but this time it wasn't because he came up short, just pushed it a little. He got the four-iron on all right but a long way from the flag and then he three-putted, from about 40 feet, maybe just less, hit his first putt six feet past. A 65 would have been really nice and what he deserved."

That final-hole three-putt proved costly for Leonard as it prevented him from lying a shot closer to the second-round leader, Darren Clarke, out in front on his own after a 66 similar to that of the American's. Clarke had moved to nine under par, two strokes ahead of Leonard, with Jesper Parnevik a further stroke adrift of the lead. The leading trio in the 1997 Open Championship had set out their store and from day two the plot between these three protagonists was well and truly hatched.

"Justin was excited to be up there and he had plenty to say over dinner. We ate in the Italian again, pizza again, and talked a lot about the way things could go at the weekend. There was plenty of chance for a long sleep because we weren't out until three o'clock.

"Of course, we were out with big Darren Clarke and he can hit the ball long, so I expected that pretty well all day we would be hitting our second shots first. Justin had his best driving day of the week so far but, wouldn't you know it, the putter went cold on him. We just could not buy a putt and it took right to the 17th before any putt of length went in. That was a putt of 25 feet or so at the par-three and it was a long time coming. The front stretch was so frustrating but Justin kept cool.

"It was a lovely sunny day, but we just kept getting the lines that little bit out and wasted quite a few birdie opportunities. We got nothing out of the two par-fives going out, this time, really through the irons more than the driving. I guess it was a frustrating day for both players. Darren played really well on the front side but it went wrong for him, too, on the back nine holes.

"For us, it was pars all the way out and then, as it always seems to go when you can't hole a putt, a couple of bogeys come along. Two wayward drives in succession, on 12 and 13, dropped Justin down the leaderboard. When we ran through the round afterwards he felt he'd really lost ground because of the putting. He told me, 'The hole just got smaller and smaller,' and he was very frustrated by that, particularly the way his putting stroke had been so good for the two previous days. He felt he'd lost a lot of ground in just the department of his game he didn't expect to."

He had indeed lost ground. A round of 72 meant Leonard now trailed the new leader, Jesper Parnevik, by five strokes. Only twice before, both times in the distant past, had such a deficit been made up. Tommy Armor did so at Carnoustie in 1931, and it was just down the links from Troon, at Prestwick, where James Barnes recovered his five-stroke margin to prevail. Could the Ayrshire coast be about to witness another great fightback?

Leader Parnevik certainly hoped not. Ever since his grave error of judgment at Turnberry three years earlier, when he attacked the final hole and bogeyed to hand the Claret Jug to Nick Price, the Swede had been looking to get his own back on the Open Championship. He did not want to be like Price and twice suffer the despair of losing the Open at the death.

However, it was not Leonard whom Parnevik went to bed on Saturday night thinking about. Second-round front-runner Darren Clarke, despite a back nine of 39, was only two strokes away from the Swede. Parnevik's rousing 66 had hauled him to 11 under par. A 71 by Clarke left him nine-under for second place, then came Leonard at six-under. There was another American harboring hopes of overhauling that formidable five-stroke deficit: Fred Couples was also six under par, to share third place with Leonard.

The most significant move, though, had been made by the player who had attracted the most attention from the gallery all week. U.S. Masters champion Tiger Woods had at last turned on all the power and finesse which had seen him storm to a 12-stroke victory at Augusta. Woods had not been able to master the traditions of Troon until round three, then suddenly everything clicked. An exhilarating 64 saw him carve his way through the field to lie nine strokes away from Parnevik. If Woods had finally worked out how to play Troon, he could be an awesome prospect in the final round. Parnevik most certainly went to bed thinking about him, too.

Not being in anyone's thoughts in particular suited Leonard and his caddie. They by no means had given up their chance of glory. Leonard placed the Claret Jug the highest of all prized possessions. He just hoped his remarkable penchant for holing putts would return; if it did, his caddie was sure the oldest major trophy could reside in Texas for the next year. Before they went to bed to sleep on Leonard's chances, however, there was—just to make a change—pizza on the menu. This time, though, the Texans did not dine alone.

"We dined at the Italian again and this time it was not so quiet. Some friends of Justin's were in just for the day. They'd watched him play and they had dinner with us. It was a really nice atmosphere at the restaurant because we ran into Jack and Barbara Nicklaus. They stopped and said hello and had a long chat. They really gave Justin a lot of encouragement. To have someone like Jack Nicklaus talk to you and have confidence in you must have been wonderful for Justin. It was pretty inspiring for me, I can tell you, and I'm sure it must have been for Justin.

"He went off to bed very relaxed. We kind of chilled out that night. I was staying with a family about five miles from Troon and I went back and had a few pints with my host. There wasn't much good in going to bed before midnight and then waking up at six o'clock with seven or eight hours before I had to go to work.

"Before the final round he wasn't five back in twelfth place but five back in third place. There weren't a lot of players in front of him. Hopefully the putter would get as hot as it was on Thursday and Friday.

"We talked over plenty of things before going out that afternoon, but the main subject was the game plan. The best thing about the week was that we stuck to the same game plan we'd worked out in our 80 holes of practice. Going out with different players, you could see there were a lot of different ways to play a hole and we decided very early in the week that there were a lot of one-iron holes.

"In the first round, for instance, the one-iron was in his hands a lot and we used it time and time again. It paid off. Instead of being aggressive at some of the holes, where you could go in the pot bunkers, we held back some. That was the most important thing on Sunday—apart from getting the putting touch back, of course—that we avoided a lot of the bunkers.

"I'll always be able to remember the final round because I've got T-shirts with all of the holes we played and the scores printed on them. It's a lasting memento for a very memorable afternoon. [Riefke was then able to offer further on his red-letter day by going through the round, hole by hole, by way of his T-shirt.]

"One of the great things about Sunday afternoon was that we were playing with Fred Couples. Justin loves and respects him and he was just a great partner to have on a day like that. It was a real laid-back day. I know it's the British Open final round but, believe me, it was just like playing a practice round. No matter whether Fred's leading or if he's in 40th place, his temperament's going to be pretty much the same. His caddie Joe and I are good friends, all four of us are good friends. So it was just a great, great pairing.

"We got off to a great start, birdied two, three and four with some good iron shots and putts. The putter was back on our side again. At five, the par-three, I remember we had a little too much club, hit the back left of the green and three-putted. At six, the second par-five, we ended up a little short of the green out of the rough. He then hit an incredible pitch shot with a sand-wedge from a pretty bare lie a few feet and made that. So we've already made great inroads into the lead, three-under for the round after six.

"Then it got better. His approach shots were just fabulous over the front nine, seven of them were inside the 12- to 15-feet mark and he made five of them. He hit less than three feet on seven, looked as though it might even pitch in, and hit to about six feet on nine with an eight iron. Two more birdies went on the card and it could have been three because his 25-footer on the eighth stayed right on the rim of the cup.

"By the turn the leaderboard told us we were just one back, but his composure didn't change. Just like on the front nine when we're making up so much ground, we're still having a lot of fun out there. Even when he's in the hunt, he likes to kind of keep it even a little lighter than normal, just to calm himself down. We were having a blast out there."

Leonard had instilled apprehension into his arch rivals with such a blistering start. Playing in the group behind, leader Parnevik, who had not helped his cause at Turnberry in 1994 by refusing to look at leaderboards, did not have to check on the board to know someone was making a charge at him. He knew it was not playing partner Darren Clarke. The Irishman had virtually forfeited his chances by "shanking" a three-iron on to the beach at the second, a resultant double-bogey giving him far too much to do.

Tiger Woods had begun quietly and found little of the form of the previous day early on. The Masters champion had even played a practice round on Saturday evening to try to keep the swing and the mentality that had earned him his third-round 64. Not only did he not find that form but he disappeared for good off the leaderboard when he ran into trouble at the eighth, the dreaded Postage Stamp. As it had done to many before him, including ultimately Greg Norman in 1989 when the Open last called in at Troon, the tricky bunkers embroidered around the par-three had taken their toll on Woods to the tune of triple-bogey. Woods's failure to lick the Postage Stamp all week showed he still had a little to learn about links golf and Open Championships.

Parnevik clung on to his lead like one of the seagulls diving and changing course above him, warding off marauders while tenuously grasping a precious prize as the Swede did his best to fend off an indomitable Leonard. After going through the turn, however, Leonard himself took some of the pressure off Parnevik, before coming determinedly back in his quest for prime place on the leaderboard.

"There was a real setback for us on ten. The hole had been a bit of a struggle most of the week and it cost us bogey after hitting into the right rough. We came up short right, chipped down and missed the putt. When Jesper Parnevik birdied eleven we were back to two shots back. We also missed the greens at 11 and 12 and he drove into the right rough at 15. But he made great up-and-downs each time.

"The 15-footer he made at 15 kept him only one behind, real crucial. We took time to work that one out because we both knew we couldn't afford to drop another shot. There didn't seem enough holes left. In it went. He really showed great character. It was amazing how the week had gone, for three of the days at least. Justin played the first nine holes brilliantly and the second nine with fantastic character, never gave up on them when some would have done.

"The 16th was a real big moment and he told me afterwards it was the moment which made the hair stand up on the back of his neck. He hit a good drive, came up short with the second shot and didn't pitch that well this time, to about 20 feet. He made that putt. He hit an awesome shot at

17, but it decided to get away a little long, left of the hole. He kinda tapped that in from 30 to 35 feet!"

The pressure of knowing he was being steadily overhauled and the perfidy of Troon's now arid fairways, its treacherous bunkering and slickened greens, finally became too much to bear. When Parnevik heard yet another deafening roar, as he played the 16th, he feared the worst. The Swede backed off his putt of four feet and had to regather himself mentally. By the time he stood over the putt again, the scoreboard operators were already making their adjustments. Leonard's birdie on 17 had taken the American to 12 under par, a stroke ahead of the Swede. Parnevik suspected that as he again aimed his putt, no more than four feet for his own birdie. When he missed the putt, the 126th Open had a new leader. This time Parnevik did check the leaderboard as he walked off the 16th green. It caused him to shudder and, as he was to admit later, "the air to go out of my sails."

Parnevik's resistance was not quite over, until he hooked his tee-shot badly on the 17th. Leonard could march to an emphatic victory, making up not only the five shots to equal the Open recovery record but three more beside that. A magnificent closing round of 65 by Leonard relegated Parnevik to second place, bogeys on the last two holes spelling a second Open disappointment in three years. The bogeys took him alongside Clarke, whose last-ditch birdie earned the Irishman a share of the runners-up spot.

The tears did not flow yet for the new Open champion. They would come a little later—when the shy Texan thought back to his family, his friends, his coach back home. But there was always his faithful caddie to share the triumph with him.

"We could still hear the buzz on the 18th tee as the leaderboard changed. There had been a huge roar from the people watching us and we were close to the 16th green so I could see from Jesper's reaction that he had missed the putt and bogeyed. That gave Justin the lead.

"We were debating on whether to hit driver or three-wood off the 18th tee. When we felt Jesper had missed the putt we decided on the three-wood. At first I thought it was going to be a mistake because the ball looked as though it had disappeared into one of the three left-hand fairway bunkers. But it had skirted the bunker and come round just on to the fairway. Until we got up there, though, we had no idea where the ball was. It was a huge relief.

"He then hit a stock six-iron to the 18th green. We don't know what's going on with Jesper on 17 as Justin hits his first putt, maybe from 40 feet, a little past the hole. At that point, as he's standing over his second putt, they changed the scoreboard to reflect what Jesper did on 17. At that point I knew what had happened—that we'd just won. He'd no idea. He told me later that at that stage he felt sure it was going to be a playoff. He could tell the scoreboard was changing but he had to concentrate on the putt.

"As we walked off the green, I put my arm around him and I said, 'Jesper just went back to ten-under; you've got a two-shot lead and he's only got the 18th to come.' Justin looked up at the scoreboard and said, 'Oh really!' He didn't show a whole lot of emotion—until Mark Calcavecchia, Lee Janzen and Steve Stricker came rushing up to him from the side of the green. They were all high-fiving him and saying, 'You've won, you've won.'

"But it wasn't until he got into the scorer's trailer that he kind of realized what had just happened. He just kept saying, 'Have I really done it? Have I really won the British Open? You were great, Bob.' He'd just shot one of the most fantastic rounds of golf and he still had time to thank me. What a guy!

"Well, the presentation was very emotional for him. He desperately wanted his folks with him to share the moments. They'd been around a lot at tournaments but he only had me to share things with for the time being, so there had to be a party to celebrate.

"He decided it should be thrown at the 17th. Corey Pavin had done something similar, which Justin had gone to, when he won the U.S. Open. They had gone to the roof of the clubhouse to party. I don't think there was any way we could have got on to the roof of the Troon clubhouse to party! So he ordered some pints—and pizzas, of course—to be brought to the 17th green. The family I'd been staying with, the Cranes, had watched him on every hole and they'd actually given up their master bedroom for me that week. They were invited and Corey Pavin came, too. We smoked big cigars. It was an absolute blast. We had a picture taken of us both pointing to the hole at 17.

"It's tradition for the caddie to get the flag from the 18th, usually the flag, not the whole pole. Darren Clarke's caddie Billy Foster grabbed the flag for me after they had holed out and handed it to me. I was kinda shy to go out and do so myself.

"Well, I took the whole thing, pole and all, on the flight home. The flight crew put it in a compartment at the front of the plane and I said to them, 'I want you to look at me and remember my face, make sure no one else takes this. It's very precious to me.' It was there when we landed. I got some strange looks and people didn't believe it was from Royal Troon in Britain—where Justin Leonard had just won the oldest major in golf and the famous Auld Claret Jug."

1998 ROYAL BIRKDALE

Mark O'Meara with Jerry Higginbotham

Mark O'Meara	USA	72 68 72 68 280 (par 70)
Brian Watts	USA	68 69 73 70 280
(O'Meara won after four-hole playoff)		
Tiger Woods	USA	65 73 77 66 281
Jim Furyk	USA	70 70 72 70 282
Jesper Parnevik	Sweden	68 72 72 70 282
Raymond Russell	Scotland	68 73 75 66 282
Justin Rose (am.)	England	72 66 75 69 282
Davis Love III	USA	67 73 77 68 285
Thomas Bjorn	Denmark	68 71 76 71 286
Costantino Rocca	Italy	72 74 70 70 286

"The guy picking the ball up, that was a tremendous stroke of fortune. What might have happened to the British Open title otherwise? I don't know. Mark chipped it up and eventually made five. I believe in all hindsight that if I couldn't have identified the ball, maybe the best Mark could have made would have been a seven. I'm not saying I won the British Open for Mark. Mark won the British Open with his great golf. I'm saying a caddie stuck to what he thought was right. I could have walked up the fairway with Mark. It was fate."

Stand by your man—and his ball

Apart from Britain's Colin Montgomerie, there was probably no one more overdue a major success than Mark O'Meara when the genial 41-year-old American began the 1998 season. By the time he finished the year, O'Meara had twice raised major trophies. First O'Meara holed the longest putt on record on the final green to win the Masters, then a nail-biting playoff victory to clinch the Open Championship title provided the second jewel in the 1998 crown for the man from Windemere, Florida.

By O'Meara's side for those two heady successes was a caddie well used to serving major champions. He was a man with a name more northern British than O'Meara's home town Windemere, the highly experienced entrepreneur in real estate and restaurants Jerry Higginbotham.

In the 1970s Higginbotham carried Ben Crenshaw's bag and in the next decade he worked for the Australian David Graham. Then the far-sighted Higginbotham decided to give up full-time caddying and move into the restaurant business in Hawaii. His south-sea island idyll, though, was shattered in 1992 when a hurricane wiped out his home and business.

Higginbotham decided to stay on the island, but when the Hawaiian Open came along in 1994 the old hankering to be on the fairways gripped him once more. He took up the bag of John Cook, a great friend of Mark O'Meara's, and a year later, when O'Meara's caddie became seriously ill, Higginbotham formed the relationship that would eventually lead to double major success for the pair.

To clinch the second part of that double, O'Meara needed lady luck—and the awareness of a "streetwise" caddie who would not be budged when it came to the rules of golf.

"I was very pleased to team up with Mark because even though he was approaching the so-called veteran stage of his career, I felt he had a lot of game left. We began our time together with a third place at the Kemper Open of 1995. That represented a rejuvenation for Mark because he'd been in a slump for a while. Suddenly he had a chance to win again. I'm not saying it was because of me he came out of the slump but I thought we cooked pretty good.

"That year he won the Honda Classic when he hadn't won for quite a while [three years]. He beat Nick Faldo coming down the stretch and that was a great experience because Faldo was still a major force at that time, high in the world rankings. Mark then won the Canadian Open that year and the following two years won four more tournaments, in fact winning twice a year for the first three years together.

"By the time 1998 came around, I just knew Mark was good enough to win a major. Sure enough, his chance came along at Augusta and he took it.

"He played so good that week. His game was just phenomenal. Mark had been working on his short-game, his chipping and bunker play, for a couple of years, hitting a lot of balls. A lot of players said he didn't have the short-game to win a major but he finally got it together. His hard work finally paid off at Augusta.

"Mark took only 101 putts that week and if you take only 101 putts at Augusta on those greens you're going to win the tournament. Another point was that the whole week we pulled perfect clubs, Mark and I. Perhaps we had two bad clubs in 72 holes. That was pretty phenomenal because the wind was blowing hard at Augusta all that week and club selection was difficult.

"On the 17th tee on the Sunday, Mark told me, 'I'm going to birdie the last two holes and win this thing.' I looked at him and said, 'Okay. That sounds pretty good to me.' He did just that.

"It was a fantastic year and a wonderful one in the majors. After winning his first major you thought he could take another one because he played so well in 1998, especially in his short-game, which until then had been his weak point."

O'Meara's newly found deftness of touch could not help him to any better than a tie for 36th place in the U.S. Open, but Higginbotham's inclination that his man could win another major was well founded as O'Meara triumphed at

Royal Birkdale and then finished tied fourth in the U.S. PGA Championship. The pair fashioned the best player–caddie relationship since Nick Faldo and Fanny Sunesson pulled off the U.S. Masters and Open Championship of 1990.

O'Meara certainly had no intention of resting on his laurels after at last pulling off his maiden major title. The quiet American had a score to settle with Royal Birkdale, anyway. He had thought the course set close to the Irish Sea on the west coast of northern England had been a friend after he clinched the European Tour's Lawrence Batley Invitational there in 1987. O'Meara had therefore returned to Birkdale in high hopes in 1991 when the Open Championship went back there. But that year O'Meara, even though he found the course to his liking again, was disappointed. He finished third behind Ian Baker-Finch at the Lancashire links, losing his victory chance with a mixture of bad luck and poor course management over the opening nine holes on the final day.

For the 1998 Open Championship, Birkdale had been given almost a total revamp. Its much-criticized greens in 1991 had all been dug up and relaid. The course had been lengthened to over 7,000 yards. Its par-fours in particular, several of them between 450 and nearly 500 yards, were going to provide a formidable challenge. O'Meara, though, was a determined man when it came to Birkdale.

The much-travelled American had played many times in Britain, also going close to major success in 1985 at Sandwich, and respected the galleries as much as they respected him. The Open Championship was a title O'Meara was more than keen to win. Lifting the Claret Jug was a dream. It was a dream he had had since his first trip to traditional links. It was a dream which provided his motivation to learn all the shots in the book—and many of those not in the book. While O'Meara had been sharpening up his short-game in 18 months he had also worked on his shot-making. That had been very noticeable when he clinched the Lancôme Trophy in 1997 at St. Nom la Breteche near Versailles, Paris, on one of his frequent visits to Europe.

As something of an Anglophile—with a surname like his he almost felt it his bounden duty—Higginbotham was pleased to be back in Britain, amongst old friends, when the Open Championship week got under way. But before he had left to cross the Atlantic he tipped off his old friends in the USA.

"I told a lot of people back home, if Mark's going to win a British Open, this is the one he's going to win. A lot of my family and friends put money on Mark O'Meara to win at Royal Birkdale. I certainly put a big bet on him. I got 40–1 and it was the easiest money I ever made. Mark never wanted me to bet on him because he thought it brought him bad luck. But, this one week, I was determined to put some money on because I was so sure he was going to win. I went in with Greg Rita [John Daly's Open Championship-winning caddie of 1995] and couldn't believe my eyes when I saw Mark posted at 40–1. I said to Greg, 'I won't have to tell Mark about the bet. I'm having some of this.' I put £100 on Mark. I won £4,000 that week.

"I didn't care about the winnings. It was just a friendly bet. Winning the British Open was the main thing. A lot of the caddies who've been around a long time, we don't really care that much about the money. It's fun to win golf tournaments and we want nice bank accounts like the pros, but the real excitement comes with major victories. I wanted this one at Birkdale as much as Mark.

"I got to Birkdale on the Sunday before, just like I do at all the majors. I walked the golf course, as I always do. I'd been doing that since my first visit to the British Open in 1983, which, funnily enough, had been at Royal Birkdale. I was caddying for David Graham and Tom Watson won. It was the first time I'd ever seen a British Open course.

"Mark and his family rolled in on Monday. He'd been over in Ireland playing with Tiger Woods and Payne Stewart, getting used to links courses at Ballybunion and Waterville. We played a nine-hole practice round with Tiger. Mark and Tiger play a lot of practice rounds together. I think Tiger Woods brought Mark O'Meara's game to its peak in 1998. A lot of people think they are just so-so friends. These guys are the best of friends and they help each other tremendously all of the time.

"They played together Monday, Tuesday and Wednesday, met up with John Cook and a couple of other friends. Mark probably knew the course better than I did. He'd nearly won in 1991 and he'd played the holes so many times. When players know the golf course so well, a lot of the time the caddies can get a feeling they're kinda just along for the ride. There was no way I was going to let that temptation come my way. In my opinion there aren't that many more important times for a caddie than at the British Open.

"It blew pretty well all the time at Birkdale that week. On the first day it wasn't such a windy day but the course seemed tricky. There were a lot of long par-fours and it was often a case of getting into position on them to attack, like needing plenty of irons off the tee. We had lots of discussion over clubs. We tried to keep ourselves in position, tried not to lose the tournament. Most of the guys I've ever caddied for, when we talk about a major, the main theme is 'Don't lose the tournament on the first day; don't shoot 79, 80 and blow yourself out. Just try to keep yourself somewhere around par.' If you know the wind's going to blow and you're going to get some of the treacherous conditions you can get at a British Open, the object has got to be keep it to around par and stay close to the field. I know it sounds like a cliché. Everybody knows that, but that's the way it is. The first round is very important in all the majors, but exceptionally so in the British Open.

"Mark stuck to that adage on the first day, a very difficult day for him even if it wasn't for everybody, just kind of plugged along. He was a couple over par, so a 72 didn't put him in any headlines in the papers, but he was pretty solid all day."

O'Meara certainly did not make the headlines, but the man whom the gallery had flocked to see did. Tiger Woods's swashbuckling 65 earned him a share of a one-shot lead with fellow American John Huston. It was an American takeover of the Open again because two more held third place, the redoubtable Fred Couples and Loren Roberts. U.S. Tour player Nick Price of Zimbabwe again contended for the Open, also sharing third place after a 66. More U.S. stalwarts followed a further stroke back, Davis Love and Brad Faxon.

Woods definitely made the headlines. His powerful play out of the Birkdale rough salvaged pars that his wayward tee-play threatened and his irons clawed birdies from the monster links from places and distances about which other players could only either dream or have nightmares. Huston matched him as he again threw down the gauntlet in a major, while Couples was making his umpteenth bid to place the Auld Claret Jug in his trophy case.

When the perfect conditions of day one were taken into consideration, O'Meara's 72, on paper at any rate, appeared a lackluster score and it kept him well down the field, out of the top 50 and only just in the top 90. As caddie Higginbotham had observed, however, a 72 did not lose you the tournament in the first round.

O'Meara's decision to accompany Tiger Woods and Payne Stewart to Ireland to practice the week before the Open took on great significance when mother nature decided to play a little havoc in the second round. The wind whipped up stronger and even snapped some of the flagpoles on top of the grandstands. Swings and tempers snapped on the course. Caddie Higginbotham refused to allow his concentration to break, however, or his faith in his player's chances of winning.

"Mark was a very relaxed man all week at Birkdale. He had his wife Alicia, his mom and his mother-in-law staying with him at a beautiful English home, cooking the food for him. He had the kids there, so it was like a home environment, and he couldn't have been in a better mood for the British Open. But he was a bit taken aback by the fantastic scoring on the first day because Birkdale's supposed to be difficult. When I arrived at the course on Friday, though, I think I might have taken 72 in the second round. It was blowing an absolute hurricane and the weather was awful. The wind was in a totally different direction to the first day. It was going to be a tough day.

"Mark seemed to blank out the bad conditions. He putted magnificently and his whole game was pretty good in the second round. A 68 was a great score. We teed off in the rain as well, but Mark kept it on the fairways most of the day and hit a lot more greens than he did in the first round. He wasn't exactly knocking the flags out but he did set up plenty of birdie chances and took a few, what you have to do to get into contention. Keeping the ball in play was absolutely crucial all week because miss a fairway and you could be history. I remember Tom Lehman telling us in the locker-room after one practice round that he'd lost six balls in the rough. You had to keep it tight and Mark did. I felt my money was on a good horse!

"His decision to get used to wind and tough conditions in Ireland the week before Birkdale came into its own in the second round because he'd been practicing over there how to keep the ball low in the wind. That was another part of his game he'd worked hard at with his coach Hank Raney, keeping the ball low in the wind. It really paid off on the Friday because we must have played most of the round in a 50-mile-an-hour wind. Now we were really in contention."

The second-best round of the Friday bedevilled by morning rain and then such strong winds in the afternoon that there was a half-hour suspension from 5:30 P.M., came from O'Meara. He was two strokes worse than the remarkable score of 66 by 17-year-old amateur Justin Rose, but the 68 did put O'Meara in contention. It hauled him up to a share of sixth place, now only three strokes behind a total outsider, Canadian-born American Brian Watts, the son of an Englishman and a German, whose main source of income came from playing in Asia, especially Japan.

If Watts caused a stir by proving to be the dark-horse leader by a stroke on three-under-par 137, then the second-placed man, only a boy really, had the headline writers in full cry. Amateur Rose became the darling of the gallery and the press as his 66 put him on Watts's shoulder. Tiger Woods lost his lead by shooting a 73, actually salvaging it with a strong finish, and he shared second place with Rose and Zimbabwe's constant Open title campaigner, Nick Price. The first round co-leader John Huston, however, crashed off the board and into obscurity with a 77.

It all seemed to be boiling up to a clash between the great friends O'Meara and Woods, a prospect that caddie Higginbotham relished.

However, as the weather somehow got even worse, that vision faded in the third round. Woods did not cope with the conditions half as well as O'Meara. Only a monumental stroke of good fortune, though, coupled with an astute move by Higginbotham at the sixth hole, kept O'Meara in with a chance of his second major title.

"Mark and Tiger did a lot of talking after the second round and I could just see Sunday night being a head-to-head between them. They'd practiced together and worked the course and conditions out together. It looked odds-on that the weekend would bring them together. I had mixed feelings. It would be nice for them to play together in the last round, but you had to consider Tiger as the chief threat to winning the British Open.

"We played with Freddie Couples in the third round, though. That was a great draw because Freddie is so laid-back and I knew that would be good for Mark. We needed everything in our favor because the wind was just howling again, seemed to be even stronger than Friday. It took everything you had even to reach the fairway off the tee on some of the par-fours. When we'd been on the range on Saturday morning, Mark, Freddie and Jim Furyk were hitting six-irons about 100 yards into the wind. The ball was coming back at us.

"The first was a real trial and Mark and Freddie both took sixes on it. That was a big blow, but Mark kept his head. He just felt that it was the same for everybody and that the whole field would be dropping strokes. He was so determined not to let the round get away from him, right from the first. Double-bogeying at the start could have finished his chances that week, but he wouldn't lie down and hung in. Freddie did his best, too, but he had a real bad time of it from the start. Mark made some putts after his bad start and got it up and down a few times. That sort of steadied the ship for him.

"But the wind was a big problem and especially at the sixth. It's another big par-four and we were being hit by a crosswind there that could put the ball anywhere. By the time we came to play the second shot we were straight into the wind and I remember giving him a yardage of 215 yards still to go. It was up the hill with a dog-leg right. It was driver-driver hole and he tried to hit the driver off the fairway, flamed it way right up in the bushes. We went up there; everybody's looking for the ball. The rough was maybe five feet tall and there are at least one hundred people stomping around in it levelling it in a lot of places as it got lain down by their feet. That only made it more difficult to find the ball.

"I yelled at a whole bunch of people who were just looking down at us, 'If you're not going to look for the ball, get the heck out of the way.' There were a lot of people milling around; the TV cameras were on us . . .

"Mark was frustrated because too many people were looking for the ball. He abandoned search. I'd put the watch on us right away when we started looking and I said to Mark McCumber of ABC, 'I have him with over a minute left, a minute and a half, in fact.' That was ABC's and the BBC's estimate as well. So I gave him the driver and a ball and he went back. It's within the rules of golf that I can stay, still searching for the ball. I'm part of the team.

"Then a guy yells, 'Mark. I've found a ball.' Mark didn't even turn round. I don't think he heard the guy in the wind. So I went up there. Mark didn't have time to get back within the five minutes allowed, so it had to be me. I identified the ball. It was a Strata. It was Mark's. I just don't know how the guy found the ball there. It was all trodden down and not where we were looking. It was up on a hill and we were looking in this other bush, where the people told us the ball had gone.

"Well, when the guy sees no reaction from Mark he picks the ball up. I think, 'Shoot. Stop everything now. He's picked the ball up.' I'd identified it. We needed to get Mark O'Meara back down there.

"There was a big fiasco on the fairway. I believe it all took 20 minutes to sort out, Mark said that. The officials said he needed to identify the ball, but that is untrue. The rule says it can be the player 'or the caddie' who should identify the ball, as we are a team. I can identify the ball, which I did in the allotted five minutes. There were still 40 seconds left when I identified the ball. The kid had picked it up and then walked on the hill. Everybody saw him pick it up. That's a done deal.

"I'm not taking any credit for anything but the one thing I did do was that I stuck there. Fred Couples saw what I was doing and told me to stick right with what I was thinking. I came down to the fairway and put the bag in the middle and told Mark not to hit a second ball because we needed to get him back down there. I said to an official, 'Hey, man. I found the ball.' The officials were not agreeing with me that I could identify it. There was a lot of controversy. There were American officials . . . it was a real fuss. Eventually I was proved right.

"So Mark got to come up, dropped the ball, it rolled down the hill to two club lengths. He dropped it twice and got to place the ball, under the rule. It was a pretty good lie. It was very fortunate that the guy picked the ball up. If Mark had had to play it as it first lay then it would have been big trouble. The guy picking the ball up, that was a tremendous stroke of fortune.

"What might have happened to the British Open title otherwise? I don't know. Mark chipped it up and eventually made five. I believe in all hindsight that if I couldn't have identified the ball, maybe the best Mark could have made would have been a seven. And it would have been a miraculous seven. He'd probably have made eight or nine.

"I'm not saying I won the British Open for Mark. Mark won the British Open with his great golf. I'm saying a caddie stuck to what he thought was right. I could have walked up the fairway with Mark. It was fate.

"Well, after that he really held it together, played fantastic golf, and his 72 was for me just about his best performance of the week in the conditions and bearing in mind what went on at the sixth. It was a minor miracle that he could get back his concentration enough to be in the second-last group going out in the final round."

As many of the great names in golf either slipped badly or perished altogether—Nick Price and defending champion Justin Leonard shot 82s, Phil Mickelson 85—O'Meara jockeyed into an even better position, two strokes off the lead and sharing second place at two-over-par. The leader for a second day was Brian Watts, the only man not over par. He was level-par, two shots better than O'Meara, Sweden's Jesper Parnevik, making his annual bid for the Open title, and Jim Furyk. Young Justin Rose, who incredibly took over the lead at one time, was a further stroke in arrears.

O'Meara's chance of a shootout with his friend Tiger Woods had been ruined by Woods's 77 which left him six strokes behind leader Watts. Parnevik partnered Watts in the final group. O'Meara played alongside Furyk. The pundits felt the title now would be fought out by O'Meara, Furyk, and Parnevik, again with Woods always likely to produce a miracle, especially as conditions became reasonably benign on the Sunday. No one considered Watts for the Championship. He had other ideas.

"Mark again got off to a shaky start and we hit trouble on the sixth again. It was the approach shot which went wrong, although this time it was a vicious kick off a slope near the green. The ball was in the bushes again but this time we found it quickly and he managed to hack out of it without too much trouble. Then he made a wonderful chip. It was bogey again but his better short-game was paying off at the right time.

"We also bogeyed the seventh but then fate took over again. At the eighth we were still well in touch with the lead, three behind if I remember correctly, but it looked as though we were going to lose ground badly after a drive into the left rough. Mark had to stand with the ball well below his feet and he missed the green by some. It looked as though we could be in bad trouble when the ball shot up a mound and ran into heavy rough. But it somehow got through, spun round at the top and caught a downslope. It trickled on to the green and Mark holed out for birdie.

"At the turn we were still two behind Brian Watts and we could see Tiger was back in the running, so we talked about needing something special down the stretch now. Mark found that something special.

"This time it was the putter that did it. He twice holed putts around the 15- to 20-foot mark on 11 and 12, and when I looked at the leaderboard, we were in front. What made things more difficult was that it was our playing partner pushing Mark all the way. Jim Furyk was only a stroke behind by that stage, in second place with Brian.

"The nerves were really jangling for me when we found the sand at the 13th and bogeyed because that put us in a tie for the lead. But it just shows how determined Mark was that day. The key to the round in the end was the 14th. The wind was right to left, tricky but not blowing so damn hard it was difficult to stand still, just tricky. He'd just made bogey on 13, a good bogey in fact, so we couldn't afford mistakes at that stage. We both decided it should be a three-iron on 14, a par-three not much short of 200 yards. We always discussed clubs.

"He hit it to about three feet. That was the shot of the day. That was the shot that got him really pumped up."

The destiny of the Open Championship looked to be in the hands of O'Meara, Watts, Furyk and Woods, who birdied the last to finish one over par and set the target. Furyk blotted his copybook and subsequently lost his title chance by bogeying the 15th, watching in dismay as his saving putt somehow clawed its way back out of the rim of the cup when seemingly well set to go to ground. O'Meara had not spotted the line in and took a time-out to discuss it with his caddie. Push really was coming to shove.

"When Jim Furyk missed his putt on 15, Mark turned to me and said, 'Hey. Did you notice which side of the hole that missed on?' There are times in the heat of the battle you don't notice things like that. The other guy misses and you're thinking about your player. Jim Furyk was running us close that day. I was worried Jim Furyk was going to win the golf tournament and Tiger Woods had been posting scores over the last couple of holes. Brian Watts was up there still. Tiger was my biggest worry. I just hadn't noticed really, not so that it really stuck in my mind's eye, which side Jim Furyk had missed on.

"I said, 'He missed low, Mark, he missed on the low side.' I just hoped I'd remembered correctly. Mark went up to his putt—and poured it right into the hole!

"The 17th could be birdie chance. It's a tough par-five but you could expect a four there. We needed one. I thought that might be just enough to win if we did. But it didn't look to be the case when he drove into the left rough. It needed something special because he couldn't get anything better on it than a nine-iron. Then it needed another nine-iron but it left a putt of 20 feet. He got it. I thought that was it. One hole to go and one ahead.

"But Brian Watts just wouldn't give in. He birdied the 17th as well. I spotted that as we were playing the last. On the 18th Mark kind of laid up and then had a long putt which, as it turned out, would have won him the title outright if it had gone in. He left it five or six feet short and that got me going. He turned round, looked over and gave me a little smile. In the past he'd looked over at me when he had a putt like that and said, 'Don't worry about it, Jerry,' and I knew it would be okay because I knew he could pour those five-footers in.

"Mark made that five-footer and he walked over and said, 'Right. Now we'll have to see what happens.'"

What happened next will take its place in Open folklore. Watts, level-par and level with O'Meara going to the last, earned the right to a playoff with one of the most remarkable bunker shots seen in the Championship, particularly under the pressure of trying to win the oldest major. The resulting par threw the pair into the second four-hole shootout in four years, the third since the format changed from a full 18-hole playoff for the title. Watts's approach from a pulled drive in the rough left his ball in a seemingly impossible lie on a downslope in the greenside bunker. He had to place his right foot on the grass at the back of the trap and his left foot in it. Watts somehow managed to squirt his shot over the wall of sand to within 12 inches of the cup, terrifying the watching Jerry Higginbotham.

"We all sat there at 18—Mark, his family and I—and watched Brian Watts play the last hole, watched him make his miraculous bunker shot. It was one of the most difficult bunker shots under pressure I've seen in my life. I thought for one awful moment that the ball was going in. It was a huge relief when it pulled up. Mark and I agreed that Brian Watts was full of courage.

"Mark said to me, 'Oh, not again.' He's been burned in a few playoffs. But he's always got a positive attitude and he quickly followed that by saying, 'Come on. Let's go out and try and win this thing. Come on, Jerry. Let's go and try and win it.'

"We got into the golf cart and went up to the 15th tee but Brian Watts didn't show up for a good while. Mark said, 'What's going on? Is he having lunch or what?' He'd wanted to have a sandwich or something but we said, 'Hey. We can't do that. This is the British Open. Let's go.' Brian eventually showed up, eating a sandwich. Brian was probably a little nervous. Mark was pretty cool. Brian hit it down the right side and I said to Mark, 'You know, the guy could be a little nervous.' Mark said, 'No. We don't think about stuff like that. We'll just think about making some putts, making some birdies.'

"It's a par-five, of course, the 15th, so Mark hit a good drive and left himself a three-wood in, just short, pitched up to exactly the same place as in regulation. Brian had recovered well and hit in closer but then made a terrible putt from fairly short. Mark had poured his right in the middle. Here we go; a shot in front.

"The next hole was playing pretty difficult, had been all week, one of the toughest par-fours we'd played all week. The wind was blowing right to left, hurting a little bit, but they both played it pretty solidly, missing birdie putts.

"As far as the playoff was concerned, the next hole, the 17th, was the key to Mark winning the Open. He hit a perfect drive, just on the left, but Brian flamed his right and into the rough. He was in four foot of rough on a side hill. Judy Rankin from ABC Sport walked over to check out Brian's ball. She was within hearing distance from Mark and I and we heard her say, 'Well, Rossy, this might be the worst lie I've ever seen in all my years of professional golf.' Here's a lady who's a 'Hall of Famer.' I thought, 'This is it. Here we go. We've got it now.' Brian could only chop out 50 feet and he was always going to drop a shot from then on. Mark was two in front then because he made a steady par, decided to lay up and took two from twenty feet.

"When we went to the 18th tee, Mark turned to me and said, 'I just can't believe how calm I feel. I've never felt so calm.' He meant it, too. I wasn't nearly so calm because I just knew that he'd won. We had the Masters and now we were going to win the British Open. You could have laid a blanket over the position his ball finished after the drive on 18 and where it had gone at the same hole earlier, so we thought we knew which club to hit. I had the same yardage as in the round, maybe five yards different. The wind had shifted a little bit and maybe it was a little bit more right-to-left and hurting.

"I wanted Mark to have the right club so I picked up the bag and walked over to Brian Watts and his caddie, put the bag down. He was in a similar spot to Mark on the fairway but first away. I heard them discussing what they were going to hit. He tried to hit a four-iron, hit a terrible shot, kind of low left all the way and he was going to be in the bunker. I walked back over to Mark, put the bag down and told Mark what he hit. Mark pulled out the four-iron but we carried on discussing it. I said I thought it was the same shot as we hit in regulation and that four-iron was not the club. He agreed and hit a five-iron just past the hole. Mark O'Meara then took two putts to win the Open Championship.

"For Mark to win two majors in one year is an achievement that not only he and I will never forget. At his age, to do that, the golfing world will never forget. I'm glad that I was part of a little bit of history."

1999 CARNOUSTIE

Paul Lawrie with Paddy Byrne

Paul Lawrie	Scotland	73 74 76 67 290 (par 71)
Justin Leonard	USA	73 74 71 72 290
Jean Van de Velde	France	75 68 70 77 290
(Lawrie won after four-hole playoff)		
Craig Parry	Australia	76 75 67 73 291
Angel Cabrera	Argentina	75 69 77 70 291
Greg Norman	Australia	76 70 75 72 293
David Frost	South Africa	80 69 71 74 294
Davis Love III	USA	74 74 77 69 294
Tiger Woods	USA	74 72 74 74 294

"I said, 'Middle of the green, two putts, and it's yours.' Afterwards he was a picture to see. He just kept saying over and over again, 'Can you believe it? Can you believe it? That's the Claret Jug!' I said, 'Yes, I know, and you deserve every bit of it because you played brilliantly.' I meant every word. The Claret Jug was there for the taking. Everyone had a chance but he was the man who grabbed it."

Local hero and new kid on the block

The 1999 Open Championship at Carnoustie, the Angus course's first staging of the major for 24 years, provided a dramatic, sometimes bizarre close to the millennium. It will be remembered alongside Tom Watson's epic playoff victory in 1975 against Jack Newton, the last time Carnoustie hosted the Championship. At times, particularly as the 128th Open drew to a close, the tournament became a comedy of errors. In the end, a local hero emerged as arguably the darkest horse ever to hold aloft the famous Auld Claret Jug, certainly in modern times.

Paul Lawrie's remarkable success after a four-hole playoff with the man who threw away his first-time victory, Frenchman Jean Van de Velde, and the winner of the 1997 Open, Justin Leonard of America, saw the oldest major turned completely on its head. Never, at least in latterday Championships, had such an outsider claimed the most coveted individual prize in golf as Lawrie came from no less than ten strokes behind the lead in the final round to clinch victory.

Perhaps it was the nature of the course, the heaviest rough and narrowest fairways anybody could remember in an Open, that had a lot to do with the player from just up the road winning through to confound everybody. Lawrie, a gritty Aberdonian whom pundits had marked down for a solid but probably fairly uneventful career, apart from picking up the occasional European Tour trophy, not only took the major but he became one of the few players who did it by way of pre-qualifying.

All this would have been startling enough, but Lawrie did it with an almost completely inexperienced caddie who had picked up his first professional bag only a few months before.

Paddy Byrne, just 23 years old, an expatriate Irishman who had been living in Dubai up until mid-February, was the bagman who walked alongside Lawrie as the Scot triumphed in the Scotch mist and rain of Carnoustie to send the largely Scottish gallery, braving the elements, into raptures. It was one of the most memorable days in Open history, even if it will perhaps remain memorable for quite a few wrong reasons, as well as the right ones.

It will be remembered as much for being the Open that Van de Velde lost rather than the one which Lawrie won. And, much harder on the victorious Scot, it will likely be remembered more for the remarkable scenes involving the Frenchman at the Barry Burn than for the supreme four-iron shot that Lawrie hit over it to finally clinch the four-hole playoff and relegate Van de Velde and Leonard to runners-up.

Paddy Byrne's memories, however, will be confined to his master's bravery and determination—and to his skill, like the weaving of a brilliant 67 on the final day when nearly everyone else was failing once again to master the tricked-up north-east coast links.

Paddy Byrne may have been the only man in the world who thought Lawrie could win the Open. In what will become a historical interview, Byrne actually surmised that Lawrie could win when questioned by a radio reporter soon after the Scot had produced a little bit of magic at the end of his round to save par on the final hole of the tournament proper.

That par was to prove crucial and the 18th hole proved to be Lawrie's key to a victory. It was a victory that will become as much a part of Scottish golfing folklore as the feats of Old and Young Tom Morris, or Sandy Lyle, the first Scot to win the Championship in the modern era. Lawrie's other record was his amazing feat in overcoming a ten-stroke deficit to win the Open, the record catch-up, which is likely to stand for many a year.

Creating history, however, was the last thing on young Paddy Byrne's mind when he was called over by a friend of his father's when he was looking at the set of European Tour players warming up at Dubai Creek Golf and Country Club in mid-February 1999. That the tour had returned to Dubai for its annual Desert Classic was a delight to Byrne, whose father had moved the family there some years before. Byrne was used to meeting tour professionals because his father played host to most of the Irish pros who visited Dubai over the years.

But it was to be a Scot with whom the Irishman teamed up that week. Lawrie was without a caddie after parting company with his bagman, so Byrne was quick to acquiesce when asked if he would like to take over for Lawrie for the week. The pair got on so well, though, that the Scot asked the Irishman if he would like to take a longer spell with a view to taking over permanently if things worked out.

When Lawrie missed the cut by eight strokes, Byrne thought his tenure would be short-lived. Lawrie persevered with the partnership, though, and that paid off in full. He won the following week and won by a country mile, seven strokes in the Qatar Masters at Doha, just a short hop down the Gulf. Lawrie's ringing of the changes—he had not only taken on a new caddie in Byrne but a new coach in great friend Adam Hunter, a former tour winner—took the quiet Scot to the next rung in his career. His only other success had come in 1996 when he took the windswept Catalan Open over only 36 holes. Stepping up a rung had silenced those who had said his win was not really a win at all because it was not a full tournament.

Over the next nine months the new trio—Lawrie, Byrne and Hunter—would step up several more rungs on the golfing world ladder . . . to triumph in the Open and go on to being one of the success stories in Europe's losing Ryder Cup team at Brookline. Lawrie's life was changed for ever as he soared from 159th place in the world rankings to becoming a worldwide household name. The rookie caddie Byrne was by Lawrie's side throughout.

"The head pro at the Creek, Peter Downie, asked me if I'd like to caddie for a Scottish friend of his, Paul. I was delighted to because it made a change from working for my dad. After the first day Paul said he would keep me for the week and maybe for the following week because it was only in Qatar. But I thought it would be a short-term relationship after we missed the cut by eight shots. In Qatar, though, it was an entirely different week. He played fantastic golf and after he'd won he asked me if I'd like to caddie for him for the whole year. I love golf and I jumped at the chance. It was quite a start, though, missing the cut by eight and then winning by seven.

"That ensured I'd have a full-time job and it was the start of a very exciting time for me. I had no idea just how exciting it was going to be, though.

"Paul played pretty well for the next few months but we hadn't qualified for the British Open and so we had to go to Downfield to the final qualifier. He didn't play great for the opening round but I knew there was going to be something for him at Downfield because he was just a whisker away from his top game. When it came to the last nine holes on the second day, thankfully he found his best game. One of the Scottish caddies, Edinburgh Jimmy, had told him he might need to be even seven-under to get through and he was only two-under at that stage. Then he knew he had to shoot four-under on the back nine to make it and that's just what he did. His pre-qualifier second round was a bit of a curtain-raiser to the week, really. I think it did him good to find his concentration and his game at that stage because Carnoustie was very, very tough and you had to be at your best."

So the 128th Open Championship got under way and Lawrie was typically out of the limelight. In fact, one of the players who had shared sixth place with him at Downfield, the young British amateur Zane Scotland, commanded far more attention than Lawrie. But, at that stage anyway, that was how the somewhat introvert Scot liked it. The family man who was commuting every day from his wife and two children in Aberdeen was not the sort who could stand much fuss.

With his splendid short-game, however, a game taught to him by his father, Jim, Carnoustie could have been made for him. His nickname on the European Tour is "Chippy," and that is not because he and wife Marian own a fish-shop. Lawrie is one of the best chippers and pitchers in the game. Soon he would show that strength and more than a little acumen with other parts of his game, too.

"We could see the course was very difficult and the first thing we talked about was just making the cut. I don't think the thought of winning the British Open ever entered Paul's head at that stage. It certainly didn't enter mine. Practice was quiet and studious, taking careful mental notes of all the tough spots, landing areas, and keeping an eye on rhythm. We just played on our own, going out with his coach Adam, who went through a few things with him. It was always going to be tough with the wind. Paul's a good wind player. He'd won his first tournament in terrific winds and when he won in Qatar it was pretty windy all the week, so a Scottish wind, which he was used to, didn't bother him. It was more a case of settling any swing doubts that Paul might have, that was important, and Adam put him right on that.

"It was going to be a huge task in front of us. Certainly it wasn't going to be a matter of how long you could hit it. The key was always going to be keeping it on the fairways. That made you wonder if some of the fancied players might struggle, even if they can hit the ball a mile, people like Tiger Woods, for instance. You had to put a lot of thought into the rough as well, use a fair bit of course management. You were in deep trouble ten yards or so off the fairway but, if you went further, you could get lucky where the rough had been trampled down. The whole week soon proved to be a case of luck if you did miss fairways, as it very often can be when there are a lot of spectators about.

"The first round was absolutely magical for me, bearing in mind that here I was in my first few months as a tour caddie; just drinking in the atmosphere, the crowds, the tents, all the buzz—here we were at the Open. Great. I'd never dreamt that this would be happening when I first agreed to take Paul's bag in Dubai. I could hardly believe it was happening to me. I'd never even watched a major live, only on television. I had to shake myself out of it, though, because there was a job to be done. It was never going to be easy out there.

"Paul played some great stuff in the first round, chipped and putted brilliantly. His short-game was great. He shot a 73 on a tremendously difficult day. That was only two strokes off the lead, so he'd carried on that last nine holes at Downfield, just as I'd hoped he would. He made very few mistakes, got it round a very difficult golf course without too many worries. He began in a very positive mood and I couldn't see him being shaken from it much. There was never anything that wasn't positive that went between us in conversation, like: 'If I don't do this I'm going to be in trouble' or 'If I can't do this I'm not going to make the cut' or 'It's going to need this or that or we're in trouble.' He was just so positive all week. That's why I think he could find the extra, like at the last on the fourth day or in the playoff. He just didn't look at anything 'unpositively.' Do our best and that's all we could do. We'd gone out very late in the day in the first round [with the exciting young English amateur Luke Donald and the in-form Australian Peter Lonard, teeing off at 3:25 P.M.] and it's easy to get distracted at the end when the crowds are all drifting away. You can even hear the mowers coming out behind you. Paul dropped shots on the 13th and 15th without particularly making big mistakes, but he just took it all in his stride."

That attitude reaped dividends because Lawrie's two-over-par 73 left him only two strokes behind the leader, another surprise package, Australian Rodney Pampling, whose early 71 made him the only pro not to shoot over par. While such headline-makers as the former world number one David Duval and the mercurial rookie Sergio Garcia found themselves perplexed by the Carnoustie set-up, Lawrie flourished on home ground. Duval produced a 79 and scathing comments; Garcia slithered into oblivion with an 89.

Lawrie was in a pack of seven in fourth place, a stroke behind the second-placed men, the little-known American Scott Dunlap and Bernhard Langer, who, despite the onset of veteranship, showed there was life in the old German Shepherd dog yet. The favorite, Tiger Woods, the European number one, Colin Montgomerie—Lawrie's role-model—and perennial Open contender Jesper Parnevik were among those who were three shots off the lead. There was no need yet to try to fetch father Jim from his holiday in Spain, but Lawrie had shown the first signs to his caddie Paddy Byrne that this was not going to be just an ordinary week; this was now certainly not just a week of making sure to avoid the cut.

"When we looked at the scores after the first round, Paul knew how well he'd done but he kept his feet on the ground. It was no good getting carried away and blowing it in the second round because you needed all your concentration out there, but playing so well when a lot of big names had struggled certainly gave him a lot of confidence and it took all the pressure off making the cut.

"He went out in the second round and played pretty well again for a 74. We bogeyed the short 13th again, just the same way as in the first round, just overshooting the green, so I felt it owed us. The 17th was a late shock when the drive found the water. He did well to only bogey it. The 17th proved pretty kind to us in the long-run, though. The dropped shots didn't unsettle Paul visibly.

"We were through to the weekend, so he'd achieved his first target. It may sound like an old cliché but he really did take things one step at a time and wouldn't look too far ahead. He just kept saying to me, 'Let's take every shot as it comes,' and that's all he did. It doesn't sound very dramatic but that's Paul. That attitude works well for him."

A second-round 74 left the Scot only four shots off the new leader, the Frenchman whose name will be etched into everyone's memory at Carnoustie 1999 as much as that of Lawrie, Jean Van de Velde. The affable, aristocratic Frenchman led by a stroke after a swashbuckling 68 took him to one over par. Opening-round front-runner Rodney Pampling disappeared, the first man in latter days to miss the cut after leading. Angel Cabrera then came following in the footsteps of Roberto de Vicenzo, Vicente Fernandez and Eduardo Romero as the latest Argentinian sensation, taking up second place a stroke behind Van de Velde. Jesper Parnevik continued his annual crusade for the trophy that had eluded him thrice before, holding third place two off the pace.

Lawrie slotted neatly into seventh place, now five strokes away from lead position. Then it was time to battle to stay on the nether reaches of the leaderboard, as caddie Byrne remembers.

"So we're well up there when it came to Saturday. It was his best golf day. He didn't play that great but he kept his head and battled really, really hard. He fought and fought and never let go, even though it would have been easy to have given in to the course like a lot of players finally did.

"Paul kept his score down to the minimum, kept it to a reasonable level when it could have blown out far worse than a 76. He was out in 40 and it could have been the same for the back nine for an 80, or even worse, because he just wasn't hitting the ball well. He didn't moan about anything, though.

"That's what I mean about being positive. Never once did we talk about anything in the negative. He even pointed out that we hadn't made double-bogey yet. That was important."

It was a commendable effort but Lawrie's presence, now well down the scoreboard, hardly caused a ripple, even with the Scottish press. Van de Velde did not seem to command much press attention either as the Frenchman's determined, if enigmatic, 71 was greeted with rather bewilderingly taciturn reports in the Sunday newspapers of his unexpected five-stroke lead. Perhaps the fourth estate could not believe what they were witnessing. As Mae West might have told them, "You ain't seen nothing yet."

Van de Velde was five shots ahead of the 1997 champion at Royal Troon, Justin Leonard, and five better than Craig Parry, as the Australian made yet another bid for a major title. There was now a whole host of hopefuls in between Lawrie and top place.

Lawrie's determination not to fall by the wayside in the third round was to pay handsome dividends. When he began the final round, though, winning was far from his mind, and from that of his caddie. They were ten strokes behind the leader Van de Velde. It was going to need a near-superhuman effort to get into the hunt for even a top placing. Ideas of lifting the Auld Claret Jug that night were a far-fetched dream. In the end, two magical four-iron shots would make that dream come true.

"Perhaps being so far behind took the pressure off a little. He thought he might be too far back to win, but it didn't stop me getting a bollocking on Sunday morning. I'd rung Paul's house the night before but made the big mistake of ringing after nine o'clock. He'd already gone to bed and he was not impressed by being called out. We just went to practice as normal on the

Sunday morning. It sounds pretty ordinary to say that we had no set plan before the last round of an Open, but it's the truth. It's the same before any round of any tournament. We don't discuss what we're going to do at this hole or that hole or how we're going to play the wind here or miss the rough there. We just go out and get on with it.

"It wasn't nearly as windy as the previous days. We were with Patrik Sjoland. He's a quiet guy, too. That suited Paul. We had a bit of a disappointment straightaway because he had a good birdie chance at the first but missed it. He birdied the third, though, the short par-four, with about a 12-foot putt, but then dropped one at the fifth. He got it straight back with a birdie at the long sixth and then sank a 25-footer at the eighth. So we were gradually getting a good round together.

"His back nine was brilliant apart from the 13th, which we again bogeyed— three times out of four for the week. He hit a great four-iron to less than four feet at the 12th. His four-iron was definitely his key iron on the last day. At that time, though, I had no idea how much of a key iron!

"Paul's finish was unbelievable. At the 14th he was in an awkward spot but pitched to about a yard again for another birdie and then he holed a 25-footer on the 17th. That really moved him up the leaderboard. When we went into the bunker on the 18th I just willed him to get it up and down so that he wouldn't spoil such a great round. He did it and I'd no idea how important that up and down was going to be.

"We just hoped it was good enough for top five. We didn't dream it had a chance of winning at that stage. Somebody told us that top four got him into the Masters next year and that was a fantastic feeling for him. It wasn't until I saw players like Craig Parry falling away on the leaderboard that it occurred to me that he might just have a chance [Byrne's prophetic radio interview confirmed that, and Colin Montgomerie predicted that his six-over-par total would be good enough for a playoff].

"Jean was five shots ahead, though, and you just never thought he'd lose it like he did. Obviously, as things wore on we had to prepare just in case we were involved in a playoff. Paul went to the practice ground with Adam and I went to the locker-room to get the gear prepared, collect balls and stuff. I was beginning to think we might be called upon, though. When I was interviewed by the BBC, I told them so.

"I think Paul actually put a lot of pressure on the players still out on the course. We were home and dry and had posted a great score, a 67, and set a reasonable target. He'd set the pace, I suppose."

Lawrie labeled his 67, the best return in the final round, "the best of my life considering how tough Carnoustie has been, with or without the wind." When Lawrie came in, however, he felt six-over was "two too many."

Even while he was in press conference, though, he was edging closer and closer to the lead. He decided he would have to practice after all, just in case.

The "pace" was to prove an obstacle neither Leonard nor Van de Velde could better. First Leonard went into the Barry Burn on 18 to finish level with Lawrie, then Van de Velde contrived to despatch his chance of victory into the rough and the water that is the infamous finish at Carnoustie.

Van de Velde had a three-stroke advantage playing the last but, after a serious misjudgment, collapsed with a triple-bogey, to finish alongside Leonard and Lawrie. On the 72nd hole, the Frenchman hit a wayward drive but found a freshly mown piece of ground quite near to the 17th fairway. Then came his fateful two-iron shot as he made a bid to carry the Barry Burn. His decision to go for the carry rather than lay up saw him founder on the scaffolding of the 18th grandstand. His ball ricocheted back off the stand and the concrete burn wall into heavy stuff. Van de Velde then snuffed his next into the Barry Burn.

There followed 20 minutes of sheer theater. First, he considered playing his ball from the burn. But then he changed his mind as the ball sank deeper into the mud during the time he took to take off his shoes and socks and roll up his trousers (afterwards he wished he had not bothered because it was the last hole anyway and the ball became unplayable while he was doing so). After at first clambering into the burn, the Frenchman took a penalty drop—only to then hit into the greenside bunker. It took a courageous putt of about seven feet for him to even make the playoff with Lawrie and Leonard.

"As far as all the happenings at the 18th are concerned, I missed the lot. I know Paul watched some of Van de Velde's shots at 18 from the practice ground and he knew what had happened to Leonard, so he must have been getting pretty worked up. But I never saw a thing and wasn't even sure what was going on until I got a call from Adam that I'd better get ready to go out again. Then Paul came up to me, perfectly calmly and said, 'We're in a playoff. Let's go.' It was as easy as that.

"We went out on the tee and had a little chat, talked about all kinds of things—football, things not concerned with golf. I tried to keep him calm and relaxed because there was a big wait on the tee. Van de Velde had forgotten his hat. He had to have it because of his sponsors, so we had to hang around for a good while so he could go back to the locker-room for his hat. Paul thrives on pressure, though, and he was totally focused once we got going.

"The playoff started and the noise around the tee was tremendous, people shouting out Paul's name. They were really urging him on. Well, none of them hit the fairway at the 15th and it was a pretty awful start to the playoff. We made a good five and put the pressure on Leonard. He holed a six-footer for his five. Van de Velde made a six because he got into trouble off the tee, so we're level with Leonard and one better than Van de Velde.

"Paul's ability to stand the pressure really showed at the next hole, the short-hole 16th. We were very unlucky to find the bunker. It was pot luck whether you got a bounce or not and the ball went in. He hit a good bunker shot to about five feet but it's downhill and left-to-right. He just missed it and made a four. They all made four, so it's still Paul and Leonard in front.

"On the 17th he got a pretty reasonable drive away and then hit a four-iron to about 15 feet pin-high left. That was another great four-iron. There was more to come. It's always going to be his favorite club now! Van de Velde was a bit further away but made the putt. Paul followed him in for birdie as well, so that was important. Leonard could only par so that meant he was one one ahead of both of them now.

"Then it was all down to the last. We knew we couldn't afford to make any mistakes still, but there was never any hint of talking negatively or trying to protect, defend anything. He hit a great three-wood off the tee.

"We had 192 yards to the pin, into the wind, cold and damp. We couldn't see exactly what Leonard had done but it looked as though he could have gone in the burn. And Jean could only lay up.

"Paul said to me, 'Four-iron?' I agreed straightaway. I had no doubts whatsoever, because it was a similar distance to the shot we'd played at the 17th. I had the utmost confidence in him hitting that four-iron well, as he had done all day. So there was never any doubt in my mind, and I said, 'Middle of the green, two putts, and it's yours.' He gave a little smile and then looked serious again. He said, 'Are you sure this is enough?' I said, 'Sure it is, it'll get you there all right.' He went through his pre-shot routine. He must have been churning inside but you'd never know to look at him.

"Well, he caught it absolutely perfectly, flew the burn easily. I knew we had it then. He had a one-shot lead, Leonard had gone into the water again and would have needed to hole his chip. Van de Velde would have had to have holed his fourth from the bunker. Even then it might not be enough.

"It was a fantastic feeling walking down the last again. The crowd could see how close Paul was. He was only four or five feet from the pin and they were going mad, all of them soaked, but they didn't care about that. Paul then put the icing on the cake by holing his putt for birdie.

"What a feeling! Here I am, a caddie for only six months and I'm with the Open champion. To be honest, I didn't dwell on it that much. I took the bag to do a job and I felt I'd done it. I hope there are going to be more weeks like that. I want him to win every week. It was a case of celebrate that night and then get on with it. You can't dwell on the past, otherwise you might lose the big picture—which is to help Paul get as high on the world rankings as I can. It got Paul into the Ryder Cup, which he played really well in. As far as I'm concerned, there's more to come from him, more chances in world events and more Ryder Cups. I hope I'll be helping him get into those kind of positions.[The pair have now parted company.]

"After the ceremony, which was obviously very emotional, I celebrated in style and I wasn't in the best of shapes when I went up to his house the next day to meet his wife and kids. We celebrated this time with a cup of tea! Then I went home. It didn't hit me first of all, but then when everyone was congratulating me, aunts and uncles, at the end of the week, it did start to sink in. We were in Ireland as well, the following week, and I was hounded by the press at the K Club. People were slapping me on the back, people I'd never met . . . the whole country was really happy about Paul's win. The Irish love a winner and I'd been with a winner. They really made a fuss of Paul. The Irish loved him.

"Paul did say a few nice things to me when he collected the Open trophy, but I'd sooner keep them to myself. He was a picture to see, though, and he just kept saying over and over again, 'Can you believe it? Can you believe it? That's the Claret Jug!' I said, 'Yes, I know, and you deserve every bit of it because you played brilliantly.' I meant every word. The Claret Jug was there for the taking. Everyone had a chance but he was the man who grabbed it."

2000 ST. ANDREWS,
THE MILLENNIUM OPEN

Tiger Woods with Steve Williams

Tiger Woods	USA	67 66 67 69 269 (par 72)
Ernie Els	South Africa	66 72 70 69 277
Thomas Bjorn	Denmark	69 69 68 71 277
Tom Lehman	USA	68 70 70 70 278
David Toms	USA	69 67 71 71 278
Fred Couples	USA	70 68 72 69 279
Loren Roberts	USA	69 68 70 73 280
Paul Azinger	USA	69 72 72 67 280
Pierre Fulke	Sweden	69 72 70 69 280
Darren Clarke	N Ireland	70 69 68 73 280

"Stevie? I can't say enough about Stevie. He's so positive out there, keeps me upbeat. We have a good time out there. If I'm playing good or bad, it doesn't matter, we're going to enjoy each other's company."

Earning your stripes

The "Stevie" to which the world's greatest golfer of the new millennium, Tiger Woods, was referring, is the tall and elegant New Zealander Steve Williams. This chapter recognizes Williams' part as he caddied for Woods at, arguably, the most outstanding Open—in terms of total dominance by one player—ever witnessed at St. Andrews. Much of the chapter is a tribute to the caddie by the player. Woods turned on the magic but he knew he had a man by his side on whom he could totally rely, should two heads need to prove better than one.

You might say that Woods was in such irresistible mood and form that he could have won the Open with his adoring mother on the bag (she was in the gallery at St. Andrews that week). Surely anyone could have done the job? However, when Woods gazed up at the final green and the infamous Valley of Sin, you understood the value of an experienced caddie. The Open Champion–elect showed the faith in which even a player of Woods' caliber has in such a bagman as Williams when he reminded the New Zealander they had to get just one more shot right. Then Williams would have done a good job for the week. The world's number one golfer might have already decided what he was going to hit in to the 18th, but appreciated that it had needed just a little more than his own presence of mind to achieve greatness at the Home of Golf.

Woods was desperate to finish with at least par. Par would take him past Nick Faldo's 18-under-par record winning total for the Open but he insisted afterwards that he was not interested in records (later he admitted it was one record he really did crave). What he wanted was to play all four rounds in the 60s. A bogey would crush that ambition.

Not only did they get the club right but Williams and Woods then lined up the putt correctly. It was close to making it for birdie but, only inches away from the cup, par was duly made. Woods had achieved his ambition with a closing round of 69. Thus he had played four rounds in the 60s—something he had not been able to do when winning the U.S. Masters of 1997 or the U.S. Open a month before, where he had broken just about every other record, or the previous year's U.S. PGA Championship. Before he started to consider that he was about to become the youngest winner at 24 years of age of the elusive Grand Slam—to win all four majors—Woods had made sure his pride was not dented by finishing bogey-bogey. Caddie Williams played his part in helping him make it an illustrious finale without any gilt being taken off the gingerbread.

Williams had taken over on the bag from Mike "Fluff" Cowan in early spring 1999. The American caddie had had his moments of major glory with Woods, by his side for the first of Woods' record-breaking performances when he won the 1997 Masters. And the highly-experienced Cowan also served during seven PGA victories.

Cowan, however, was hardly a shrinking violet. A man who rarely pulled a punch, the broad-shouldered, blanched-mustachioed doyen of caddies could often be outspoken. He rarely hesitated when asked an opinion about anything. In the end, clubhouse scuttlebutt had it, Cowan talked once too often. The parting of the ways came for him and Woods.

In March 1999, Woods turned to Williams. He was a true golfing caddie in the old mold, able to "eyeball" yardages while, alternatively, being an easy-reader of yardage books. A former two-handicapper who once dreamt of a pro career himself until, at 13, he decided he wanted to be a professional caddie instead. That was after a heady experience for a teenager, which he often related, accompanying one of golfing's greats: "I caddied for Peter Thomson [five-times Open Champion, including the "hat-trick" in 1954, '55 and '56] in the 1976 New Zealand Open at Heretaunga and at the end of the tournament he gave me 150 dollars, his golf bag and a lot of golf balls. In those days, I was getting 50 cents a week pocket money, so I thought there must be something in this caddying lark."

The New Zealander had seen service with another one of the world's highest profile golfers during a career in which he had already gleaned a wealth of experience at top events. He was Greg Norman. The Great White Shark watched Williams working with Ian Baker-Finch when they played together and asked the Kiwi caddie to join him in the early '80s. They stayed together for several years before American Pete Bender took over [see Turnberry Open 1986]. Williams then came to Woods after 12 years on the bag of Raymond Floyd, another major winner.

In fact the man from Paraparaumu, still playing off a handicap of six, was plucked from working on the seniors tour with Floyd, so it was a whole new ball game. Just before his first tournament with Woods, the Bay Hill Invitational in Florida, Williams explained how lucky he felt he had been: "I haven't slept for the past three nights. It was great to work for Greg Norman in the past but this is going to be even more thrilling." Williams added that he had been quite happy working with Raymond Floyd and certainly hadn't joined in all the caddie "frenzy" after Cowan was sacked. "Out of the blue I got a message from Tiger's coach Butch Harmon, saying Tiger wanted to talk to me. I just about fell over. I mean, here was Tiger Woods asking me—not me asking Tiger Woods! What makes it really satisfying is that almost every American player has an American caddie and Tiger has gone for—a Kiwi."

After accompanying Woods to his second major title, the 1999 U.S. PGA Championship, caddie Williams helped his man scale new heights in 2000.

The New Zealander had already come up trumps when Woods won his second major. With a rampant Sergio Garcia snapping at his heels at Medinah and only a stroke adrift, Woods had needed to hole a brave six-footer on the 17th after overshooting the green to stay one in front and ultimately go on to pip the young Spaniard. The putt was made by using two heads instead of one, as Woods revealed afterwards: "I knew it didn't break as much as it looked. My caddie said it was inside-left, and I thought 'perfect.'" A miss and Woods would have ultimately been in a playoff. Williams had proved his worth in one small confirmation of a putt.

By the time the pair arrived at the Home of Golf for the Millennium Open, Woods had chalked up his third major, shattering the U.S. Open winning-margin record, taking the honors by 15 strokes at Pebble Beach, a record, indeed, for any major in any era. The pairing of Woods and Williams, however, was about to reach even dizzier heights.

Williams had already caddied at St. Andrews Open Championships and also at Dunhill Cup tournaments at the legendary Scottish links. So he knew all about the minefield of pot-bunkers and the pitfalls of finding them not only on your fairway but, if you went even just a fraction astray, on adjoining fairways, too. It may have been Woods firing the glorious drives with ultimate accuracy to avoid the notorious bunkers, 112 of them, most of which had been renovated with even steeper faces, all week. But Williams held the compass!

Winning a British Open at St. Andrews is every golfer's dream and Woods had more than a dream to make come true. In 1995 long before John Daly's glory hour, Woods had finished his final round and his week ended rather unfulfilled. He had qualified for the major by virtue of the first of his record three consecutive U.S. Amateur victories the year before, and came to St. Andrews as the clear favorite for the Silver Medal, awarded to the top amateur finisher in the major. Things did not go according to plan, however, and he was not only beaten to the Silver Medal by the diminutive English youngster Steve Webster but also had to settle for third-best amateur behind the giant Scot Gordon Sherry. A tie for 66th place was small beer for Woods and he left that legendary little corner of Scotland vowing it would be different when he returned.

Before returning in triumph, though, there was plenty more frustration for Woods as far as the British Open was concerned.

The following year at Royal Lytham and St. Anne's in England, Tom Lehman's year, delight came before disappointment as he did clinch the Silver Medal as best amateur by finishing tied 22nd. He also headed such golfing luminaries as Tom Kite and Ben Crenshaw, outdid Phil Mickelson and Corey Pavin, and finished 10 places and two shots better than the player soon to establish himself as his great friend and mentor, Mark O'Meara.

In 1997 Woods showed the world his potential after turning professional. He left everyone in his wake at Augusta to win the Masters by the greatest margin and took a creditable tied 19th place in the U.S. Open. Scotland, Royal Troon and the Auld Claret Jug beckoned.

With a huge gallery on opening day, he played steady golf until the 11th hole ruined his first round. A drive into the infamous gorse bordering the right of the fairway left him only able to hack out. Then bravado cost him dearly as he tried to recover with a two-iron, failed, and only made the green with his pitch-shot fifth, running up a seven. Only two birdies in the last three holes kept him five strokes behind joint leaders Darren Clarke and Jim Furyk. In the second round his nemesis came a hole earlier. After overshooting the 10th green, the Troon gorse again became his tormentor. With his ball close to a gorse bush he tried to hack out. He hit a branch on the way down, causing his club to slip under the ball, hardly moving it. Another swish left him short of the green still. Visibly fuming, he then overhit his next to send his ball careering through the green. An eight went on the card—quadruple-bogey—and that should have ended any chance he had of giving the chief protagonists a run for their money. His 74 left him 13 strokes behind the second round leader Clarke, languishing in a tie for 49th place. His only comfort was to at least qualify for the weekend.

But then Woods at last showed his Augusta form, hauling himself back into contention with a course record-equaling 64, which proved to be the best round of the week. Tiger had decided to go on the attack, and he treated another immense Troon gallery to an exhibition of swashbuckling golf. It could have cost him at least another 74 as he dueled again with the gorse but instead he finished 10 shots better than that, seven-under-par, transforming his position to eighth. That left him eight strokes behind new leader Jesper Parnevik but with a chance of victory if he could turn on another 64.

Royal Troon, though, and the deadly little "Postage Stamp" par-three eighth, had other notions. It was the innocent short hole that had caused so much woe to many that finally sealed and delivered Tiger his fate. Needing two to get out of the bunker, he then three-putted for a triple-bogey. It drew the Tiger's claws and he never really raised his game from then on in. Another 74 plummeted Woods to just a share of 24th place, 12 shots adrift of the all-conquering Justin Leonard.

A year later and Woods' greatest Open frustration yet left him desperately close to handling the Auld Claret Jug as his friend Mark O'Meara carried off the spoils after a playoff with Brian Watts. This time final-round heroics left Woods agonizingly within an ace of joining the playoff.

He had thrown down the gauntlet at the start of the Royal Birkdale week in England with a memorable 65 which once again showed him at his aggressive best. Woods took only 30 shots going out, inspired by a magical save at the second where he had driven into an awful spot he labelled "a terrible place, one of those lies that might mean you can move the ball only four feet." Reminiscent of what he would achieve at St. Andrews later, Woods powered into the heavy stuff so strongly he nearly launched himself as well as the ball, which sprung out like a terrified mole intent on finding another hole, this one set in a green 120 yards via a bunker. It was one of the shots of the week and earned Woods the unlikeliest of pars to set him on his way to his blistering 65. That gave him a share of a one-shot lead with John Huston.

Woods had not ironed out his inconsistency, however, and a second round 73 pegged him a stroke off the pace set by Watts. Worse was to come, though. A 77 on Saturday dogged by strong winds left Woods six strokes behind leader Watts. Refusing to be bowed, Woods predicted a 64 would win it—a score in an Open with which he was not unfamiliar—and he was dead-on. His 66, finished with a typical joyous punch in the air as he birdied the last, fell one stroke short of playing off. Frustration hit new heights as Woods had to settle for third place.

The last Open of the old millennium did nothing to bring Woods much cheer. He opened with a 74 and got into the running with a 72 as everyone but the remarkable Jean Van de Velde felt the wrath of Carnoustie. From only three strokes and tied fourth behind the French leader at the halfway stage, however, Woods slipped seven adrift of the Frenchman after three rounds even though hanging on to fourth spot. A share of seventh place, four strokes away from the three-way playoff won by Paul Lawrie, after closing with his third 74 of the week, proved that Woods had not been able to master a formidable layout set up by the Royal and Ancient. It was a week, however, for surprises. And Woods as a winner would not have been a surprise!

But his time for holding aloft the famous Auld Claret Jug was coming.

Woods began the week of his return to St. Andrews for the new millennium Open as the shortest odds favorite for many a long year and, over four rounds of mere zephyrs and sunshine, he would not disappoint the punters.

On Thursday, the gallery waited for the target to be set by Woods, but they had a long wait. With his putter cold, he had to stay patient when the birdies did not come along straight away. Woods only came alight around the turn. First he holed from 12 feet on the ninth after he and Williams had decided on a pitching wedge in. Two heads then again proved better than one when the pair coaxed in a 10-footer for a second birdie, Woods taking two putts from all of 50 yards after gaining the green with the drive on the 10th. Then the 12th green was hit for two putts from only 30 feet. Once the long 14th green had been navigated in two, birdie was almost a formality and then an astute nine-iron to 10 feet on the 15th earned a fifth birdie. But it was not just birdies on the minds of Woods and Williams.

It had taken Woods a great deal of patience to get into contention and he did not want to throw it away at the most famous hole in Open golf, the Road Hole 17th at St. Andrews. Woods found the rough, though. His approach looked no laughing matter but, remarkably, perhaps proving his confidence that week, he was seen chuckling with caddie Williams before hitting the shot which physically cost him his balance.

His ball—in a tough lie 160 yards from the front of the green—came out just as he wanted it to and left him with a putt from the right of the hump in the middle of the green. When it hovered close, caddie Williams was so relieved and full of admiration at a resultant formidable save, he could not resist clapping. Amazingly, Woods reported later that his caddie and he were telling each other jokes before he played the shot into the 17th.

There was disappointment when Woods had to settle for only par on the 18th, but a 67 announced his intent. Only Ernie Els headed him—by a single stroke—and the world waited for the Tiger to pounce.

For years the golfing world had waited for the Bear to claw. But now the Golden Bear, Jack Nicklaus, was giving way to a new order. As Nicklaus tearfully finished off what could be his last Open, Woods was just preparing for his round. The new golfing number one and his trusty caddie Williams watched as Nicklaus mounted the Royal and Ancient steps for possibly the last time in a major. It was as if the Tiger had set aside a special moment to salute the Bear, although Woods confided afterwards that he had merely gone to the first and the warm-up green early to get the feel for the round.

The world did not have to wait long for the Tiger to pounce once Woods began his second round in further benign conditions. To glean his sixth birdie of the Championship, it needed a deft sand-iron to eight feet at the first hole. On a stunning putting day, Woods' hours of practice and concentration with his putting before and during the Open paid rich dividends as he and caddie Williams lined them up and the maestro popped them in. At the fourth he didn't need Williams' opinion because his nine-iron shot landed only a foot from the cup.

The only danger then was lethargy. Waiting on the fifth tee, Woods even contemplated sending out for a pizza for him and his caddie as they stood by for half-an-hour, he related afterwards. But the concentration never wavered. Woods found a subtle touch to take two putts from just off the long fifth green and when he rammed in a 12-footer to again birdie the ninth, he was in an ascendancy that would take him to the Auld Claret Jug.

Putts of similar length went in at the 12th and 14th and then it was time again to hang on to his score. The Road Hole still had to be mastered to ensure he would command a big lead. And, besides, he had not made bogey yet. In fact he had gone 60 holes in majors without a bogey. Pride brought out the best in him when he still had not made the 17th green in two. He produced one of the shots of the Championship, a wily chip which saw his ball roll back from the slope before settling about eight feet from the hole.

Woods had spent a long time on the practice area with his caddie Williams, preparing for such a shot, made more difficult because of the hard ground. The time he spent covering all eventualities at St. Andrews showed how much the perfectionist he was, as his New Zealand bagman knew all too well. But it needed both their wits to achieve the coup de grace, after Woods' brilliant approach chip. Left with a putt which broke twice—from right to left and then left to right—par was by no means a formality, even with Woods' hours and hours of putting practice and improvement in posture on the greens, now paying off. When the putt went in, Williams came close to clapping his master for a second day.

A 66 took Woods to 11-under-par and into a three-shot lead over the little-known David Toms. The Millennium Open was over, bar the shouting.

Perhaps Woods sensed it. Certainly it was time to pay a glowing accolade to his bagman Williams, digressing about having almost a sixth-sense with each other. How Williams had helped in the crucial second round: "I think that it's something that has come about over time. We've gotten to know each other. He has got to know me really well, how I like to play on a golf course, what my thought process is going to be. He can just read me—to the point where he knows when to say something, when not to say something. And we genuinely like being around each other. I think that's what makes for a wonderful partnership, especially one that lasts for a long time.

"A couple of times on tee shots today, when I wanted to play a different shot, he got in my head a little bit and said: 'Look at this option; consider this.' I think that's what he's good at. And he doesn't force it on you. If I want to go with my shot I go with it. I'm the one holding the club. But he knows enough about golf to go ahead and tell me what he's thinking; what he thinks is the best play, when asked. You can't ask more of a caddie than that."

There was a shock in store for Woods though, early in the third round. It hardly caused a flutter among the pundits but it did frustrate him immensely.

222

A three-putt from only 25 feet on the second caused him his first bogey for 64 holes of major golf. The only way to respond to that in Woods' book is to get the shot back. He almost insisted his putter send ball to ground on the next hole. It obliged from 12 feet for birdie.

With the rest of the field given just a glimmer hope, though, that Saturday may just be the bad-round-day of the week, Woods needed to re-establish his authority. He did so with a six-iron of utmost quality at the short eighth, needing a mere putt of 18 inches at the 175-yard hole. When he slotted in a 15-footer on the ninth, challengers wondered why they had even entertained any idea that Woods might falter.

Another three-putt, from about 80 feet after gaining the short par-four 10th green from the tee, this for par, of course, rankled but did not cause any loss of concentration. When he ran in successive birdies from the 12th to the 14th, Woods and Williams were already on the way to an even bigger lead than Nick Faldo and Fanny Sunesson had enjoyed to take into their final round 10 years previously.

The 17th had to be negotiated to protect a six-shot lead, one better than Faldo's 1990 advantage, but the Road Hole would not relent. Woods again three-putted to drop his second shot of the week, this time from only 20 feet, although it was again a putt of more than one break to it.

As he did at the beginning of the round, though, he struck back. Biting his lip and refusing to be upset by an untimely bogey, Woods and Williams concurred on a four-iron off the final tee, giving plenty of scope for a full pitch in. That paid off as he birdied the last by holing out from 10 feet after studiously mapping out with the faithful Williams.

Woods may have missed out on Faldo's 17-under-par 199 three-round record by a stroke, but his 16-under-par total with another 67 had really scattered the field, earning him a six-stroke advantage.

A birdie on the last had taken David Duval, for so long the world's number two behind Woods, into the final twosome as the second-placed man, six shots behind the leader.

And Duval at least, had not entirely given up the ghost on the Claret Jug and the Millennium Open. The man with the wrap-around sunglasses, fighting a niggling back problem all week, found the birdies and Woods did not. The lead was cut to four strokes. Ernie Els, coming back into the picture yet again, also reduced it by that margin.

Woods was playing with his foes like a cat with a mouse, however, and struck with a vehemence on the fourth, holing a 20 foot putt to move to 17-under-par, just a stroke off Nick Faldo's record.

It was a signal for everyone at last to run up the white flag, although they probably could have done so after round two. Duval made mistakes to enhance the lead again, and Els in the end had to battle for a share of second place—his third in the year's majors—with the Dane Thomas Bjorn. Whether it was Woods' birdies on the 10th, two putts from 80 feet this time after gaining the green, 12th, two putts from 30 feet after driving the green, and 14th, two putts from 20 feet after hitting the par-five green in two, that finally ground down Duval is a matter of conjecture. Certainly he chose the wrong option by trying to float up and over the Road Hole bunker instead of pitching out sideways. His demise was painful to watch as he ran up an eight, taking four shots to emerge from the dreaded sand which ended Costantino Rocca's forlorn lingering hopes five years previously.

Woods himself will not remember the Road Hole with any fondness for he again tripped up at it, having to settle for a third bogey of the week, two of them coming at the 17th. This time his six-iron approach was always going to finish up short after a drive that was hardly his Sunday-best.

Thus there was work to be done if Woods was not to provide his own anticlimax by finishing poorly, when the engraver had already etched his name on the Auld Claret Jug. After a few frustrating minutes while a streaker spoiled the march up the 18th and the acknowledgment to the tumultuous gallery, the all-important par went on the card.

At 24 years old Woods was a Grand Slam champion. The Tiger had earned his stripes—and so had his conscientious caddie.

Williams was to accompany Woods to further glory in 2000 as they added the U.S. PGA Championship title to those of the U.S. and British Opens. Without that sudden breeze at the 12th at Augusta, which helped his ball into the water and took the wind out of his sails in the Masters opening round, maybe Woods could have been the first to achieve the full Grand Slam—winning all four majors in one year. As it was, he was the first player since Ben Hogan in 1953 to win three majors in one year.

Woods' grip on the world rankings number one spot was so vice-like he could probably have retired at the end of 2000 and still not have been overtaken on top for at least a couple of years! Over the year, Woods trebled his lead on the world rankings to nearly 18 points, an unassailable and unprecedented position. In 22 official ranking events he placed in the top five no less than 19 times, heading the U.S. PGA Tour money list for the third time in four years. By the time the 2001 season began, Woods' world ranking points average showed 28.80 compared to the second-best man in the world Ernie Els, whose average was 11.45. Els, the "Big Easy" from South Africa, was used to playing second fiddle, though. He had finished runner-up to the Tiger in three of the 2000 majors. Reducing Els to also-ran was a mammoth achievement in itself. The genial giant South African had been tipped three years earlier as the man who might prove the threat to Woods' world dominance. Ernie just never got a look in.

Tiger passed the ten million dollars mark for the year and that meant a huge cut for caddie Williams. One newspaperman back home totted up the percentage and suggested the Kiwi might just about be the highest paid sportsman in New Zealand. Woods won a staggering 10 individual titles. Nine of them came on the U.S. Tour, in which he played only 20 times. He came right out of the blocks at the start of the 2000 season, winning the U.S. Tour's opening event, the Mercedes Championship in Kapalua. That meant the Tiger had won five consecutive tournaments, the first to do so, again, since Ben Hogan, who achieved the feat in 1948. That set the scene for the year, doubly so because Ernie Els finished second. It was one of the few times Els got a sniff at toppling the Tiger, losing a thrilling finale in a sudden-death playoff. Woods just seemed determined to trample on the previous century's achievements by the golfing greats, adding title after title, including defending his NEC Invitational World Championship. He rounded off his wonderful year by helping retain the World Cup for America. Woods also finished second four times on the U.S. Tour and third once, the only real hiccup coming when he surprisingly gave best to Darren Clarke in the Andersen Consulting World Championship Matchplay final. With team triumphs in the President's Cup and with David Duval in winning the World Cup in Argentina, Woods was almost invincible.

The jewel in the 2000 crown, though, was undoubtedly the British Open and his claim to not only the Auld Claret Jug, but the Open Championship scoring record—achieved at the Home of Golf, St. Andrews. Woods revealed at the end of his brilliant season: "I really wanted that record. I didn't want to just share it."

Tiger worked his magic. Williams quietly got on with what he considers is the best job in the world.

Said Woods of his companion of the fairways: "Stevie? I can't say enough about Stevie. He's so positive out there, keeps me upbeat. I get on him; he gets on me. We have a good time out there. If I'm playing good or bad, it doesn't matter. We're going to enjoy each other's company. It's a positive for me and can't but help me."

A colorful band

S o there you have it—a few more tales from the caddies. They are a colorful band. Gone now are the likes of "Mad Mac," the eccentric who used to stalk the fairways in an old macintosh, wearing a pair of spectacles with no lenses in them to line up putts. He is the caddie who, when asked what line his master's ball might take, uttered the immortal riposte, "I think it's slightly straight, sir." Gone is "The Prof," an entrepreneur who dabbled in the stock market and a man who had the mental prowess to do the *Times* crossword in an hour—without using a pen! Gone is "Halifax Wingy," an extraordinary man who, despite having only one arm, accomplished his caddying tasks with reasonable aplomb—until losing his hook in the rough one day. Gone is "Johnny Blank," the piratical-looking caddie with one eye and a patch. Gone are the grizzled and dishevelled characters that used to make up the caddying circus. In their places have come the men with similar strange sobriquets, "Squirrel," "Ferret," "Gypsy," "Seagull." The caddies are no longer quite so gnarled. But they can still tell a yarn or two, like the diminutive "rake-rat" who squeezed himself into a golf bag and was placed by his comrades in a luggage rack while his train crossed over a border, because he had lost his passport. He gave himself away when he broke wind loudly, mistakenly thinking the suspicious border guards had gone away.

My favorite all-time caddie story, however, concerns Tom Weiskopf's former caddie Albert Fyles. He is the brother of the late, legendary Alfie, Tom Watson's bagman in the '70s and '80s, who would, I am sure, have had fine tales to tell for this book from the 1980, 1982 and 1983 Opens.

Albert was a remarkable caddie because he overcame a terrible speech impediment to become Weiskopf's right-hand man at Troon in 1973. His stammer often got him into trouble, however, not more so than when meeting up with one of his masters, Butch Baird. That was because Baird had a stammer to match Albert's! Baird thought Albert was making fun of him when he introduced himself and was nearly fired on the spot. The pair soon worked things out, though, until, as the caddies term it, "the bell rang," when their first tournament together began in earnest.

As is the ritual nowadays, players are expected to reveal their make of clubs and ball before teeing off in a tournament, all to do with marketing. When the official asked Baird his make of ball, the pro replied, "It's a ta-ta-ta-ta; it's a ta-ta-ta-ta; a ta-ta-ta-ta-ta . . ." The enquirer lost patience. He turned to Albert and said, "I can't wait around all day. What sort of ball is your pro using?" Albert gasped, "It's a ta-ta-ta-ta-ta; a ta-ta-ta-ta-ta . . ." The frustrated official turned on his heel and flounced off, never recording the fact that Albert and his pro intended using a Titleist for the tournament.